Smarter: Lessons from the New Science of Learning

What does cognitive psychology really tell us about how people learn – and why does it matter for both teachers and learners?

This book offers a deep dive into more than half a century of research into learning, examining evidence from psychology and neuroscience to help educators and learners create more effective and efficient methods of teaching and learning.

Drawing on behavioural, social, and cognitive aspects of learning, as well as recent developments in cognitive neuroscience and instructional design, this book offers a clear, accessible, yet critical look at the science of learning, grounded in cognitive psychology and written with educators in mind. It explores how learning happens, what helps it stick, and why it so often goes wrong. It examines learning in the classroom and into adulthood, highlighting how our ability to learn changes throughout the lifespan.

Full of examples, case studies, and helpful definitions, this book offers a valuable guide to learning for educators working across all phases. It shows that learning is more than remembering, and that context and meaning are crucial for the development of knowledge.

Marc Smith is a chartered psychologist, Associate Fellow of the British Psychological Society, freelance writer, and former secondary school teacher. He is the author of *The Emotional Learner*, *Becoming Buoyant*, and *Psychology in the Classroom* (with Jonathan Firth).

Smarter: Lessons from the New Science of Learning

Marc Smith

LONDON AND NEW YORK

Designed cover image: © Getty Images

First published 2026
by Routledge
4 Park Square, Milton Park, Abingdon, Oxon OX14 4RN

and by Routledge
605 Third Avenue, New York, NY 10158

Routledge is an imprint of the Taylor & Francis Group, an informa business

© 2026 Marc Smith

The right of Marc Smith to be identified as author of this work has been asserted in accordance with sections 77 and 78 of the Copyright, Designs and Patents Act 1988.

All rights reserved. No part of this book may be reprinted or reproduced or utilised in any form or by any electronic, mechanical, or other means, now known or hereafter invented, including photocopying and recording, or in any information storage or retrieval system, without permission in writing from the publishers.

For Product Safety Concerns and Information please contact our EU representative GPSR@taylorandfrancis.com. Taylor & Francis Verlag GmbH, Kaufingerstraße 24, 80331 München, Germany.

Trademark notice: Product or corporate names may be trademarks or registered trademarks, and are used only for identification and explanation without intent to infringe.

British Library Cataloguing-in-Publication Data
A catalogue record for this book is available from the British Library

ISBN: 978-1-041-04780-3 (hbk)
ISBN: 978-1-041-04779-7 (pbk)
ISBN: 978-1-003-62986-3 (ebk)

DOI: 10.4324/9781003629863

Typeset in Melior
by codeMantra

Contents

	Introduction: towards a new science of learning	1
1	Remembering, knowing, and understanding	8
2	Wired to learn	21
3	From salivating dogs to the new science of learning	37
4	How memory works	48
5	Why we struggle to remember	66
6	Context matters	85
7	How the brain constructs knowledge	101
8	Knowledge is power (just not always)	113
9	Why learning should be hard (but not too hard)	128
10	Routes to remembering	144
11	The forgotten variable: emotions and learning	160
12	Balancing minds, metacognition, and motivation	174
13	Designs for learning	192
14	Smarter learning	209
	Index	215

Introduction
Towards a new science of learning

This book is about cognition. Cognition, according to Ulric Neisser, is the activity of knowing: the acquisition, organisation, and use of knowledge. It is something that organisms do, and in particular, something that people do. For this reason, the study of cognition is part of psychology, and theories of cognition are psychological theories (Neisser, 1976, p.1). I emphasise this to firmly establish learning within the discipline of psychology, and the branch of cognitive psychology specifically. By doing this, I am fully aware that I reveal a bias towards my own discipline, while also accepting that the science of learning has multiple influences, many of which I'll touch on throughout the following chapters.

Retaining the messiness of cognitive psychology and learning

Neisser is generally considered one of the founders of cognitive psychology, the school of thought that emerged during the 1950s, although its origins date from much earlier. His 1967 book, entitled simply *Cognitive Psychology*, is considered the seminal work within the discipline. It wasn't the first with that title, however. That honour goes to Thomas Verner Moore, who published his *Cognitive Psychology* in 1939. While we might attempt to tidy up the history of psychology through categorisation and chronological sorting, it remains messy, with many schools of thought overlapping and influencing each other. They also may contradict themselves at times. This book intentionally retains some of the messiness, which might frustrate the reader, but I believe it better represents the history of learning science by retaining much of its nuance. There are a few absolutes here, and no theory, model, or framework is beyond at least some criticism.

Cognitive psychology's remit is wide, encapsulating memory, attention, perception, and all the facets of learning. Cognitive psychology has produced models of memory and attention inspired by real people (such as those with severe memory impairments and people displaying superior memory), but it has also looked to computers and micro-processing to help understand how humans might process, store, and recall the vast inputs encountered each and every day. On the flip side, machine learning models and artificial intelligence algorithms use what cognitive psychology has brought to the table, resulting in a complex reciprocal relationship. Cognitive psychologists have also carried out an awful lot of experiments, emphasising the view that psychological phenomena should be studied using scientific methods.

Cognitive psychology or cognitive science?

You might be more familiar with the term cognitive science than cognitive psychology, especially if you've been keeping up with trends in teaching and learning over the past decade or so. In education, there does appear to be a preference for the former term, even though there is very little practical difference. The distinction between cognitive psychology and cognitive science is a little peculiar. Cognitive psychology concerns itself with the study of mental processes, particularly those related to memory, attention, perception, and language. Cognitive science, on the other hand, adopts a much wider view, incorporating cognitive psychology, philosophy, neuroscience, anthropology, computer science, and linguistics. But cognitive psychology also studies many of these areas, and often it's hard to disentangle them. In current education discourse, we tend to find that the only relevant area of cognitive science is cognitive psychology, and the main topic is memory. But we hear much more about cognitive science than we do cognitive psychology.

Around 2014, the UK Department for Education began referring to cognitive science, avoiding the term psychology at all costs. Although there was some suspicion pertaining to government ministers' lack of knowledge surrounding what they were promoting, or perhaps a desire to emphasise the science element and, therefore, increase its perceived legitimacy (cognitive psychology is science, by the way). Whatever the reason, it can lead to some confusion, especially as all the evidence used to promote cognitive science in education has come from cognitive psychologists (with a few educational psychologists thrown in for good measure, although these terms are also often used interchangeably). Perhaps I'm a little defensive of my own discipline, and ultimately, it doesn't really matter how we choose to label this specific brand of science. George Miller, another early pioneer of cognitive psychology, preferred the term cognitive sciences, highlighting its interdisciplinary nature. My preference for the term cognitive psychology once again reveals my bias, but I still often use them interchangeably. And do so throughout this book.

A new science of learning

Memory is the most vital part of learning, so it's hardly surprising that those of us involved in teaching and learning lean into it. Without memory, there is no learning. However, by placing so much emphasis on memory, we can easily neglect other important influences. Learning science (or the learning sciences) is more ambitious than cognitive science, with a much wider remit. Definitions differ, however, and it's difficult to pinpoint the exact areas covered by this rapidly emerging field. The Learning Sciences Research Institute at the University of Nottingham, for example, focuses on many aspects of psychology, while other research centres might focus on educational technology, computer science, anthropology, or the philosophy of education. At the University of York, much of what learning science covers is encapsulated within the Psychology in Education Research Centre. Such departments, schools, and research centres are interdisciplinary, bringing together a wealth of interests and expertise to focus on one goal – the science of learning.

Despite the plethora of research into learning, education is playing catch-up, and even now, some of the psychological models and theories it promotes are reaching their sell-by date. What's changing is that many of the models and theories that have remained disparate for decades are now coming together, thanks to the efforts of an emerging body of learning scientists. Cognitive load theory is a good example of this – many of its component parts have existed since the dawn of cognitive psychology (some for much longer). Schema theory, cognitive load, retrieval practice, distributed learning, etc., have been around for a long time. The only difference is that now learning scientists are viewing them as part of a combined effort to understand how learning happens.

Learning or education?

Education is a far more contentious issue than learning, seeing as it also reflects the prevailing values of the time, what society and governments deem necessary for people (mainly young people) to learn, and passing trends. Reading, writing, and mathematical skills are certainly vital to the individual, wider society, and economic systems, yet many would also argue that education is much more than the learning of these skills. What about sociability, self-regulation, empathy, and compassion? Furthermore, some systems might consider it vital to instil a feeling of patriotism and national identity. This is what sociologists often describe as the hidden curriculum. We don't simply learn subjects at school; we also learn how to behave, how to treat other people, and how hierarchical structures operate. Schools are micro-societies, often mirroring the outside world. Perhaps schools also help to acclimatise young people to the world of work in which they will spend most of their lives.

School subjects do, of course, play their role, with some being viewed as less or more important. The sands of education shift over time, while learning, as wide-ranging as it is, remains relatively stable. More recently, the teaching profession has become concerned (some might say too concerned) with finding solutions that work; solutions that are supported by experimental data. But sometimes it feels we simplify the complex too much or eradicate nuance to the extent that we might assume such things are unchangeable and infallible. Indeed, I co-wrote a book in 2017 entitled *Psychology in the Classroom: A Teacher's Guide to What Works*. A more accurate, yet much less catchy, sub-title might have been *A Teacher's Guide* to *What Should Work* (given the stability of variables and the control of potential extraneous variables and considering pupils' individual differences, motivations, sleep quality, anxiety levels, and whether they'd eaten a healthy breakfast). This is even before we question the differences between the types of studies and their methodology that proclaim to offer workable solutions. Notions of how people learn, and the most effective methods, certainly aren't static. Cognitive psychology and the wider cognitive sciences can provide models and theories. Neuroscience can inform us of what is happening in the brain as we learn, as well as why learning becomes more difficult with age. But with each study, every laboratory experiment, naturalistic examination, and case study, we discover more. That's how science works.

Knowledge is another tricky concept. The principal goal of education is to create knowledge, in all its many guises. But whose knowledge? Are we talking about objective truths or those infamous alternative facts? Knowledge can be objectively inaccurate, but that doesn't stop it from being knowledge. This distinction is perhaps more important now than ever, particularly in a world of social media, fake news, misinformation, disinformation, and powerful people willing to use and weaponise knowledge. Cognitive psychology certainly has its darker side.

This book is, therefore, about learning rather than education. The examples I use in the following chapters are intended to apply to everyone engaged in learning, be they teachers, children in a classroom, employees on a training course, or someone learning a new language for their upcoming holiday. To some extent, therefore, I've attempted to isolate learning from education, annoyingly side-stepping the often-volatile debates that surround the latter. I'm not here to change education, and it's doubtful a book like this could. The aim is to inform, to offer up what the science of learning has discovered, and how this can help us create beneficial learning environments.

Terminology

Early cognitive psychology relied heavily on the computer metaphor – the notion that the human mind could be compared to the workings of a computer. While this reliance has waned over time, the terminology has endured. We, therefore, talk of information or data and how it is accessed, stored, retrieved, and so on. This language fails to fully acknowledge the complexity of the human cognitive architecture (and, yes, that's another term from cognitive psychology), and how unlike a computer it really is. There are many terms and phrases psychology has adopted over the years, and I think we are yet to settle on any that fully and faithfully acknowledge this complexity. Definitions are often fuzzy, such as 'mind', which doesn't exist in any objective way. We can describe it as the product of brain functioning. Or we can use the brain in place of the mind or refer to the brain-mind. But when we hear the word 'mind', we instinctively know what it means, even if we can't fully define it. In a similar way, if I say that the human cognitive architecture processes and stores information before retrieving it from storage, we understand the meaning even though the language feels inadequate. We are not computers, far from it, but the terminology helps us comprehend things about us that seem incomprehensible. For this reason, I defer to this terminology throughout the following chapters, while remaining mindful of its shortcomings.

Engagement is another term that divides opinion. What is it to engage in learning? How might a teacher know their class is engaged? This is a term I would often encounter when teaching, especially during an observation lesson. We tend to use proxies for engagement (as we do for many aspects of learning). An observer might see a classroom of students quietly working through a task or listening to the teacher and use these behavioural cues to imply engagement. Perhaps we place an emphasis on silence in the former and eye contact in the latter, but we know from experience we can all look as though we are engaged when in our own heads we've drifted off (meetings spring immediately to mind here). Our attention wanders, perhaps to something in the environment or something within our heads – our minds have a tendency to wander. But just because we cannot necessarily see engagement, this doesn't mean we are not engaged. In laboratory settings, researchers might use eye-tracking or brain scanning technology to measure engagement, but that's impossible in real-world situations. When I refer to engagement in the following chapters, I am most often referring to the objective, experimental kind. If I use it in a more general way, I'm referring to proxies that hint at a degree of engagement.

Cognitive psychology acknowledges that learning is more than memorisation, yet many of its detractors use this argument to reject its role in teaching and learning. The reasons for this are, I suspect, multifaceted. One potential explanation is that cognitive psychology is often still anchored to the past in some people's minds. Models of memory are looking a little tired and worn; there are too many boxes and arrows, and they appear to emphasise the role of remembering useless information like random numbers, letters, or nonsense words. This, combined with the outdated view that the human brain works like a computer, has understandably led many to reject it. But there's more to it than that, I believe. Recent adopters of cognitive science have a tendency to display what can best be described as missionary zeal. Many of these new supports have come from the teaching profession and have arrived with the desire to sweep aside the vestiges of progressive teaching and replace it with something they view as more evidence-based. However, there is also a tendency towards a narrow view of cognitive psychology, emphasising the role of short-term, working, and long-term memory and the need to rehearse information until our eyes bleed (metaphorically speaking). In such an environment, it's hardly surprising that they encounter resistance. While psychologist and educationalist Guy Claxton has attempted to raise many of these concerns, I can't help thinking that all he has achieved is to add fuel to the fire and further divide so-called progressives and traditionalists (Claxton, 2021). This book isn't an attempt to address these concerns directly, yet it challenges some of them inadvertently.

The purpose of this book

I've attempted to disseminate research into learning and offer a broad, flexible framework by which we can learn more effectively. At the heart of the framework lie three guiding principles:

- Memory is the bedrock of learning. Without memory, we cannot learn.
- Learning requires the effective management of cognitive resources. The human brain, while highly efficient, has limitations, and we need to consider these when learning a new task.
- What we know helps us to know more. Prior learning, therefore, can be seen as an investment in future learning.

The book is intended to be approached in its entirety and chronologically. Like learning itself, earlier chapters build a foundation while later ones introduce some nuance and attempt to challenge common misconceptions. For this reason, I have kept much of the repetition that other books might reject.

Confronting learning myths

Teaching and learning have always been fertile breeding grounds for so-called learning myths. During my teaching career, I often spent training days or after-school workshops being introduced to methods with zero evidence base. While some intrigued me, I was equally frustrated with others. The knowledge I'd received during my undergraduate psychology studies meant that many of these methods made little sense within cognitive psychology. I also often found myself teaching psychology students material that ran counter to what these training sessions taught teachers. It often felt as though the teaching profession was promoting techniques that had no chance of succeeding.

One such method involved learning styles. Or, more precisely, the matching hypothesis. This is the notion that educators should match their teaching style to the students' learning style. These styles most often take the form of visual, auditory, and kinaesthetic (the so-called VAK method). Yet despite the popularity of the method, the evidence supporting it is close to non-existent. And we've known this for over two decades. Furthermore, the myth is also alive and well in higher education (Newton, 2015). Maybe educators are conflating learning styles with learning strategies (Hattie & O'Leary, 2025). An aim of learning science is to correct such misunderstandings and offer evidence-based alternatives. Hopefully, the following chapters can help to do this.

Sources, further reading, and acknowledgements

While researching this book, I thought carefully about how best to select sources. Research articles have been chosen from established, peer-reviewed journals, and I have tried to minimise bias as much as is humanly possible. If there is a weakness to a study, I have tried to articulate it; if there is an opposing viewpoint, I have tried my best to consider it. While I have kept sources to respected peer-reviewed journals and academic texts, inspiration and signposts have come from wider reading, including books, blogs, and articles from mainstream sources. There is a list of further reading at the end of some chapters, authored by people I respect and whose judgement I trust. Most are seasoned education professionals with many years of teaching experience, and I'm grateful to all of them, regardless of whether our wider views of the education landscape align.

References

Claxton, G. (2021). *The future of teaching and the myths that hold it back*. Routledge.

Hattie, J., & O'Leary, T. (2025). Learning styles, preferences, or strategies? An explanation for the resurgence of styles across many meta-analyses. *Educational Psychology Review*, *37*(2), 31. https://doi.org/10.1007/s10648-025-10002-w

Neisser, U. (1976). *Cognition and reality*. W.H. Freeman and Company.

Newton, P. M. (2015, December). The learning styles myth is thriving in higher education. *Frontiers in Psychology*, *6*, 1–5. https://doi.org/10.3389/fpsyg.2015.01908

Remembering, knowing, and understanding

> Learning is a change in long-term memory.
>
> – Kirschner et al. (2006)

The above quotation is as succinct as it is problematic. It's accurate within our current understanding of memory and learning. It's problematic because it reduces learning to something to be remembered. Like all quotes, it's out of context, and context is something the following chapters are going to take up a large amount of space discussing. The view that learning is a change in long-term memory was, in 2018, adopted by Ofsted – the Office for Standards in Education, Children's Services and Skills, with jurisdiction over state-run educational institutions in England. It's also a definition that you'll come across in everything from education blogs to teacher conferences. While not universally accepted, it is rather popular. It might be accurate and succinct, but is it a useful definition of learning?

The quotation is specific to a type of learning, the kind that takes place in schools and other centres of education. In contrast, take the following definition: Learning is a mechanism by which organisms can adapt to a changing environment (Anderson, 2000, p.3). The context of the latter definition is much wider than the former, yet much less useful for the teacher working with a group of seven-year-olds or even a university lecturer approaching a lecture theatre filled with eager young undergraduates. The former might imply that learning is little more than remembering, yet learning involves much more than changes in long-term memory. The latter is concerned with survival. Although not the same, both are related. Let me explain.

If there is one teacher from my schooldays that comes easily to mind, it's Mr Jarvis. Mr Jarvis taught English, and even back then (the early 1980s), his style of teaching and general view of the world seemed old-fashioned, even though he couldn't have been very old. Most of all, he seemed to revel in punishing his unruly pupils with lines, and I often found myself on the receiving end of probably the most mind-numbing sanction imaginable. Most teachers would keep it simple – write *I must behave in class* 200 times. Not Mr Jarvis. He was a little more inventive when it came to doling them out. I recall spending my evenings writing line after line of *I must endeavour to remember to furnish myself in all necessary scholastic requisites,* my hand cramping and fingers aching. I cared little for what the sentence meant, and I'm not sure how much of it I understood. But that didn't stifle my ability to copy it down accurately. And I can still recite it word for word from heart more than 40 years later.

Was this a type of learning? That I can still recall those lines implies they led to a change in my long-term memory, and I know I'll still be able to recite them as I draw my final breath. A fitting epitaph, perhaps. The purpose of the lines was an attempt to encourage me to behave in class, not some higher intention, like making me a better learner or, indeed, encouraging me to *endeavour to remember*... etc. The sentence could have been written in German or Icelandic, Klingon or Dothraki – it wouldn't have prevented me from copying the sentence 200, 400, or 600 times. I could still recite the lines with little prompting. Mr Jarvis could have told me to write 200 lines of gibberish, and I would still have been able to accomplish the task.

The lines did something because I can still recall them. I can think about the task and immediately imagine the individual words and the sentence, as if plucking a star from an infinite sky. Repetition led to long-lasting retention – a change in long-term memory. But what did I learn? Initially, the lines taught me the words and the sentence, the letters and spaces, and the sounds as they echoed inside my mind. Over time, they have come to mean something else; I now know what the sentence is about and the definitions of the individual words. Not only do I remember them, but I also understand what the words mean. But this understanding took time and, at first, I neither understood the words on any concrete level nor really cared all that much about them. The ability to recite them by heart, however, became a curious badge of honour, proof that we had found ourselves on the wrong side of Mr Jarvis's ire.

It's not only the words but also the memories attached to the lines. Attached to the words are recollections of my teenage years, of Mr Jarvis and his classroom in the old mansion house building with its huge sash windows overlooking the playing field. And then a nudge, like a billiard ball striking its target, reminding me that his wife sometimes taught French when our regular teacher was off sick or at a meeting or training course. Then another memory. Our regular French teacher informed us on our first day at secondary school that she didn't like children, a disclosure that turned out to be frighteningly accurate. These are all memories, but they are not the same type of memories. Neither do they constitute learning in its strictest sense. Indeed, I can't recall when or where or from whom I learned most of the things I know. And much of what I was taught in school has vanished completely. I have knowledge of many things, and sometimes I can recall them when I decide to or when presented with the appropriate cues. Memory, like learning, is contextual, often tied to time and place (so-called context-dependent memory). I can't think of the lines without also conjuring up the image of Mr Jarvis and his classroom.

This anecdote from my schooldays is simply that, a nostalgic jaunt to illustrate the complex nature of learning and memory. It should not be taken as proof that this is how memory works, but it can add to the overall concept of remembering, knowing, and understanding. In this respect, memory is more than simply being able to recall things. From a much wider perspective, it also has survival value. But our memories also serve a subjective purpose, the answer to the age-old question of who we are on an individual and collective level.

What, then, is it to learn something?

If I asked you to pause for a moment and think about all the things you've learned in your life so far, you'll quickly realise that you'll need longer than a moment. You may have been drawn to your schooldays, to the subjects you studied, and exams completed. Perhaps you asked yourself, what qualifications do I have? But your learning will have begun long before you sat any formal test and even before you attended your first day at school. You have learned to walk and to talk, as well as countless other early developmental skills. The early years of formal education would have focused on reading and writing, basic mathematical skills, perhaps some science, and more creative endeavours. You will also have been learning about how to work with others, behave in a manner deemed appropriate, and become accustomed to routine. You would have practised fine motor skills, the correct way to hold a pen or pencil, and the motions of the hand when creating letters on a page.

Later, you will have learned the skills necessary to carry out tasks related to your profession and might have gained higher qualifications as a means to realise your aspirations. Somewhere along the way, you might have learned to ride a bike, drive a car, tie a tie, and tie shoelaces, to cook – the list goes on. You might be a little stumped about whether you actually learned some things. Did you learn to be an extrovert or an introvert, resilient, conscientious, curious, creative, or a general pain in the neck? We certainly know we learned some things, because we can recall the often-painful journey we undertook to gain skills and knowledge; struggling with algebra or French grammar or tumbling to the ground when learning to ride a bike. Of course, learning French grammar isn't the same as learning to ride a bike, but they are still examples of learning. You need to hold the rules of French grammar in memory, but riding a bike is more about teaching our body to balance, to pedal, to work the brakes, and remain mindful of the wider environment. You may well forget your French grammar in later life, but you'll never forget how to ride a bike. Learning a new language and learning to ride a bike result in the formation of new neural pathways, pathways that grow in strength as we practice saying the words, writing them down, or listening to conversations. Or engage our limbs in the repetitive actions of cycling. Sometimes, however, we're not even aware we've learned something, because the mechanisms involved are beyond our conscious experience.

There are, therefore, many types of learning, some formal and intentional, others unconscious. We might choose to learn, or others might compel us to, and this is going to impact how we learn. We may also learn certain behavioural responses with no intention or coercion. This includes what we call conditioned responses, such as reacting to bells and whistles. Many reflexes, such as leaping out of the way of a sudden obstacle, seem pre-wired into our biology. We might learn to fear dogs because of a negative experience with one in the past. We then unconsciously generalise a specific incident with a particular dog to all dogs in every situation (no explicit instruction required). Interestingly, we can also intentionally learn to overcome these fears through methods developed to treat an array of psychological conditions.

We also learn unconsciously from others, a phenomenon known as social learning. We learn to behave in a certain way from our parents, peers, and characters from fiction in both positive and negative directions. Research has discovered, for example, that young drivers take more risks when they are carrying passengers of a similar age, but not ones that are significantly older (Simons-Morton et al., 2019). People's behaviour is therefore linked to learning and maturation and might come about through experience, exposure to other people's behaviour, or as a wider response to living in a complex society. Role models are important for this type of learning to take place, be they positive or negative.

Some learning is, therefore, implicit, or latent. There are many things we learn without knowing we've learned them. They appear to bypass conscious memory completely. The products of this implicit learning may reveal themselves in our attitudes, behaviour, or opinions. They may even lie dormant until we need them.

Learning and memory

It's impossible to describe learning without relying heavily on explanations of memory. As we'll see, learning requires the ability to remember. If we have significantly impaired memory function, perhaps because of brain trauma, learning is often much slower and sometimes impossible. For this reason, much of this book will focus on memory processes and what we currently understand about how memory works. But learning isn't just about our ability to recall information, the primary metric by which we know if we have learned something. One important debate in memory research concerns the distinction between recognition and recall. Recognition is the ability to remember something as familiar. We might, for example, see someone and recognise them as someone we know, even if we can't recall their name or from where we know them – it's a feeling of familiarity, void of context and detail. Similarly, a song might come on the radio, and we think *I know this song*. However, we can't recall either the name of the song or the artist.

Recollection, on the other hand, is when we recall something. It's the conscious retrieval of an item, often complete with contextual details. This might include the moment we first encountered the item. Perhaps you heard a song on the radio at a particularly significant time in your life. In education settings, we might be asked about, say, the events leading up to the First World War. Answering the question requires us to recall this information, not simply knowing that we know it. Compare this to a multiple-choice question where we are presented with five possible answers to a question. One of the possible answers will, hopefully, appear more familiar than the others, but we won't need to recall it to answer; we simply need to tick the box next to the item that creates a feeling of familiarity. We can think of these two processes as related to remembering (recollection) and knowing (familiarity), although the processes involved are rarely so clear-cut and the differences are more likely to appear on a continuum (Ingram et al., 2012).

We often see these distinctions made in memory research. Say I was to present you with a list of words to memorise and, after a brief interval, ask you to recall them. Chances are you'd recall some. However, if after memorising the words I gave you a list that included both the words you memorised and some other unrelated words and then asked you to identify what was included in the original list, chances are you'd correctly identify more of the words. You might not have remembered all the words, but you will have acquired a familiarity with them.

These differences explain why we can't always put a name to face (or name the title and artist of a song we recognise). How often have you declared, it's on the tip of my tongue? This is precisely what memory researchers call this experience: The tip-of-the-tongue phenomenon, or TOT. It reflects the different processes our brains utilise to both store and recall information. In Chapter 4, we'll dive more deeply into the science of memory.

What is knowledge?

Learning and memory are, therefore, deeply entwined. In this respect, the quote at the beginning of this chapter is spot on. When we learn, long-term memory changes, as do the connections between neurons – new connections may form or existing connections may strengthen. Some of these connections allow me to recall Mr Jarvis's lines effortlessly, others create a feeling of familiarity. If someone were to ask me, do you remember Mr Jarvis's lines? I would be able to answer quickly and confidently, without having to actively recall them. This familiarity represents knowing, but how does this knowing relate to knowledge? And what is knowledge anyway?

Within formal education settings, there is often much talk about knowledge and knowledge rich, but often notions of what knowledge represents differ depending on where individual and collective biases lie. This is a book primarily concerned with cognition; it views knowledge within a cognitive paradigm. I'll, therefore, sidestep social, cultural, and ideological views concerned with these complex matters, although there is a legitimate need for debate over who chooses the knowledge included in a knowledge-rich curriculum. Because of my side-stepping, the definitions presented here might appear somewhat clinical, but they are chosen for the best fit within the overall aim of this book.

I've hopefully established that learning cannot happen without memory. Equally important is the notion that not all types of learning are the same, and neither do they serve the same purpose. Knowledge is another one of those notions that we tend to understand instinctively without having to give it much thought. So, let's begin with a couple of definitions, just so we are all on the same page, so to speak. Put simply, knowledge is all the information in one's memory (McCarthy & McNamara, 2021). Information, in this respect, is used in a broad sense as an individual's personal stock of information, skills, experiences, beliefs, and memories (Alexander et al., 1991). We might have knowledge of childhood experiences, motor skills, historical dates, mathematical formulas, and so on. All these things represent knowledge. Knowledge is all that we know to be true, but also what we believe to be true, so knowledge also encompasses memory and learning errors, misremembered facts, false information, and misinformation (the last two are perhaps particularly pertinent in the current climate). We might have knowledge of how to ride a bike and of French grammar, but we might also have knowledge that the Earth is flat, and the moon landings were faked. Your knowledge of how to ride a bike is accurate, your knowledge of French grammar might be accurate, but we can safely say that the final two are undoubtedly false, despite them being examples of knowledge (at least within the parameters we have set). The knowledge we have (prior knowledge) is therefore going to impact every aspect of our lives, regardless of its accuracy. A belief in a flat Earth, for example, will impact our ability to understand gravity and the motions of the planets. It's going to impact how effectively we learn.

Knowing how and know that

I know *how* to ride a bike, but I know Wellington is the capital of New Zealand. These are distinct types of knowing and require different types of learning. Canadian cognitive psychologist Endel Tulving distinguished between noetic consciousness (knowing) and autonoetic consciousness (remembering). Knowing is our awareness of information about the world. It relies on the memory of general knowledge or facts. From a cognitive science perspective, knowing is a feeling of familiarity, that we have encountered the information before, even though we may not be able to bring it immediately to mind (Tulving, 1985). For example, you know what the capital of France is, but it is only as you read this sentence that you actively recall Paris. Remembering, on the other hand, involves a vivid recollection of the past, often accompanied by a sense that we are travelling back in time and re-experiencing it. Understanding involves comprehending the underlying principles, meanings, or reasons behind a concept. To understand something, you need to connect ideas and see how parts relate to a whole. It allows for analysis, application, and creativity in using information. We might know Paris is the capital of France (a fact), but understanding the historical, geographical, and cultural significance of Paris enhances our knowledge.

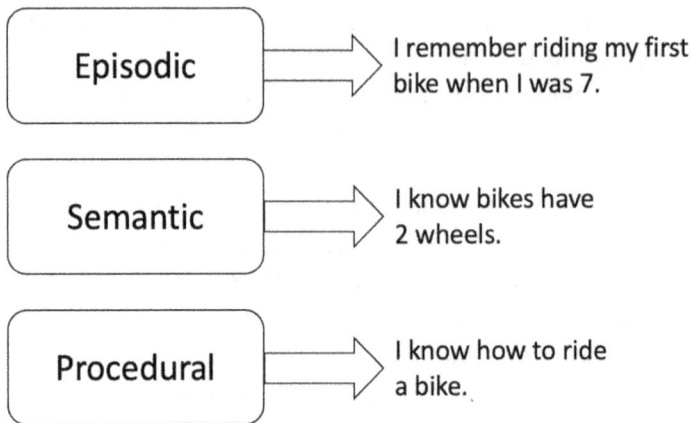

Figure 1.1 Three types of knowing (based on Cohen and Squire, 1980).

Let's look at another example. I have vivid memories of when I first rode a bicycle. I was seven years old and living in New Zealand. I borrowed a bike from my friend Wayne, and we rode up and down his driveway. At first, I wobbled and fell off a few times, but eventually got the hang of it. I knew then and know now that bikes have two wheels. Most importantly, I know how to ride a bike. These three things constitute different types of memory and, therefore, different types of learning. Tulving calls the first type of memory episodic. It's an episode of my life that I can recall. The second, he calls semantic. This is my knowledge of bikes – that they have two wheels. The third is procedural. It's the ability to ride the bike based on what my body has learned to do. The first two, Cohen and Squire, describe as declarative or knowing that. The third, they call procedural, or knowing how (Cohen & Squire, 1980). I know a bike has two wheels (declarative), but I know how to ride a bike (procedural). We'll return to these distinctions in Chapter 4 (Figure 1.1).

Knowing and understanding

If knowledge is all the information we have stored in long-term memory, does this knowledge represent the product of learning? The short answer is yes, because even incorrect knowledge has led to a change in long-term memory, which (according to the quote at the beginning of this chapter) is what learning is. Let us, then, assess your learning, as well as your confidence in it.

Consider the following questions. On a scale of 1–10 (where 1 is I definitely don't know and 10 is I definitely know), gauge how confident you feel in your ability to answer them correctly.

- What is the capital of France?
- What is the world's largest land mammal?
- What was the middle name of Wolfgang Mozart?

- What year was the Battle of Hastings?
- The Velocipede was a nineteenth-century prototype of what?
- Which actor starred in The Matrix?

Chances are, you've picked 1 or 10 for most of these. You either know the answer or you don't (or you believe you know the answer, but your answer might be wrong). Curiously, you might know who starred in The Matrix but cannot bring the name to mind (the TOT phenomenon). Whatever your answer, the destination is certain, and the answer is right or wrong.

Now, imagine you have to explain the following concepts to someone with no knowledge of the concept. Again, rate your confidence on a scale from 1 to 10.

- Climate change
- Vaccines
- Depression
- Memory.

You may have opted for 10 on some of these, but I suspect your confidence is lower than for the first list. And now for the disappointing part – you've probably over-estimated your ability to explain most of the topics in the second list. You may, of course, have specialist knowledge, in which case your high confidence score would be justified.

Although we might not describe ourselves as experts, we are pretty confident in our ability to explain a range of topics, from climate change and vaccines to politics. Some of us are more confident than others, and many of us will have witnessed spats on social media or face-to-face public forums when a layperson feels confident enough to question the views of someone considered an expert on the topic. There were suddenly an awful lot of virologists during the COVID-19 pandemic, and many of them had no training in virology, medicine, or any other related discipline. They did believe, however, that they had found the truth and that this truth had been overlooked by the international scientific community, which had been working flat out to better understand the virus. This is an extreme example, but it isn't uncommon.

Our confidence in our understanding of many things usually far outweighs our ability to explain them. The first set of questions are facts with a right or wrong answer – you either know a velocipede was an early bicycle prototype or not. What if I asked you to name the capital of Australia rather than France? You might know this instinctively, but you might be thinking, *I know it's not Sydney.* There are historical reasons the capital of Australia is Canberra, and not Sydney or Melbourne, and knowing these reasons may help us recall the correct capital. I know Mozart's middle name was Amadeus, not because I have a particular interest in classical music, but because I recall Falco's *Rock Me Amadeus*, which reached number one in the UK charts the year I left school. What about the Battle of Hastings? I know it was 1066, and that it was the beginning of the Norman conquest of England. I know I know the answer (I have knowledge of it), but I don't know how I know it. Chances are, I learned it at school, but it's one of those dates that many people (certainly in the United Kingdom) appear to know instinctively. Regular exposure to school, television, and books imprints the date onto our minds. If you're in the United States, the date might mean little to you, although 1776 will. 1789 will have greater significance for the French people than 1066, so what we remember is often tied to culture, history, and nationality. Despite knowing the date of the Battle of Hastings, however, if I were asked to explain the event in any depth, I would probably struggle beyond the basics.

There are other questions I could ask. Some you would know, some you won't know, while others you may think you know with 100 percent accuracy but actually don't. If I asked you to estimate the memory span of a goldfish, you might confidently answer three seconds. This is an example of a factual error, in that goldfish have perfectly adequate memory spans and can even be trained to perform tricks (Sibeaux et al., 2022). Similarly, we may know that the Great Wall of China is visible from space. Only it's not – just ask an astronaut. Often, our factual errors occur through misunderstanding or comprehension issues. But they may also occur because of our inability to distinguish reliable sources from unreliable ones. At other times, we might accept something as fact because it fits with our beliefs, a well-known phenomenon called confirmation bias.

Now, look again at the second set of questions. How would you explain, say, climate change or vaccines to someone? Go on, try it. I used to think I was pretty knowledgeable about climate change and global warming until I had to explain the concepts to someone else. I could describe the basic idea of climate change, but my answer lacked depth – lacked actual knowledge of the topic (if you're a science teacher, you'll be much better at it than I am). What really betrayed my lack of knowledge was when I was asked questions about it or asked to clarify particular areas. My ability to elaborate was woefully lacking. Before I had to explain it, I would have given myself an 8 or 9. After, it would have been much lower.

The problem with explanatory tasks is that there is no defined endpoint, and we don't really know how much we know (or don't know) until we begin our explanation. If you've dedicated your life to explaining climate change to the public, studying it, researching it, and teaching about it, then your initial confidence rating is justified. But most of us aren't environmental scientists and climatologists, so we overestimate our understanding. This disparity between what we think we know and what we actually know is a cognitive bias called the illusion of explanatory depth (Rozenblit & Keil, 2002). The illusion of explanatory depth holds that we have less knowledge about a topic than we think we do, a bias that's revealed when we are expected to explain it. Explanation requires elaboration, while facts do not. Explanation involves remembering, but elaboration is more than recall.

Knowledge is therefore not synonymous with understanding, although we can assume that any attempts at a knowledge-rich curriculum will also require students to understand that knowledge. Nevertheless, students may often have limited opportunities to make sense of or understand what they learn due to the emphasis often placed on memory and the neglect of understanding. From a scientific standpoint, assessing understanding is difficult, while establishing simpler forms of learning (such as facts) is relatively straightforward, which is perhaps why curricula often prioritise knowledge over understanding. As we can see with the illusion of explanatory depth, many of us know a lot of facts, but bringing these facts together to understand them is a much more cognitively complex task than recalling snippets of information.

The confusion between knowledge and understanding isn't confined to the layperson. According to Joanna Huxster, even in peer-reviewed literature, researchers often conflate knowing with understanding (Huxster et al., 2018). The difference is like someone telling us they know about music because they can name all the instruments in an orchestra. Just because I've watched a YouTube video about quantum physics or the life of Emily Brontë, it doesn't automatically follow that I have learned anything about either, even though I might be able to reel off some pertinent facts about them. Defining the difference between knowledge and understanding might at first appear superfluous, but if we are going to design curricula that do more than create superficial knowledge, it's worth taking the time to investigate these differences.

Huxster describes knowledge as an atomistic epistemic state, meaning that knowledge is focused on singular, discrete pieces of information. Understanding, on the other hand, represents a holistic epistemic state, or the ability to grasp a body of facts and how they relate to each other. Understanding goes beyond knowledge, requiring the individual to work with learned information while remaining flexible to new information. Someone with a knowledge of climate change, for example, will know that the Earth's climate is warming, and that carbon dioxide is a greenhouse gas. They also know that human activity contributes to greenhouse gas emissions. These pieces of knowledge can be acquired through various means, including reading, listening, and memorising. We can then assess this knowledge using, for example, a multiple-choice test or other methods requiring limited answers. Understanding, however, requires the learner to grasp how these facts are interconnected. To assess if the person understands climate change, we'll have to employ a different assessment method, one that requires a more elaborate answer, such as the following tasks:

- Explain how increased greenhouse gas emissions led to global warming.
- Explain how different human activities contribute to greenhouse gas emissions.
- Explain the scientific process through which climate scientists reach their conclusions.

- Analyse how climate change impacts various systems, such as sea-level rise and extreme weather.
- Evaluate the validity of different claims about climate change.

An individual with a knowledge of climate change, therefore, might be able to recite facts and figures, but they may struggle when presented with new information or counterarguments. In contrast, someone with an understanding of climate change could apply their knowledge to new situations, critically evaluate new claims, and articulate their understanding in their own words.

As learners, we often draw generalisations based on specific examples or observations. This might be a student studying examples of mathematical problems or a trainee surgeon observing a superior carry out a heart operation. This approach, generally referred to as induction learning, involves identifying patterns or rules from observed data or specific instances and using those patterns to make predictions about new, unseen data – the key route towards understanding. A rookie surgeon won't learn everything about open-heart surgery through observation because there are a multitude of scenarios that might arise. Rather, they will take what they have learned and use it to inform future judgments. Becoming a surgeon takes many years of study, observation, and practice – you can't become skilled by watching a video or googling *how do I do a heart bypass operation on my 80-year-old gran?* When we learn, the process must consider what it is we are learning. Google won't turn me into a heart surgeon, but neither will sitting in a classroom and being told how to do a heart bypass surgery. It can teach me something about heart surgery, but I'll also need to accumulate hours of observation time and hands-on practice.

Remembering, knowing, and understanding are collectively part of the learning process. At each stage, long-term memory changes. Memorising English monarchs will change my long-term memory, as will learning multiplication tables. But learning is also concerned with what we do with this information. My ability to reel off every king and queen of England is a nice party trick but has very low utility unless I can connect this information to wider aspects of history. Learning multiplication tables, on the other hand, allows me to become more efficient regarding mental arithmetic. Mr Jarvis's lines changed the structure of long-term memory, but how useful that change was remains unknown.

We can describe these stages in different ways or build complex hierarchies, from simple forms of learning to ascending levels of complexity. However, from a cognitive science perspective, each stage will result in a change in long-term memory. We can describe these changes in respect to depth of processing, a term coined by psychologists Fergus Craik and Robert Lockhart in the 1970s (Craik & Lockhart,1972). Within levels of processing theory, memorisation would constitute the shallowest form of learning. We could, for example, memorise a list of made-up words and recite them verbatim or write them down. This would constitute a type of learning, but it's of very little use on its own. The focus here is on how the information looks and sounds, rather than an attempt to integrate this information into the information we already have. Shallow processing doesn't require any attempts at critical thinking or elaboration. Intermediate processing requires a little more effort and results in better learning. We might, for example, be expected to recognise relationships and structures rather than surface features. This level would include identifying spelling or phonetic patterns in language (such as 'e' rules, as in hat and hate), or grouping similar items together, such as sorting animals into mammals, reptiles, and amphibians. The deepest level of processing requires the learner to make connections between new and prior learning, engage in critical thinking, reflect on their own learning (or employ metacognitive strategies), as well as engage emotionally with the to-be-learned information. We can see how the increasingly deeper levels map onto memorisation and understanding. We'll look more closely at Craik and Lockhart's theory in Chapter 4 and at how we engage emotion in Chapter 11. In Chapter 13, we'll look at how we can incorporate this model into instructional design.

Chapter summary

- The view that learning is a change in long-term memory, while accurate, represents an oversimplification and might not be particularly useful for educators.
- Memory and learning are deeply intertwined, in that the former is vital if the latter is to be successful. Repetition, while resulting in permanent changes in long-term memory, does not always lead to understanding.
- Remembering, knowing, and understanding are three related but distinct concepts. Remembering involves the conscious retrieval of information with context, knowing is a feeling of familiarity, and understanding goes beyond recalling facts to involve grasping relationships and applying knowledge.
- Knowledge is defined as all the information in one's memory, including facts, skills, experiences, and beliefs, even if inaccurate.
- The illusion of explanatory depth is the cognitive bias where individuals overestimate their understanding of a topic, revealed when they attempt to explain it in detail.
- Learning includes formal, informal, intentional, and unconscious learning, such as social learning and conditioned responses.
- Levels of Processing Theory posits that deeper processing, involving making connections to prior knowledge and critical thinking, leads to better learning and understanding compared to shallow processing focused on memorisation.

Further reading

Kirschner, P. A., & Hendrick, C. (2020). *How learning happens: Seminal works in educational psychology and what they mean in practice.* Routledge.

Sloman, S., & Fernbach, P. (2017). *The knowledge illusion.* Pan.

References

Alexander, P. A., Schallert, D. L., & Hare, V. C. (1991). Coming to terms: How researchers in learning and literacy talk about knowledge. *Review of Educational Research, 61*(3), 315. https://www.jstor.org/stable/1170635

Anderson J. R. (2000). *Cognitive psychology and its implications.* New York: Worth Publishers.

Cohen, N. J., & Squire, L. R. (1980). Preserved learning and retention of pattern-analyzing skill in amnesia: Dissociation of knowing how and knowing that. *Science, 210*(4466), 207–210. https://doi.org/10.1126/science.7414331

Craik, F. I. M., & Lockhart, R. S. (1972). Levels of processing: A framework for memory research. *Journal of Verbal Learning and Verbal Behavior, 11*(6), 671–684. https://doi.org/10.1016/S0022-5371(72)80001-X

Huxster, J. K., Slater, M. H., Leddington, J., LoPiccolo, V., Bergman, J., Jones, M., McGlynn, C., Diaz, N., Aspinall, N., Bresticker, J., & Hopkins, M. (2018). Understanding "understanding" in public understanding of science. *Public Understanding of Science, 27*(7), 756–771. https://doi.org/10.1177/0963662517735429

Ingram, K. M., Mickes, L., & Wixted, J. T. (2012). Recollection can be weak and familiarity can be strong. *Journal of Experimental Psychology: Learning Memory and Cognition, 38*(2), 325–339. https://doi.org/10.1037/a0025483

McCarthy, K. S., & McNamara, D. S. (2021). The multidimensional knowledge in text comprehension framework. *Educational Psychologist, 56*(3), 196–214. https://doi.org/10.1080/00461520.2021.1872379

Rozenblit, L., & Keil, F. (2002). The misunderstood limits of folk science: An illusion of explanatory depth. *Cognitive Science, 26*(5), 521–562. https://doi.org/10.1016/S0364-0213(02)00078-2

Sibeaux, A., Karlsson, C., Newport, C., & De Perera, T. B. (2022). Distance estimation in the goldfish (Carassius auratus). *Proceedings of the Royal Society B: Biological Sciences, 289*(1984). https://doi.org/10.1098/rspb.2022.1220

Simons-Morton, B. G., Bingham, R., Li, K., Hu, C., Buckley, L., Falk, E., & Shope, J. (2019, April). The effect of teenage passengers on simulated risky driving among teenagers: A randomized trial. *Frontiers in Psychology, 10.* https://doi.org/10.3389/fpsyg.2019.00923

Tulving, E. (1985). Memory and consciousness. *Canadian Psychology/Psychologie Canadienne, 26*(1), 1–12. https://doi.org/10.1037/h0080017

2 Wired to learn

We are born to learn. From the moment of birth, our brains are gathering information and processing huge amounts of data. We are learning about movement, separating human features from non-human ones, exploring our bodies, and exploring the world. Of course, all living organisms learn – recent evidence even suggests that amoebae are capable of very simple learning, despite not having a brain or any form of central nervous system (De la Fuente et al., 2019). But the sophistication embodied within the human brain makes us unique among the many creatures with which we share this planet.

Learning is part of the human evolutionary journey and functions to protect our species and extend our capacities and capabilities. Our prehistoric ancestors would, for example, need to learn where to find food and remember where they found it. They would have needed this information to make plans, such as knowing when food would be plentiful or become scarce. Early nomadic hunter-gatherers would most likely have detected the change in the seasons and used this knowledge as a sign that it was time to move on. Later, they would have learned to make tools, grow crops, produce art, and develop methods of writing and mathematics. All this information would be remembered, acted upon, and shared with others. As our brains grew and cognitive capacities increased, our lives became more complex and sophisticated, ultimately leading to higher levels of thinking and further adaptation to the neurological system.

This journey led to the development of innate mental structures, hard-wired systems that interacted with the environment and made learning happen. These systems include memory structures that allow us to retain and recall information. Once our ancient ancestors developed the ability to do this, the world unfolded before them, and they could engage in intentional foraging for food, storage of that food, and, eventually, toolmaking, farming, and a multitude of other skills. It then became possible to pass these skills to the next generation, who would adapt them and pass the knowledge to others. But memories of the near and distant past also allow humans to predict the future. Our ancient ancestors would have needed to know about the changing seasons, that winter makes food more difficult to come by, developing methods of food storage and preservation. This type of thinking would have required not just the ability to predict, but also the imagination and creativity to invest in and develop new techniques. Our ability to imagine is, itself, reliant on memory systems. Our imagination uses what we know, often in highly creative ways, but we still need to know something to imagine something else.

These innate structures also include language systems, as well as structures that allow us to perceive animate and inanimate objects, and ones that encourage us to differentiate between pro-social and anti-social responses to situations (who we perceive to be good or helpful and bad or harmful). We are even born with the innate ability to understand simple arithmetic. These systems develop even before birth, yet it is within the first months following our emergence into what William James called the blooming, buzzing confusion that this innate, or core, knowledge really takes flight.

David Geary approaches knowledge from the perspective of evolutionary psychology (Geary, 2008). Evolutionary psychology represents the marriage of evolutionary theory with classic cognitive psychology, positing that many psychological traits, such as memory, perception, emotions, and social behaviours, are adaptations that evolved to solve recurring problems faced by our ancestors in their environment. Many of the traits are said to have been acquired during the Pleistocene epoch between 2.6 million and 11,700 years ago. Early humans at the time lived in small groups of hunter-gatherers during a time when we see the greatest leaps in human evolution. This includes the first instances of tools for working stone, wood, ivory, as well as weapons for hunting. It's during this time (known to evolutionary psychology as the Era of Evolutionary Adaptation) that we first see the creation of symbolic art and sculpture, implying that human cognitive capacities had evolved to use and apply imagination.

Geary suggests that human knowledge can be divided into two types: biologically primary knowledge and biologically secondary knowledge. The first type of knowledge is evolutionary and assumes that humans have evolved to acquire knowledge. Some knowledge, therefore, is part of our evolutionary journey. This includes our ability to learn to listen to and speak our native language, engage in general problem solving, and the ability to recognise human faces. Such knowledge is modular, in that it would have developed independently of each other and at different times in human history. For example, the ability to recognise faces may have developed at different time than our ability to problem solve. Biologically, primary knowledge is also generic-cognitive, in that it represents a basic skill that can be applied to a variety of domains. Problem-solving skills, for example, represent the use of means-end strategies, or knowing where we currently are in a task, knowing where we need to be, and reducing the difference between the two. According to this view, biologically primary knowledge can be learned by most people, but it can't be taught.

Biologically, secondary knowledge, on the other hand, represents acquired knowledge. This includes the type of knowledge that's taught in schools, colleges, and universities. This knowledge isn't modular and is largely domain-specific. For example, humans haven't evolved to solve algebraic equations or to read. These things, according to Geary, require explicit teaching to acquire. This implies that teaching, in most cases, must take the form of explicit instruction. According to this view, therefore, we can teach algebra, but we can't teach critical thinking.

Geary's view has many admirers, including advocates of cognitive load theory, which I'll discuss in later chapters. It isn't without its critics. Some of these criticisms are also levelled at evolutionary psychology more generally, while others are directed at Geary's theory specifically. Many of the more general criticisms come from evolutionary biologists who see evolutionary psychology as too deterministic and lacking empirical rigour. The speculative nature of the discipline means that evolutionary psychologists often reach conclusions that have little empirical support. Furthermore, to narrow the acquisition of biologically primary knowledge to a specific epoch in human history can be seen to oversimplify the dynamic and ongoing nature of human evolution when seen through the lens of evolutionary psychology.

Another criticism levelled at evolutionary psychology comes from cognitive psychology and neuroscience. If we view the human mind as modular, as evolutionary psychology does, composed of domain-specific computational modules, this leads to all sorts of problems when it comes to the brain's ability to adapt to changing circumstances and experiences. The notion of biologically primary and biologically secondary knowledge is often seen as at odds with established notions like neural plasticity. Critics argue that evolutionary psychology often neglects the role of culturally mediated behaviour (Peters, 2013; Ward, 2012). One example would be that of cognitive abilities. As we'll see, some activities (such as learning a musical instrument or a foreign language) can induce physical changes in the brain, including growth in areas such as visual-spatial, verbal, and mathematical skills. Reconciling such evidence with that of a modular mind as described by evolutionary psychology can be seen as problematic.

Specific to Geary's theory, cognitive scientist Guy Claxton argues that it's little more than a mash-up of notions culled from evolutionary theory and the last 60 years of cognitive science (Claxton, 2021, p.174). Claxton calls into question Geary's assumption that all forms of learning and problem-solving that are not controlled are achieved effortlessly. Many tasks (including those involving hard-wired systems), suggests Claxton, still require a great deal of effort. Finally, Claxton questions Geary's proposal that academic learning becomes more difficult over time, leading to a drop in motivation and engagement. One criticism levelled at evolutionary psychology more generally is that it tends to ignore individual differences, and this is perhaps what Claxton is referring to here. While many learners lack motivation and remain reluctant to engage as their learning becomes harder, not all do. Indeed, some thrive in such environments. This is particularly the case with older, more independent learners.

Despite disagreements between evolutionary psychology, evolutionary biology, and cognitive neuroscience, there is little debate over the innate nature of many human abilities. It's well understood that within only a few months following birth, infants know that some objects only move if acted upon by an external force, while other objects (people and animals) can move without being physically pushed or pulled. They also understand that objects cannot simply vanish and cannot be in two places at once. But how do we know infants know this? By observing the behaviour of infants under experimental conditions, researchers have found babies act surprised when objects appear to violate the laws of physics (a phenomenon known, unsurprisingly, as cognitive surprise).

Eye-tracking technology determines where babies look and for how long they maintain their gaze. By doing this, researchers can measure the degree of surprise. At only a few weeks old, babies already possess deep intuitions of the physical world and show shock when their experiences don't live up to their expectations. However, although babies may possess a vast knowledge of the world, they don't know everything, and it takes a few months for them to understand how the physical world works. To do this, they behave like scientists, testing their hypotheses and learning from their observations. At first, babies know that objects fall when dropped, and they'll test this hypothesis again and again by continually dropping things, much to the frustration of their parents. Then, they will begin to understand that some objects can be supported by other objects. When they place a toy on a table, they understand the table is going to support it, but if they push the toy to the edge of the table, at some point, it's going to fall. While the toy stays put when placed on top of the table, through experimentation, they'll soon realise that this is not the case when they place the toy on the underside. But not all objects act like this, and from very early on (the first year of life), infants understand that not all objects are the same. Babies don't show surprise that some objects walk around and move by themselves in ways inanimate objects don't. By about ten months old, infants are attributing personalities to these objects.

If we show a baby a scene in which an adult throws a child to the ground, they turn away from the person and much prefer an adult who helps the child up. However, they can deduce that, sometimes, doing harm is unintentional. One study conducted by Marine Buon and colleagues from the French National Centre for Scientific Research found that 29-month-old toddlers and 10-month-old preverbal infants could discriminate between the actions of someone whose behaviour was positive (comforting in the study) and a person whose behaviour was negative (harmful). Not only could they tell the difference between positive and negative behaviour, but they also displayed a preference for the person who displayed the positive behaviour (Buon et al., 2014). It appears they have already formulated some understanding of what it is to be mean or nice, or good or bad, long before they have developed any concrete notions of these concepts or have the vocabulary to describe them. This might imply that, from a very early stage, infants can distinguish between bad behaviour and good behaviour. But there are still many unanswered questions that cannot be scientifically and systematically investigated, so any discussion over whether people are born good, bad, or indifferent is somewhat pointless. Indeed, the debate over whether people are born good or bad is best left to those willing to overlook the inability to reach such conclusions scientifically.

Perhaps the most interesting area of investigation concerns infants' knowledge of numbers. We might assume that mathematical skills are learned. This is true to a point, yet from a very early age, babies appear to understand numbers instinctively, albeit at a very simple level. For example, if we repeatedly present babies with slides showing two objects, they eventually get bored. Yet, if we add a third object, they will stare at the scene for longer, implying they have detected the change.

By manipulating the size, density, and nature of objects, we can better investigate infants' understanding of number. If we show infants several objects and accompany the objects with a sound, say 'tu', they show greater interest in the scene if the repetition of the sound matches the number of objects. So, if I were to present an infant with four cubed blocks and the sound 'tu, tu, tu, tu', they would show greater interest in the scene than if the sound had only two repetitions. Babies, therefore, appear to possess the ability to recognise and approximate numbers without the need to count.

But can babies calculate? If a nine-month-old baby watched me hide an object behind a screen and I then took a second object and placed that behind the screen, the baby should assume there are two objects behind the screen – simple enough. However, if I were to remove one object without the baby knowing and then lift the screen to reveal the remaining single object, the baby would show surprise. One object would be missing. If I lifted the screen and revealed both the original objects, the baby wouldn't show any interest. Infants only a few months old know that $1 + 1 = 2$, and if it doesn't, the baby displays surprise. The infant knows what is behind the screen because it has created an internal mental model of the hidden scene and holds that information in a system known as working memory. There, the baby can manipulate by adding or removing objects (working memory is going to play an important role in the chapters to come).

Evidence points to arithmetic as being innate, and newborn babies appear to perceive numbers within a few hours of life (this is also true for other animals, including monkeys and corvids, such as crows and magpies). Infants certainly refine these skills over time, but the necessary apparatus is there from birth. Both numbers and objects, therefore, represent core knowledge, those faculties that are present at birth and allow for the development of more complex thought.

Nowhere can we see this rapid acquisition of skills more than in language learning. Babies appear to learn to speak effortlessly and naturally, provided they are raised in an environment where language is spoken. At only a few days old, when babies hear the sound 'a', they open their mouths in a way that corresponds with the sound. If they hear the sound 'e', they will move their mouths differently. Even before they have knowledge of their own mouths, babies are trying to create the sounds they hear. In one interesting study, Stanislas Dehaene and Ghislaine Dehaene-Lambertz scanned the brains of babies while they slept and listened to speech. They discovered that the same brain regions were active in three-month-old babies as in adult brains when they heard speech in their native language, suggesting that brain organisation doesn't have to wait for experience to accumulate to process language – the ability already exists (see Dehaene, 2021).

For us to learn our own language, we need the ability to categorise the sounds that make it up (called phonemes). Newborn babies can distinguish between all speech sounds and are actually more sensitive to these sounds than adults. For the first 12 months or so, this sound discrimination is determined by the sounds the infant experiences in the environment, but beyond about 12 months, they lose the ability to distinguish between sounds they are not exposed to. We can illustrate this process by looking at the Japanese language. Native Japanese speakers cannot distinguish between L and R sounds because the Japanese language doesn't contain such sounds. But Japanese babies can distinguish between L and R; only they lose the ability to do this once the sensitive period has passed (about 12 months). Similar findings have been discovered in other languages. This is an example of a sensitive period of development. It was previously called the critical period, but it's become clear that the window of opportunity is left a little open. We know children raised in environments where they don't experience spoken language make much slower gains when they attempt to speak later, while some never get to grips with spoken language at all. This is one reason reading to even very young children is so important for their later development. What we see is that children who begin their schooling with a good grasp of language tend to do better academically, while those with poorer language skills rarely catch up to their more competent peers. We'll look at some of the reasons for this in Chapter 8. As for adults, learning becomes harder later in life, but it's not impossible, as we'll see later.

Learning, therefore, arises through an interaction between innate structures and new environmental inputs. We are born knowing how to speak, but we need to experience a world in which language is spoken if we, ourselves, are going to learn to speak.

The human brain

The brain is at the centre of all learning. This incredible feat of biological and evolutionary engineering weighs in at around 1.4 kg and has 86 billion cells, or neurons, and around 100 trillion connections. As we learn, these connections grow, and stronger connections represent better learning. Neurons enable different parts of the brain to communicate with each other. But the brain not only contains neurons. Astrocytes, or star cells, support the nervous system by providing nutrition and regulating what can pass into the brain from the rest of the body, while oligodendrocytes wrap around neurons and provide support, enabling the neurons to transmit information quickly. Our nervous system, like that of other animals, can adapt continually to changing circumstances. It can also find new ways of learning even after experiencing damage. When we learn something new, our brain changes. The more we use our brain, the more it changes. This means that the more we repeat an action, the stronger the connection becomes and the less likely the connection will weaken. It's certainly the case that plasticity decreases with age, just not as much as we once thought. Even the adult brain has an enormous capacity for change, regardless of sensitive developmental periods and increasing years.

Knowing that our brains are wired to learn is rather comforting for those of us who might find learning new things either difficult or daunting. Your brain is learning now. With each word and sentence you translate into a form you can understand, store, and later recall, you are altering your complex neural network by encouraging some of those 86 billion brain cells to talk to each other. Our neurons are basically electrical devices, like tiny batteries, communicating via electrical events known as action potentials. Neurons don't touch each other, but there is a tiny junction between them known as a synapse. The action potential causes the neuron to release a chemical messenger called a neurotransmitter. Types of neurotransmitters include glutamate, serotonin, and dopamine, and they carry different messages from one neuron to another. They can also help (excite) or hinder (inhibit) the receiving neuron from firing its own action potential.

The more we repeat an action, such as practice chord progressions on the guitar or memorise French vocabulary, the stronger the connections between these cells. A stronger connection leads to greater stability and resilience, so we are less likely to forget what we've memorised. In addition, during this process, neurons are often forced to grow new branches and axons (or nerve fibres). These then surround themselves with a sheath of fat composed of lipids and proteins called myelin via a process known as cortical myelination. Myelin insulates and protects the axons while allowing electrical impulses to travel quickly and efficiently. Cortical myelination is determined both by genetics and the environment, with genetic factors accounting for up to 66 percent. However, there remains a significant environmental component. Environmental factors are most noticeable during the earlier stages of brain development – so-called developmental myelination. While myelination peaks in infancy, it continues well into early adulthood in some brain regions, at which time the process is sensitive to environmental stimuli. One study found that mice housed in an enriched environment during peak myelination displayed both increased levels of myelin and improved motor function (Goldstein et al., 2021). Of course, humans and mice are very different, and it's questionable as to how much we can learn from animal studies.

As technology develops, so do the tools we can employ to learn more about what the brain is doing when we learn. The most notable development includes sophisticated brain scanning equipment, such as magnetic resonance imaging (MRI), that literally permit scientists access to the living brain, revealing secrets kept for thousands of years. Once, we had to wait for death before we could open a person's skull. But a dead brain is very different from a living one. Now scientists examine brain scans of the living and attempt to identify structures within the brain that appear to be responsible for different types of learning. Seeing the brain as it learns not only benefits scientists – doing so can also benefit learners. Often, we are motivated to exercise or eat a healthy diet because doing so allows us to see the changes when we look at ourselves in the mirror. This can be a powerful motivator. Of course, we don't learn German or Spanish in order to stare admiringly at the changes in our brains. Learning a language has practical utility, and many of us decide to study because we hope to put our new learning to use. But you might decide to learn a new skill to keep your brain active and in the hope that you can remain mentally agile well into old age. You might embark on a course of study later in life at your local college for the pure joy that often comes from learning. Whatever you decide to learn, rest assured that your brain will change for the better. And we can see it happening.

Neuroscientist Eleanor Maguire is perhaps best known for her studies into the brains of London taxi drivers. The capital's cabbies are required to pass an incredibly gruelling test (known as The Knowledge) if they are to be granted a licence to operate one of the city's distinctive black cabs. Maguire discovered that the brains of those who successfully completed The Knowledge had changed between beginning and completing the course. Most notably, the hippocampus (an area of the brain most associated with memory) was larger. (Maguire et al., 2000). This is neuroplasticity in action. We can see what learning does to our brains, just as we can see changes in our bodies when we embark on a healthier lifestyle. But you don't have to be a London cabbie to increase the size of your hippocampus.

At the Swedish Armed Forces Interpreter Academy, recruits who have shown a particular flair for language learning are enrolled in an intensive ten-month course. The languages chosen are very different from Swedish and include Arabic, Russian, and Dari, a Persian language spoken in Afghanistan. They begin their training with no knowledge of the language but are expected to be fluent by the end of the training period, a seemingly impossible task. The days and weeks are long, and the work is hard, with lessons running continually from morning to evening and into the weekends. They must learn between 300 and 500 new words each week. The pace of learning is said to be the fastest of any language course.

Johan Mårtensson and his co-researchers from Lund University were interested in how the course altered the physical brain structure of those completing the course. The researchers used MRI to scan the brains of recruits and included medicine and cognitive science students from Umeå University as a control group. They wanted to see if learning a language changed the brain in ways other types of learning didn't. The researchers then took a second scan after they completed the course. While the control group participants showed no change to their brain structure, parts of the language students' brains had grown. Particularly relevant was an increase in the hippocampus (just like the London cabbies). Other areas also displayed cortical thickening (or brain growth), such as the Inferior Frontal Gyrus, an area involved in the mapping of new words (Mårtensson et al., 2020). This last point is particularly interesting because other studies have found that bilingual and multilingual people are less prone to age-related cognitive decline. Learning new languages seems to protect the human brain in old age.

We are not blank slates

We can see that learning leads to observable physical changes. The brain is designed to learn and does this very effectively. But how much of this learning ability is present at birth, and how much is received from the environment? American behavioural psychologist John B. Watson viewed humans as born tabula rasa, a blank slate, devoid of innate mental content. In one of his most famous quotes, he declared, Give me a dozen healthy infants, well-formed, and my own specified world to bring them up in and I'll guarantee to take anyone at random and train him to become any type of specialist I might select – doctor, lawyer, artist, merchant-chief and, yes, even beggar-man and thief, regardless of his talents, penchants, tendencies, abilities, vocations, and race of his ancestors. He did, however, admit to some over-reaching, concluding that I am going beyond my facts and I admit it, but so have the advocates of the contrary, and they have been doing it for many thousands of years (Watson, 1928). History has proven Watson wrong on many counts, while the school of thought he helped to build (behaviourism) was waning by the late 1950s. Not all behaviourists thought like Watson, and we need to give credit where it's due. The Radical Behaviourism of B. F. Skinner held that behaviour wasn't just about the environment, recognising the influence of innate factors such as genes. Nevertheless, with a shift from behaviourism to a more cognitive psychology, along with advances in brain science and computer modelling, it became increasingly difficult to support the view of humans as blank slates.

Despite the criticism, the blank slate idea remains a popular one, perhaps because we all have a desire to believe we have significant control over our life path. This debate is often described as one of nature versus nurture, although today we have a greater understanding of such things, and it now seems all too obvious that the people we become arise through an interaction of innate tendencies and the external world, less nature versus nature and more nature and nurture. We aren't, therefore, born being able to do everything, but we do have the apparatus in place to learn how to do many things. We are, after all, the result of millions of years of evolution and adaptation, from simple single-celled organisms to modern-day homo sapiens. There are, however, certain traits and dispositions that appear more innate than learned, such as personality and intelligence.

Intelligence and personality

These innate systems have developed to allow us to function in an ever-changing world. In a practical sense, learning helps us function within complex modern societies. Learning to read and write greatly increases our chances of obtaining employment, not to mention day-to-day activities such as completing forms, reading, and understanding instructions or ordering a new washing machine online. Learning is also related to our wider goals, our desires, and aspirations for the future. If, for example, I want to become a metal worker, I would need to learn from someone who was skilled in metal work; if I wanted to become a medical doctor, I'd need to start my journey early, secure the appropriate school qualifications before entering university to begin formal medical training. Writers learn their skill both formally (perhaps as part of a college or university course) and informally by reading books and experimenting with the written word. But often we simply have the desire to learn something new for its own sake.

Innate, hard-wired structures are, therefore, going to impact to some extent on how well people learn. However, environmental factors will also play their part. A good example of how innate and learned structures interact is intelligence, or IQ. Exactly what IQ represents is a topic of some contention, but we know that scores on tests of intelligence correlate with many positive life outcomes. There's also a relationship between IQ and exam success. It's not my intention here to provide an in-depth analysis of the pros and cons of intelligence testing, only to highlight the role of IQ in potential learning outcomes.

There is certainly a genetic component to intelligence, anywhere between 40 and 70 percent. When plotted on a graph, IQ forms a very pleasing bell curve, with the top of the curve representing the average (a score of 100). This is what we call a normal distribution. In this respect, IQ is the same as shoe size, birth weight, and height of a population; some people have small feet, while others have very large feet. In the United Kingdom, the average shoe size for men is 10, or about 28 cm. Forty years ago, the average size for men in the United Kingdom was 8. Despite the increase, the distribution remains the same. The same may well be true for IQ, a phenomenon known as the Flynn Effect. Humans might be more intelligent than they were 40 years ago, but the distribution remains the same. There are, however, some aspects of IQ testing that we need to consider, such as emotional state. Anxious people score lower on IQ tests than less anxious people, for example. Furthermore, certain personality traits may help to counter the potential negative effects of low intelligence.

People tend to have an intuitive understanding of what intelligence means, but what is it from a learning sciences standpoint? Intelligence refers to the structure of human abilities and the way they differ between individuals. Intelligence is linked to memory of all flavours, and there is certainly a relationship between the capacity of a specific type of memory (called working memory) and how well people do on an intelligence test. Just like other aspects of psychology, researchers develop models that attempt to describe the differences between people in terms of their cognitive abilities.

The most influential and rigorously tested of these models is the Cattell-Horn-Carroll theory (or CHC), an amalgamation of two previous models, one developed by Raymond Cattell and John Horn, the other (known as the three-stratum theory) developed by John Carroll. Cattell and Horn proposed that general intelligence (often referred to as g) comprises fluid intelligence (Gf) and crystallised intelligence (Gc). We can think of Gf as the processing power – how well we reason and how well we adapt to new environments or solve novel problems (it's the nuts and bolts of intelligence). Gc, on the other hand, is our accumulation of knowledge, including general knowledge and procedural knowledge (such as riding a bike). The two are related, with Gf being an important factor in the speed at which Gc knowledge is accumulated. So, if a person is high in fluid intelligence, they learn quickly and adapt better to novel situations. Not surprisingly, Gc increases with age, whereas Gf peaks in late adolescence and then declines steadily, which might explain why it takes longer to learn new things as we age.

John Carroll proposed that intelligence is composed of three strata that take into account numerous individual differences in cognitive ability. People, for example, might be particularly skilled in recognising faces, dealing with complex calculations, or writing fiction. Some people might simply be better at learning things and be able to pick up new skills or consolidate novel information faster and more efficiently than others. Carroll, therefore, separated intelligence into general (strata one), which represents general intelligence, or g; broad (strata two), which represents crystallised and fluid intelligence, as well as memory and processing speed; and narrow (strata three), which are highly specific to the task in hand, such as spelling or mathematical ability. Some theories divide intelligence further, such as the theory of multiple intelligences developed by American developmental psychologist Howard Gardner. Unfortunately, there doesn't appear to be a great deal of evidence in support of the theory, a criticism accepted by Gardner himself.

Another potentially innate quality that might impact learning is personality. Intelligence and personality research are two areas covered by psychometrics, the view that we can measure certain aspects of the human condition. You may well have taken a personality test at some point in your life, perhaps as part of the selection process for a job or by following a link on Facebook or other social media sites. Many are based on the most popular measure of personality, the Myers-Briggs Type Indicator (or MBTI). Despite its popularity, the MBTI is notoriously unreliable and its scientific credentials somewhat dubious.

Academic researchers prefer to classify personality in terms of five main traits, known simply as the Big 5. These five traits are: openness to experience, conscientiousness, extraversion, agreeableness, and emotional stability (formerly referred to as neuroticism). Because emotional stability represents our ability to regulate emotions, including levels of anxiety, scoring low on this trait may well lead to lower IQ scores. However, scoring high on conscientiousness, the ability to remain methodical, be well organised, and perform at our best in highly structured and predictable environments, may help to compensate for low IQ.

Lifelong learners tend to score high on measures of agreeableness, conscientiousness, and openness to experience. Regarding openness, the intellect and imagination components appear to be the most important. People scoring high on openness are imaginative and creative, but prone to boredom. This means they require a constant supply of new ideas and experiences. Agreeable people are trusting, friendly, and cooperative.

It's important to point out that traits appear as a continuum, so some people might be more open or conscientious than others. Extraversion, for example, is one end of a scale that includes introversion, but most people fall somewhere between these two extremes.

Personality, like intelligence, has a large heritable component. By heritability, we mean a measure of how much of a difference we see in a population can be accounted for by genetics and how much is determined by the environment. Watson and other behaviourists tried to claim it was all about the environment, an assumption that has proved wrong. Take language, for example. A person might have a very high IQ, but a genius level of intelligence will not help much if they are raised in an environment where they never hear people speak.

Where does this leave us when we consider our own learning? Most people neither know their IQ nor their personality type, and there's no reason we should be in possession of this information before embarking on learning a new skill or acquiring new knowledge. If you consider yourself a lifelong learner, we can assume you're a curious person, open to new experiences and with a desire to learn. Successful writers often have little formal training in writing, yet their desire and determination are enough. Often, however, the things we want to learn need to be built from the foundations up. When I began learning German, I couldn't dive in and attempt to learn entire conversations or read novels in the German language. I started small with short phrases and common words and built up from there. When I was a teenager, I bought a book about black holes. The problem was that my understanding of physics was negligible, and I didn't even really know what astrophysics was. Needless to say, I don't think I understood most of it and finished the book, still not knowing very much about black holes. We might be born with all the apparatus needed for us to learn, but learning takes time. There are no quick fixes – few shortcuts that can turn us into a genius overnight. This is because learning takes time to embed, as our brains require repeated exposure, elaboration, rest, and even a certain amount of forgetting for knowledge to form.

Cognitive decline

Higher levels of learning correlate positively with brain health, reducing rates of cognitive decline (Almeida-Meza et al., 2022). Our ability to retain information follows a developmental trajectory. Due to a phenomenon known as infantile amnesia, you're not going to recall very much about your past until you're at least three or four years old. This is thought to be because infant brains are still developing and aren't yet able to fully form new memories. Simple memory systems, however, do provide the necessary apparatus to help the infant learn important skills like walking and talking and many of the skills described earlier. These systems equate to what Geary describes as biologically primary knowledge, even though the modular nature of these evolutionary adaptations poses a problem for neural plasticity.

It's thought that our memories, and therefore our capacity to retain new information, steadily increase until our twenties before declining, becoming most noticeable in our 50s and 60s. Much of this decline is related to the speed at which the brain can process information. Not all research agrees, however, and a 2022 study found that processing speed may not decline significantly until about 60; it's just that as we age, we become more cautious, and this might impact how quickly we make a final decision (von Krause et al., 2022). Younger people appear to favour speed over accuracy, while older adults are willing to take longer to complete a mental task if the extra time results in getting it right.

Nevertheless, our brain does slow down, and cognitive decline is an inevitable side-effect of the ageing brain; it's going to occur to some degree even in people who never develop dementia (around 10 percent of people aged over 65 will, sadly, succumb). Cognitive decline is believed to be caused by decreased neurogenesis in specific areas of the brain. Neurogenesis is the process by which new brain cells form. One particular area that appears to be involved is the dentate gyrus, situated deep inside the hippocampus. You'll recall from the London cabbie study that the hippocampus is a region of the brain associated with memory. Stem cells in the dentate gyrus somehow lose their ability to produce new neurons.

This might sound quite worrying, especially for those of us who fully intend to be learning new things long into old age. We are, of course, living much longer than we did a 100 years ago. In Britain in 1900, life expectancy was 47 years for men and 50 for women, although these figures are skewed because death in childhood was still common. By the 1950s, men could expect to live until around 65, rising to 79 in 2015 (and 83 for women), although the COVID-19 pandemic resulted in a fall in life expectancy by a few months. Cognitive decline, including dementia and Alzheimer's, is therefore more common today than a hundred years ago because we are living longer. But all is not lost.

It wasn't all that long ago that we assumed the mature brain was pretty much static and unchanging. The prevailing wisdom was that by late childhood, around seven or eight years old, the brain was fully developed following a period of rapid synaptogenesis, the formation of connections between neurons. We now know that a second period of brain development takes place during adolescence, often continuing into our early 20s. More importantly, by the mid-1980s, scientists concluded that even the mature brain is still creating new neurons because they had found stem cells there (in mice, at least). A stem cell is an immature, unspecified cell, a blank canvas from which different specialised stems can form. Stem cells can keep dividing, just so long as they're alive (they are self-renewing). Each stem cell can give birth to more stem cells, and each stem cell can become multiple types of more specialised cells, such as neurons, astrocytes, and oligodendrocytes. In order to slow cognitive decline, the brain needs to keep producing new neurons.

Thankfully, your desire to learn throughout your lifetime may well provide some protection from this mental downturn, and the human brain's ability to adapt and grow new connections may slow, but continues. The more we learn, even in adulthood, the better the brain becomes at learning more. These adaptations, like learning itself, are cumulative. But what we learn makes a big difference when it comes to cognitive decline, with some things having a greater protective quality than others. Italian researchers, for example, found that learning a second language can reshape critical brain networks in older adults and slow cognitive decline (Bubbico et al., 2019). Similarly, a team from Switzerland found a slower rate of mental decline in volunteers aged 70 and over who played a musical instrument (Mansky et al., 2020).

We know from the London cabbie study that learning can change the structure of some brain regions, most notably the hippocampus. But what impact can learning have on these all-important myelinated connections? White matter is found in the central nervous system, the deeper tissues, or subcortical areas of the brain. It comprises the myelinated axons, and it's these that give the white matter its colour. Heavily myelinated axons can transfer signals faster than those with thinner coverings and are also better protected from damage. This means they also lead to faster and more efficient learning. Myelin sheaths degrade over time, however, resulting in reduced transfer speed. This demyelination might be one reason for cognitive decline. But if learning can lead to an increase in myelin density, can we slow this mental decline by learning new things as we age?

In a study from 2022, researchers set out to investigate the impact of a six-month piano training programme on the brains of elderly but healthy musically naïve participants (Jünemann et al., 2022). The focus of the study was the fornix, a white matter tract connecting the hippocampus to other brain regions. The researchers used fibre density as a measure to investigate the microstructure of the fornix, providing an indication of the density of the axons within a given area. Fibre density doesn't directly measure myelin, but changes in fibre density could imply changes in the number or diameter of myelinated axons within the fornix.

The researchers randomly assigned 121 participants between the ages of 62 and 78 to either the piano training or lessons on music listening and culture. Both groups engaged in their assigned programme for one hour a day, plus 30 minutes a day of homework. At the end of the six-month period, those in the piano training group displayed a stabilisation in fibre density, while those in the control group displayed a reduction. So, while the piano training didn't appear to increase myelination, it did manage to prevent it from shrinking, often seen as an inevitable consequence of cognitive decline.

What can we then conclude from these studies? The overriding takeaway is that learning is good for our brains, even if we choose to take up a new skill later in life. Every unique experience will change the structure of the human brain, but some have a protective quality while others don't. Reading a book about an ancient civilisation will certainly add to our store of general knowledge but won't necessarily alter the structure of the brain in the same way learning to read does. Learning to play a musical instrument or a foreign language appears to both add to our store of knowledge and alter neural pathways that may very well slow brain ageing.

So learning isn't confined to childhood, nor should it be. Lifelong learning is essential if we want to remain healthy into old age and slow down the seemingly inevitable decline in cognitive function. Of course, learning is not the only factor, and remaining physically active and maintaining a healthy diet are also very important for all-round physical health and psychological well-being. Young learners have an obvious advantage over older ones. For starters, their brains are still developing rather than declining. But older learners also possess qualities related to learning that younger learners lack. I'll come back to some of these advantages in later chapters.

Chapter summary

- Humans are innately wired to learn from birth, with our brains constantly gathering and processing information. This innate capacity for learning is a key aspect of human evolution, serving to protect our species and enhance our abilities.

- David Geary distinguishes between biologically primary and biologically secondary knowledge. Biologically primary knowledge is evolutionary, developing naturally and often modularly (e.g., language recognition, problem-solving), while biologically secondary knowledge is acquired through explicit teaching and is often domain-specific (e.g., algebra, reading). This distinction is not without its critics, who question the rigidity of the modular mind and the role of culture and neural plasticity.

- Infants possess remarkable innate abilities, including an understanding of basic physics, simple arithmetic, and the ability to differentiate between positive and negative social behaviours.

- Brain structure and connections change in response to learning experiences (neural plasticity). Studies on London taxi drivers and language learners at the Swedish Armed Forces Interpreter Academy illustrate how learning can lead to physical changes in the brain, such as increased hippocampus size and cortical thickening.

- Lifelong learning can positively impact brain health and potentially slow cognitive decline.

- Learning is an interaction between nature and nurture in the learning debate. Genetic components, including intelligence and personality, play an important role, as do non-genetic, environmental conditions.

References

Almeida-Meza, P., Richards, M., & Cadar, D. (2022). Moderating role of cognitive reserve markers between childhood cognition and cognitive aging. *Neurology*, *99*(12). https://doi.org/10.1212/WNL.0000000000200928

Bubbico, G., Chiacchiaretta, P., Parenti, M., Di Marco, M., Panara, V., Sepede, G., Ferretti, A., & Perrucci, M. G. (2019). Effects of second language learning on the plastic aging brain: Functional connectivity, cognitive decline, and reorganization. *Frontiers in Neuroscience*, *13*(May), 1–13. https://doi.org/10.3389/fnins.2019.00423

Buon, M., Jacob, P., Margules, S., Brunet, I., Dutat, M., Cabrol, D., & Dupoux, E. (2014). Friend or foe? Early social evaluation of human interactions. *PLoS One*, *9*(2). https://doi.org/10.1371/journal.pone.0088612

Claxton, G (2021). *The future of teaching and the myths that hold is back*. Routledge.

De la Fuente, I. M., Bringas, C., Malaina, I., Fedetz, M., Carrasco-Pujante, J., Morales, M., Knafo, S., Martínez, L., Pérez-Samartín, A., López, J. I., Pérez-Yarza, G., & Boyano, M. D. (2019). Evidence of conditioned behavior in amoebae. *Nature Communications*, *10*(1), 3690 https://doi.org/10.1038/s41467-019-11677-w

Dehaene, S. (2021). *How we learn: The new science of education and the brain*. Penguin.

Geary, D. C. (2008). An evolutionarily informed education science. *Educational Psychologist*, *43*(4), 179–195. https://doi.org/10.1080/00461520802392133

Goldstein, E. Z., Pertsovskaya, V., Forbes, T. A., Dupree, J. L., & Gallo, V. (2021). Prolonged environmental enrichment promotes developmental myelination. *Frontiers in Cell and Developmental Biology*, *9*. https://doi.org/10.3389/fcell.2021.665409

Jünemann, K., Marie, D., Worschech, F., Scholz, D. S., Grouiller, F., Kliegel, M., Van De Ville, D., James, C. E., Krüger, T. H. C., Altenmüller, E., & Sinke, C. (2022). Six months of piano training in healthy elderly stabilizes white matter microstructure in the fornix, compared to an active control group. *Frontiers in Aging Neuroscience*, *14*. https://doi.org/10.3389/fnagi.2022.817889

Maguire, E. A., Gadian, D. G., Johnsrude, I. S., Good, C. D., Ashburner, J., Frackowiak, R. S. J., & Frith, C. D. (2000). Navigation-related structural change in the hippocampi of taxi drivers. *Proceedings of the National Academy of Sciences*, *97*(8), 4398–4403. https://doi.org/10.1073/pnas.070039597

Mansky, R., Marzel, A., Orav, E. J., Chocano-Bedoya, P. O., Grünheid, P., Mattle, M., Freystätter, G., Stähelin, H. B., Egli, A., & Bischoff-Ferrari, H. A. (2020). Playing a musical instrument is associated with slower cognitive decline in community-dwelling older adults. *Aging Clinical and Experimental Research*, *32*(8), 1577–1584. https://doi.org/10.1007/s40520-020-01472-9

Mårtensson, J., Eriksson, J., Bodammer, N. C., Lindgren, M., Johansson, M., Nyberg, L., & Lövdén, M. (2020). White matter microstructure predicts foreign language learning in army interpreters. *Bilingualism*, *23*(4), 763–771. https://doi.org/10.1017/S1366728920000152

Peters, B. M. (2013). Evolutionary psychology: Neglecting neurobiology in defining the mind. *Theory & Psychology*, *23*(3), 305–322. https://doi.org/10.1177/0959354313480269

von Krause, M., Radev, S. T., & Voss, A. (2022). Mental speed is high until age 60 as revealed by analysis of over a million participants. *Nature Human Behaviour*, *6*(5), 700–708. https://doi.org/10.1038/s41562-021-01282-7

Ward, C. (2012). *Evolutionary psychology and the problem of neural plasticity* (pp. 235–254). https://doi.org/10.1007/978-94-007-1951-4_11

Watson, J. B. (1928). *Psychological care of infant and child*. W.W. Norton Company, Inc.

From salivating dogs to the new science of learning

To understand the evolution of the new science of learning, we first need to investigate its modern beginnings. As Neisser points out, the study of cognition is part of psychology, and theories of cognition are psychological theories (Neisser, 1976, p.1). From psychology emerged a broader cognitive science, an area of investigation that would eventually include multiple disciplines from neuroscience to artificial intelligence. From its beginnings, psychology has always included the study of learning, so we can never separate it from a broader learning science. Psychology as we now understand it began in Germany in the late nineteenth century, and I'll return to some of these early pioneers later. First, however, I want to skip ahead to the first part of the twentieth century and the beginnings of the behaviourist project, from where some of the earliest formal theories of learning originate.

Early behaviourism was a school of thought that rejected everything that couldn't be directly and objectively seen. This meant that internal thought (or cognition) was off limits. The concept of the mind was all but rejected, at least in terms of a legitimate area of study. The only valid data was that which could be seen, and learning isn't visible, unlike the behavioural responses that learning elicits. Only by observing your behaviour will I know you have learned to ride a bike, play the piano, or can recite your times tables. Contemporary behaviourist thought does acknowledge the role of cognitive states, but my focus here is on the behaviourism that dominated up to around the 1950s and what it can tell us about how organisms learn.

Behaviourism's roots lie with the work of Russian physiologist Ivan Pavlov, who chanced upon a curious form of learned response while investigating salivary secretions in dogs. Pavlov found that salivation not only increased when the dogs knew they were about to be fed, but they also salivated when they saw the trappings associated with the event. This included the laboratory assistant charged with feeding them. Pavlov could then associate, say, the sound of a bell with the food, so that when the dogs heard the bell, they would salivate. Although, contrary to popular belief, Pavlov most often used a metronome (Todes, 2014). This might take several episodes of pairing the two, but eventually, by eliciting a sound just before presenting the food, the dogs would salivate in anticipation of their meal. This kind of learning is variously referred to as stimulus-response learning, Pavlovian conditioning, or classical conditioning. If you're a dog owner, you'll have witnessed this type of learning firsthand. Perhaps the sound of a tin opening results in an over-excited pooch who associates the sound with being fed and who then looks confused and disappointed on discovering that the contents of the tin aren't what they expected. These associations may even become more sophisticated as your pet learns to associate certain sounds (the word 'walk' or 'walkies', for example) with the opportunity to get out of the house. When I was a child, we temporarily solved this problem by spelling out the word 'walk', only to discover that our excitable spaniel would eventually make that connection too. Although, and I can't stress this enough, she hadn't learned to spell.

We can see these same learned responses in humans. In one of history's most infamous psychological studies, behaviourist John B. Watson and his assistant Rosalie Raynor instilled fear of an object in a child who had never displayed such a fear. The object in question was a white rat, and the child was known only as Little Albert. Although accounts of the experiment differ, it's generally understood to have gone like this: On presentation of the rat, Watson would stand behind the child and strike an iron bar with a hammer, resulting in Albert displaying signs of distress. The more Watson and Raynor paired the rat with the distressing noise, the more Albert feared it, eventually resulting in the child being fearful of pretty much anything white and fluffy, including beards and fur coats (Watson & Rayner, 1920).

Luckily, for the local children at least, Watson became embroiled in a scandal at Johns Hopkins and was forced to leave. He did, however, then begin a new and very successful career in advertising (make of that what you will). What is also relevant is that such fears can be unlearned, although this revelation may have come too late for poor Albert. Inspired by Watson's work, Mary Cover Jones discovered that by pairing an anxiety-provoking object with something pleasant, children will eventually no longer fear it (Jones, 1924). This discovery formed the basis of subsequent behaviour therapies used to treat phobias.

B. F. Skinner distinguished between what he termed respondent behaviour (triggered automatically by a stimulus in the environment, such as a sound) and operant behaviour, behaviours that are triggered voluntarily. The salivating dog can't help but salivate, but in other instances, animals might volunteer a certain response because they have learned it will lead to a desirable outcome. Say, for example, we place a pigeon in a cage and at one end of the cage place a button that, when pecked, will release a food pellet. The pigeon will most likely randomly peck at different areas of the cage (because that's what pigeons do). Eventually, however, it will accidentally peck the button and release food into a tray. At this point, the bird hasn't associated the pecking with the button, so it just continues randomly pecking. The more the pigeon pecks the button and retrieves food, the stronger the connection becomes until the bird learns that pecking the button will guarantee food. Now, if the bird flaps its wings and the mischievous researcher releases food into the tray, the pigeon may well eventually associate the flapping of wings with the delivery of food. Skinner called this phenomenon pigeon superstition, although it applies not only to pigeons (Skinner, 1948).

Talking of pigeons, Skinner also developed a pigeon-guided weapons system using behaviourist principles. This was during the Second World War, when the Americans were trying to work out how they could more effectively bomb enemy positions. Fortunately for the pigeons (who would, by the way, not survive the mission), the military decided not to move forward with Skinner's plans.

Like the pigeon who accidentally chanced upon a means to acquire food, Edward Thorndike viewed this type of learning as a process of trial and error. He built puzzle boxes for use with cats, whereby the task was to operate a latch that would open the door. When the cat freed itself, the researchers would reward it with a piece of fish. Initially, the cat would behave randomly while attempting to escape the box, but would eventually, and purely by chance, work the latch and escape before helping itself to the fish. Thorndike would then place the cat back in the box, and the process would repeat. With each repetition, the cat became more adept at escaping. In one particular instance, a cat took around five minutes to escape in the first trial, but after around 20 trials, it was about five seconds. This process became known as *Thorndike's law of effect* and was crucial in distinguishing classical from operant conditioning (Thorndike, 1933).

Classical conditioning, therefore, relies upon certain instinctual behaviours and pairs them with an environmental stimulus. We can see this effect in action in the training of dogs, especially so-called clicker training. A clicker is a small device that emits a 'click' when operated and can be used in place of a metronome in Pavlov's classic studies. We witness a similar type of behaviour in humans, too; fire alarms, school bells, and ambulance sirens all trigger a behaviour; if we are driving along a road and we hear a siren, we prepare to pull over. If we are in a building and the fire alarm sounds, we prepare to leave and make our way to the nearest exit – the behaviour is automatic. Automatic behaviours require fewer cognitive resources to operate, which, as we'll see later, can have a powerful impact on learning.

The major problem with behaviourist explanations is that, in emphasising only observable behaviour, they exclude internal thought processes. Are humans simply stimulus-response machines, or are they highly complex decision makers? Surely, human action is often planned and can serve several different goals, most of them conscious. Edward Tolman was conducting his own studies on learning in rats at the same time as the behaviourists, so we tend to place him in the behaviourist camp. However, in retrospect, Tolman was one of the first cognitive psychologists, mainly because his findings implied that reinforcement wasn't always necessary for learning to take place. In one of his most influential studies, Tolman had rats attempt a maze. In one condition, he reinforced the rats every time they found their way through the maze to a food box, while in a second condition, the rats received no reinforcement. A third group of rats received no reinforcement for the first ten days but received reinforcement after the eleventh. Results found that the first group learned the maze quickly and made very few errors, while the second group (the no reinforcement condition) never reduced the time to complete the maze and moved around with very little aim. The third group, however, made no apparent progress during the first ten days, but then displayed a sudden decrease in the time to find the food on day eleven, catching up almost immediately with the first group. Although it wasn't observable, the rats in group 3 had been learning their way through the maze during the first ten days, but the learning was latent, that is, hidden or behaviourally silent. The learning itself wasn't observable until day 11, when they were given the incentive of the reinforcement. Tolman concluded that reinforcement was important in relation to the performance of the learned behaviour, but not necessarily for learning itself. This is often referred to as place (or sign) learning in that the rats learn expectations as to what part of the maze will be followed by which other part of the maze. These expectations Tolman called mental maps (Tolman, 1948).

The rats in Tolman's studies could also adapt to a changing environment. When their usual route was blocked, they found alternative routes and shortcuts, while if the maze was rotated, they could still find the food from different starting locations. In one study, researchers flooded the maze immediately after the rats had learned it, and the rats would swim to the food with no more errors than when they had walked (Restle, 1957). In addition to the processes involved in learning, these studies also highlight the need to adapt and remain flexible to new experiences. When it comes to humans, this adaptive behaviour might include the ability to bounce back when we fail or when things don't go according to plan, or to find efficient solutions to new problems.

But humans are very different from rats, and these studies rarely apply to us. Harold Stevenson did, however, examine latent learning in humans (Stevenson, 1954). Stevenson had children (some as young as three) explore a series of objects to locate a key that would open a box. But the environment also contained non-key objects and items that were irrelevant to the task. The question under investigation was: would the children learn the locations of the unrelated items during their search for the relevant ones? Would the children display latent learning? The short answer is yes; when the children were asked to find the irrelevant, non-key items, they were relatively faster in doing so when the objects were in the explored environment. The researchers also noted that latent learning increased with age.

How would latent learning work in the real world? Say we have moved to a new town and each morning we catch the bus to work and return in the evening. On one particular pleasant morning, we decided to walk to work rather than taking the bus. Now, although we haven't specifically learned the route, our bus journeys have allowed us to create an internal map, along with geographical markers. We have learned the route latently, and it's only when we need to use the information that the learning can be evidenced through our behaviour. The reinforcement (or reward, if you like) is goal-directed, that is, reaching our destination on time. We didn't consciously learn the route while sitting on the bus day after day, but we did learn it. We just didn't know it until that learning needed to be used.

Beyond behaviourism

There is a tendency to think that behaviourism dominated psychology until the 1950s, but this was really only the case in the United States. Its influence certainly spread far and wide, but in the United Kingdom and mainland Europe, it didn't have the same iron-fisted hold. While British psychology was more influenced by the biological models of Donald Hebb than Watson and Skinner, in Germany, researchers had clung, to some extent, to their early roots in experimental psychology. This German movement became known as the Gestalt school and had more in common with what would become cognitive psychology than behaviourism.

The Gestaltists argued behaviourists failed to consider the idea of ripeness: the readiness to make a discovery or solve a problem, based on relevant knowledge, skills, and previous experience. Rats and pigeons are biologically ill-equipped to carry out the tasks that researchers set them, they argued, so it's no surprise their learning seems pretty random and slow. Wolfgang Köhler worked with 'almost ripe' chimpanzees on problem-solving tasks, providing them with a variety of items that could help them obtain food suspended from the ceiling and just out of reach. The chimps would stack boxes on top of one another or attach two small sticks together to create a longer one, implying their learning was based on insight rather than trial and error (Köhler, 1925). Unfortunately, psychology in Germany narrowed significantly during the 1930s, as researchers were expected to use their skills and knowledge to justify the notion of German biological superiority, and many, including Köhler, left to find new academic posts in the United States. What many of them found, however, was a community entrenched in behaviourism, making it difficult for them to find positions in American universities.

In the United States, Harry Harlow was also training monkeys to solve problems and found that training them on different but related sets of problems accelerated their improvement – the more they learned, the better they could apply what they had learned to other problems (Harlow, 1949). Harlow called these 'learning sets' and the more sets the monkeys were equipped with, the faster they learned. This notion would much later be expanded to humans with respect to the advantages of prior learning. However, certain aspects of Harlow's research remain controversial, specifically his studies into social isolation, which were both cruel and no doubt unnecessary. Furthermore, we must remain mindful that studies in non-human primates don't always transfer well to humans, just as studies on rats and cats can't tell us all that much about our own behaviour or learning capabilities.

Psychology's coming home: the cognitive (counter) revolution

While research focusing on non-human primates has been useful, such findings rarely translate well to humans. Rats, cats, and salivating dogs are even further removed, yet the behaviourists were sure that behaviour was behaviour, regardless of the animal the behaviour pertained to. Indeed, despite the occasional exception, the behaviourists didn't study the species they were attempting to explain the behaviour of, unlike its predecessor, the experimental psychology that arose in German universities in the late nineteenth century. By the 1950s, the picture was changing. The growing frustration among many American researchers that internal factors were, in a way, off limits, coupled with the advent of the microprocessor, was at the forefront of this change. In the United Kingdom, Donald Broadbent was already developing his own model of learning, a model that would have far-reaching consequences. These early proponents of cognitive psychology were asking themselves, what if learning is less stimulus-response and more information processing?

This period is often referred to as the beginning of the cognitive revolution, the emergence of cognitive science that would rapidly sweep aside the vestiges of behaviourism. However, it was more accurately a counterrevolution, a return to the early German laboratories of the late nineteenth century. As Neisser points out, when psychology emerged as a separate discipline a hundred years ago, it was extensively concerned with such matters as sensation, perception, association, imagery, and attention. The principal goal of psychological science was the analysis of 'mental processes', which usually meant cognitive processes (Neisser, 1976, p.1).

George Miller, one of cognitive psychology's earliest proponents, stated that the counterrevolution began on the 11th of September 1956, the second day of a meeting of the Special Interest Group in Information Technology at the Massachusetts Institute of Technology, or MIT. The meeting included talks that would later combine to form a new interrelated discipline, the name of which depended, initially at least, on the institute concerned. At Harvard, it was called Cognitive Studies, while at Carnegie Mellon, it went by the name of Information Processing Technology. Eventually, the name used by the University of California, San Diego was the one that stuck: Cognitive Science. However, Miller, writing in 2003, admits that he much preferred the term Cognitive Sciences, in the plural, because several disciplines were involved, some working in isolation, while others were more interdisciplinary (Miller, 2003).

The talks that took place at the MIT meeting gave a taste of the areas that the new discipline would cover: Allen Newell and Herbert Simon introduced their computer-based logic machine, while others gave talks on sensory psychophysics and computer simulations of Hebb's neural cell assemblies. Noam Chomsky introduced delegates to his transformational grammar and demolished Skinner's attempts to apply behaviourist principles to language learning, breaking the behaviourists' grip on the discipline of psychology and paving the way for new subject areas such as Artificial Intelligence. George Miller spoke of how to avoid the bottleneck created by limitations of short-term memory, a topic that is as fresh today as it was in 1956 – it's also going to play a very important role in our journey.

In the United Kingdom, much of the work on cognition was carried out by a small yet very active group at the Medical Research Council's Applied Psychology

Unit at the University of Cambridge (now the MRC Cognition and Brain Sciences Unit). They included Sir Frederic Bartlett and Donald Broadbent (both of whom served as directors of the unit) and Alan Baddeley, who, along with Graham Hitch, would develop probably the most influential model in memory research (the working memory model). Bartlett had resisted the lure of behaviourism despite much of his most influential work taking place during the 1930s, while others (including Miller in the United States) would try but fail in their pretence to be seen as behaviourists. Again, all these names will become more familiar to you as we move through the following chapters.

In his 1958 book Perception and Communication, Broadbent would summarise a wide range of research on perception, attention, memory, and performance, much of it carried out by members of the unit at Cambridge (Broadbent, 1958). Perception and Communication is one of the seminal texts of cognitive psychology, not least because of Broadbent's attempt to present research within an information processing framework. The model Broadbent proposed was a model of attention, yet it was to form the foundations of later memory models and notions of both perceptual and cognitive load (the pressure placed upon the limited human cognitive system when carrying out tasks of increasing complexity). One particularly relevant notion (to us at least) was Broadbent's assumption of a short-term memory system that can temporarily store limited amounts of information and assist in its processing. I'll return to some of this early work in later chapters, as it encapsulates much of what we currently understand about how learning happens.

The shift from behaviourism to cognition was in part because of both frustration and technological advancement, and the information processing model is one result of this. The frustration arose because internal processes such as memory and perception were seen as off-limits to behaviourists – if it couldn't be directly observed, then it wasn't a legitimate area of study. Learning, therefore, could only be implied. To be fair to the behaviourists, even today, we accept that learning is beyond observation, and we can only observe the results of learning. However, as Miller notes, by the mid-1950s, it had become apparent that behaviourism couldn't succeed, while according to Chomsky, defining psychology as the science of behaviour was like defining physics as the science of meter reading (Miller, 2003). Those who had resisted behaviourism knew it was bound to fail, eventually. But there was another important factor at play: technology. The invention of the microprocessor has provided frustrated psychologists with a model to explain the internal workings of the human mind. What if, they asked, the architecture of a computer is analogous with that of the human mind, with inputs and outputs and processors that drive learning? If we look at some of the early models of memory and attention, it becomes clear that these were based on what early cognitive scientists understood about how computational machines work (see Figure 3.1). Today, this view is at the heart of artificial intelligence.

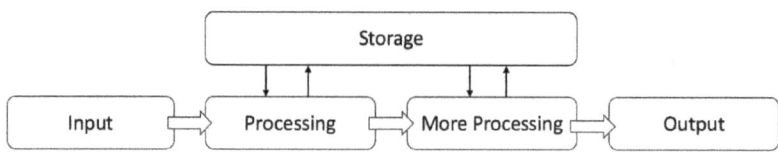

Figure 3.1 A simple information processing model (adapted from Neisser, 1976).

Over 50 years on, the computer analogy isn't holding up too well – computers don't have emotions, they don't get distracted or bored like humans, so perhaps we were mistaken to believe that we could compare them in such absolute terms. According to computational neuroscientist Romain Brette, computers are programmable things. Brains are not – at least not literally (Brette, 2022 p.4). Even our everyday experiences don't match those we see in computers. I know that when I save the document containing these words, it will be an exact copy of the one I access tomorrow, or next week, or next year, barring a glitch that corrupts the entire file. The same isn't the case for my memory. I know that recollections of my past aren't entirely accurate, and some bear only a faint resemblance to the event they pretend to have captured. If my brain were like a computer, I would rarely forget or misremember (and I do both – often).

Yet despite such reservations, cognitive models based on the computer analogy have proven useful, even though they can never account for every human idiosyncrasy. Although many models may well be wrong, if we can use them in constructive ways, we can forgive their shortcomings. These cognitive models of memory have perhaps been most useful for learning, although those concerned with attention are also vital, as we'll see later. Models have provided the impetus to test different notions of learning and combine them into theories of, for example, instructional design – the way we can arrange our teaching and learning to more appropriately take into account what the science is telling us. It's not perfect, but then science rarely is, but if these changes lead to improved learning (at least within the criteria we adopt), then it's good enough for our purpose.

While animal studies were popular among behaviourists, cognitive psychologists preferred human participants and computer models. Nevertheless, animal studies like those of Wolfgang Köhler can still provide useful information. The observation of animal behaviour might suggest that there is hierarchy to learning, from simple classical conditioning to more complex rule learning and problem solving. We can, therefore, see how simple forms of learning, such as classical conditioning, provide the foundations for more complex learning; lower notions of learning represent behaviourist aspects, while higher ones represent cognitive forms. This, then, implies that what we can learn is, to some extent, dependent on what we have already learned. For example, by learning general rules, we can then apply them to different situations. In other words, learning becomes transferable. This transfer of learning applies both to simple stimulus generalisations and more complex situations requiring advanced problem solving.

Cognitive psychology and constructivism: a complex entanglement

It wasn't only cognitive psychology that was at odds with behaviourism. During the early twentieth century, Jean Piaget in France and Lev Vygotsky in the Soviet Union were looking into the development of thinking and learning. Born in the same year (1896), the two men would never meet (Vygotsky died in 1924; Piaget died in 1980), but their ideas would be influential in the development of modern cognitive science. The theory that would eventually emerge became known as constructivism.

Constructivism views knowledge as actively constructed and influenced by what the learner already knows. This construction happens as the result of processes that organise and reorganise mental structures (Piaget called these processes assimilation and accommodation). Learning is, therefore, an active or dynamic process. Cognitive psychology, on the other hand, views knowledge as represented in the mind and explained in terms of mental models and memory structures.

At first sight, it might appear that cognitive views of learning are incompatible with constructivism, but as we'll see, as an interconnected science of learning emerged, it became clear that learning was much more than the storing of information. Information has meaning and context, and learning isn't static. Errors require correcting and updating mental maps. Early cognitive psychology and, to some extent, early attempts to quantify learning by the likes of Ebbinghaus (more on Ebbinghaus later) didn't always consider the dynamic nature of learning. Constructivism, on the other hand, views learning as shaped by context and experience. Modern cognitive science, however, incorporates many constructivist elements, including the role of connectionism and neural networks, embodied cognition, and the way knowledge is shared across people, tools, and the environment.

The emergence of learning science

Behaviourism, Gestalt, and cognitive psychology, along with the constructivist framework, influenced the way we currently view learning. However, cognitive science and computing changed the way thinking and learning were studied. While learning had been cogitated about and discussed since antiquity, the emergence of an empirical science of learning that evolved from psychology shifted the emphasis considerably. Add to this the rapid development of brain scanning technology, and we can begin to understand how and why our understanding of how people learn entered a phase of rapid expansion.

However, academic research into learning remained far removed from education as an applied profession. Research into learning was (and still is) largely focused on learning in artificial settings and with participants who are often far removed from the people we see in real-world classrooms. Real learning environments are messy, whereas laboratories are highly controlled. This creates a contested terrain (Hoadley & Haneghan, 2011). What, then, is the purpose of learning science? Is it to encourage a shift from education as an applied profession to empirical research or the marrying of research and an applied profession? Furthermore, is education an intellectual discipline, an application area for other disciplines, or a crossroads for intellectual inquiry?

These questions formed the basis of the emergence of learning science throughout the 1980s and 1990s, culminating in the publication in 1999 of How People Learn, the product of a two-year study conducted by the Committee on Developments in the Science of Learning and Educational Practice. How People Learn went some way to legitimising the link between scientific research and educational practice, paving the way for a more cohesive learning science (Bransford et al., 1999).

So, what is learning science? Learning science studies how people learn and how they can be supported. It is not a discipline in its own right, but rather a community of researchers and practitioners. The people involved tend to retain their allegiances, be that to psychology, education, anthropology, philosophy, or computer science (to name just a few). The following chapters tend to lean towards cognitive psychology, but also include aspects of other disciplines within the broader learning sciences.

This chapter has attempted to map the history of learning research, from the early days of psychology to the emergence of an interdisciplinary science of learning. The following chapters will return to many of the topics covered here in an attempt to apply them directly to how people learn. In the next chapter, I'll look at how memory research has helped shape our views of learning.

Chapter summary

- Learning science can be traced to the beginnings of modern psychology, from the early German laboratories of the nineteenth century through behaviourism and the cognitive revolution of the 1950s.

- The shift from behaviourism to the emergence of cognitive psychology was driven by frustration with the limitations of behaviourism and the advent of the microprocessor, which provided a new analogy for understanding the human mind as an information processor.

- The cognitive counter-revolution resulted in the emergence of cognitive science as an interdisciplinary field encompassing psychology, neuroscience, and artificial intelligence, among others.

- Constructivism emphasises the active role of the learner in constructing knowledge based on their existing understanding and experiences. Modern cognitive science integrates many constructivist elements.

- Learning science aims to understand how people learn and how they can be supported, bridging the gap between academic research and educational practice. Learning science is not a single discipline but rather a community of researchers and practitioners from various fields.

References

Bransford, J. D., Brown, A. L., & Cocking, R. R. (Eds.). (1999). *How people learn: Brain, mind, experience, and school*. National Academy Press.

Brette, R. (2022). Brains as computers: Metaphor, analogy, theory or fact? In *Frontiers in ecology and evolution* (Vol. 10). Frontiers Media S.A. https://doi.org/10.3389/fevo.2022.878729

Broadbent, D. E. (1958). *Perception and communication*. Pergamon Press. https://doi.org/10.1037/10037-000

Harlow, H. F. (1949). The formation of learning sets. *Psychological Review*, *56*(1), 51–65. https://doi.org/10.1037/h0062474

Hoadley, C., & Van Haneghan, J. P. (2011). The learning sciences: Where they came from and what it means for instructional designers. *Trends and Issues in Instructional Design and Technology*, January, 53–63. https://steinhardt.nyu.edu/scmsAdmin/uploads/006/742/Hoadley-VanHaneghan-draft.pdf

Jones, M. C. (1924). The elimination of children's fears. *Journal of Experimental Psychology*, *7*(5), 382–390. https://doi.org/10.1037/h0072283

Kohler, W. (1925). *The mentality of apes*. (E. Winter, Trans.). Harcourt, Brace.

Miller, G. A. (2003). The cognitive revolution: A historical perspective. *Trends in Cognitive Sciences*, *7*(3), 141–144. https://doi.org/10.1016/S1364-6613(03)00029-9

Neisser, U. (1976) *Cognition and reality*. W.H. Freeman and Company

Restle, F. (1957). Discrimination of cues in mazes: A resolution of the 'place-vs.-response' question. *Psychological Review*, *64*(4), 217–228. https://doi.org/10.1037/h0040678

Skinner, B. F. (1948). 'Superstition' in the pigeon. *Journal of Experimental Psychology*, *38*(2), 168–172. https://doi.org/10.1037/h0055873

Stevenson, H. W. (1954). Latent learning in children. *Journal of Experimental Psychology*, *47*(1), 17–21. https://doi.org/10.1037/h0060086

Thorndike, E. L. (1933). A proof of the law of effect. *Science*, *77*(1989), 173–175. https://doi.org/10.1126/science.77.1989.173.b

Todes, D. P. (2014). Ivan Pavlov: A Russian life in science. Oxford University Press.

Tolman, E. C. (1948). Cognitive maps in rats and men. *Psychological Review*, *55*(4), 189–208. https://doi.org/10.1037/h0061626

Watson, J. B., & Rayner, R. (1920). Conditioned emotional reactions. *Journal of Experimental Psychology*, *3*(1), 1–14. https://doi.org/10.1037/h0069608

How memory works

Henry was born in 1926 in Manchester, Connecticut. After an accident on his bicycle when he was seven years old, Henry developed epilepsy, originally resulting in major partial seizures that developed into major tonic-clonic seizures by the time he was 16. Until the age of 27, Henry was employed on a factory production line but had to leave his job when the seizures became more frequent. He was then referred to William Beecher Scoville, a neurosurgeon based at Hartford Hospital, Connecticut, who operated on Henry in 1953. His surgery was extensive, with Scoville removing about two-thirds of his medial temporal lobes in both hemispheres. The surgery, known as a bilateral medial temporal lobectomy, led to the removal of parts of Henry's hippocampus and most of his amygdala, as well as other brain regions. The surgery was a success in that it led to partial control of his seizures, but also resulted in specific deficits, including severe anterograde amnesia. This meant that Henry couldn't commit any new events to explicit memory. In other words, Henry was unable to make new memories. He also suffered moderate retrograde amnesia, robbing him of the memory of his life in the one or two-year period prior to the surgery or up to 11 years before that. However, his memory impairment was highly selective. He could still learn new motor and perceptual skills and could retain information about most events and facts for a brief time. He could also mentally rehearse and manipulate what he had just heard, in much the same way you or I can, just as long as nothing distracted him. In tests, he displayed almost perfect memory for the 40-second memory period of the study and could remember a three-digit number for up to 15 minutes.

Henry's case was first reported in 1957 by Scoville and the British-Canadian neuropsychologist Brenda Milner. He continued to be studied until his death in 2008. Indeed, Henry was a vital part of the search for a link between brain function and memory and had an important role to play in the development of cognitive neuropsychology as a discipline. What this wealth of information has highlighted is the complexity of memory formation and how memory appears to be spread throughout the cortex. Most notably, however, studying people like Henry has provided researchers with important details about the role of certain brain structures, in particular, the hippocampus, the area of the brain involved in the consolidation of short-term and long-term memory and spatial memory, as you'll recall from the study into London cab drivers. It may also play a role in our ability to imagine, including predicting and planning our future. When Henry was asked what he believed would happen tomorrow, he answered, whatever is beneficial – he appeared to have no information available that would inform him of the possibilities available, no database to consult when asked what he would do the next day, week, or in years to come. Often, when asked to make a prediction about his personal future, Henry would pick out an event from a distant memory. At other times, he would not respond at all (see Squire, 2009, for a full discussion of Henry's case).

What does Henry's case tell us about learning? First, it informs us that memory is vital for learning. It also tells us that not all memories are the same, and that memory is as important for looking forward through time as it is backwards. But the examination of Henry's impairments had much wider consequences – it heralded a shift in the way we think about and study human behaviour. Henry's case came to light at a very interesting juncture in the history of psychology. Behaviourism was under attack from what would eventually become cognitive psychology. Both schools were interested in how all animals, including humans, were able to learn and the conditions that bring it about. The history of our understanding of learning is, therefore, also the history of psychology. Henry could learn, but this learning was primarily the result of simple stimulus-response associations, the pairing of a stimulus to an action (like Pavlov's dogs discussed in Chapter 3). As we saw, this type of learning was studied extensively by behaviourists, yet other aspects of Henry's impairments, such as his inability to create new memories, were beyond the limits of what the behaviourists considered their legitimate remit. It would be up to cognitive psychology to offer some explanations for these deficits, ultimately leading to the development of explanatory models of both memory and learning.

Henry's wasn't the only case of its kind, but it was perhaps the most famous. One of the most important observations was that memory and learning are deeply entwined, but also that there are different types of learning and different types of memory. Furthermore, memory isn't centred in one particular region of the brain but is distributed across the cortex. There's a misconception that theories of memory developed solely from the notion that the human brain can be compared to a computer, yet many of the models developed since the advent of cognitive psychology have deferred to studies of people like Henry. While philosophers and early psychologists were interested in processes like memory, it wasn't until the 1950s that they began to develop the models we now recognise.

What is it to remember?

The most important aspect of learning is the process by which we retain newly learned information. Henry's severe memory impairments meant he couldn't learn anything beyond a few very simple actions. Henry couldn't describe what he'd done the day before, or even a few minutes before he was asked. He also couldn't anticipate what he might do the following day. Without memory, functioning at even a rudimentary level becomes increasingly problematic.

Earlier, I asked you to think about all the things you've learned so far in your lifetime. What if I asked you to think about all the things you have committed to memory? The two are certainly related, but is this second task more difficult? You won't remember much of your very early life, and your first concrete memories will probably arise around the age of four or even later. Despite this, however, those four years or so will have been filled with learning. Once you develop the ability to create concrete memories, there will be many that stand out, while others are more difficult to recall. Others, still, will have seemingly disappeared entirely. Memory isn't like a video camera; it doesn't capture everything we experience. And what we do recall is more likely to be a vague echo of the event rather than an accurate representation. We also forget things, and the reasons for this aren't always clear. We, then, need to consider what memory is, what purpose it serves, and how it relates to learning.

Memory structures are innate systems essential for survival, and different systems most likely evolved at different times as early humans existed in and were acted upon by the environment. The ability to retain information, such as experiences and learned skills, and to draw on this information at a later time, will have taken different forms at different stages of our evolution, from simple to more complex. Our ancient ancestors would have needed to remember where they could find food and when it was time to move on. Later, they would have recalled these journeys as stories that they could then relay orally from generation to generation to feel a connection to their past. As farming developed, humans would have needed to learn how to grow crops, raise livestock, and live off the fruits of their labour, teaching the next generation all they had learned to ensure later generations thrived.

Thus, memory systems evolved, but they didn't all evolve at the same time or in the same way in different species. These systems certainly became essential for survival, providing us with the capacity to retain often complex details and to use those details over and over again while the memories themselves increased in both complexity and sophistication. Around five-and-a-half thousand years ago in Mesopotamia, writing emerged and with it the potential for humans to offload much of the information their ancestors had acquired, preserving it for future generations.

Memory also fuels creativity and imagination, the ability to bring to mind advances in art, literature, and technology, and to release these thoughts into the world. Memory allows us to imagine societies, political ideologies, legal systems, economies, and a great deal more besides. It allows us to communicate through writing, language, music, and, yes, even interpretative dance. None of this would be possible in the absence of memory.

While research into memory accelerated during the so-called cognitive revolution, the study of memory dates back much further, at least to antiquity, even if it rarely moved at a predictable pace. Certainly, the likes of Aristotle, Plato, Cicero, Augustine, and Locke had much to say about memory, and it was in Ancient Rome that the art of memory evolved. During the Medieval period, this art of memory remained highly valued, and the ability to display advanced memory ability was integral to the merit and worth of a person (Collins, 2001). A good memory was associated with a person's ability to construct logical arguments, to understand scripture and laws and know how to conduct oneself. But there was also a growing interest in the details of memory and forgetting, and how and why something learned today could be forgotten by tomorrow. In his lecture to the Royal Society of London in 1682, the English polymath, Robert Hooke introduced an early model of memory. His model includes many components that aren't too far removed from those developed in the 1950s and 1960s, including aspects of encoding and attention. Hooke also introduced the idea that newly learned information decays over time if not refreshed, a notion that would receive greater prominence two centuries later (Hintzman, 2003). Similarly, French philosopher Maine de Biran writing in 1804, proposed that memory, rather than being a single entity, is composed of three forms that operate independently from one another (Maine de Biran, 1929): Representative memory (the conscious recall of facts and events), mechanical memory (learning of habits and skills), and sensitive memory (affective modifications). Although the details of de Biran's categories of memory have changed over the years, there remains a general consensus that memory is non-unitary – remembering involves the activation of regions throughout the brain.

These early accounts of memory are certainly enlightening but lack empirical support. They did, however, influence methods of instruction, particularly during the late nineteenth and early twentieth centuries. But our main focus here is the emergence of cognitive psychology in the 1950s, and this is where we see the evolution of empirically supported models of how humans retain vast amounts of daily information.

Hopefully, you'll instinctively understand what I mean when I use the word memory, but that doesn't mean formal definitions aren't useful, particularly when getting to grips with the nitty-gritty of memory research. There's also a great deal to be said for using metaphor, and over the years, memory has been described in lots of ways. Memory is a warehouse, a filing cabinet, a house, the rooms within a house, a junk box, a tape recorder, a library, and a garbage can. Plato and Aristotle described memory as a wax tablet, while Plato also likened it to a bird aviary. Formal definitions are certainly less poetic. The Oxford English Dictionary defines memory as the faculty by which the mind stores and remembers information, while William James, writing in the late 1800s, defines it as a knowledge of an event, or a fact which is out of conscious awareness currently, implying that our memories of things exist even if we can't or have little desire to recall them. Psychologists Endel Tulving and Fergus Craik describe memory as the ability to recollect past events and bring learned facts and ideas back to mind. Other explanations are less detailed, as in …memory means stored information: nothing more and nothing less (Murray et al., 2017, p.5).

The generally agreed-upon definition among researchers goes a little like this: the faculty of encoding, storing, and retrieving information (Squire, 2004). This latter description includes the processes by which people remember – that information is encoded (transformed into a form that can be stored), then stored in this newly created form, which can then be recalled (or retrieved). The process of encoding, storing, and recalling information lends itself to the information processing approach, likening the cognitive system to a computer, and highlighting the flow of information through that system. A process known as consolidation takes place after encoding, and I'll discuss this in more detail later.

Not all definitions are so precise, nor do they link directly to the processes involved in encoding, storing, and retrieving. For example, cognitive psychologist Daniel Willingham describes memory as the residue of thought. This is a description of memory well-known to teachers and educators and favoured by many within the teaching profession. Willingham has gained a substantial following since the emergence of his highly influential book *Why Don't Students Like School?* (Willingham, 2009). Although neglecting the nuts and bolts of the process, Willingham emphasises the important role of thinking in creating permanent memories by highlighting rehearsal mechanisms. Memory, in this respect, is what's left over when we think about something; the more we think about something (or the more we repeat an action), the greater chance that it's going to stay put in long-term memory.

The structure of memory

Formal definitions of memory hint at what the memory system may look like. In addition, our experience of memory allows us to have a fairly accurate grasp of what's going on when we try to learn something or attempt to recall what we've previously learned. We, therefore, think of memory as either long-term or short-term, even if we have little or no formal understanding of the science of memory. It's likely we also understand memory in terms of duration, or how long something is going to last. Unsurprisingly, information in short-term memory doesn't stay put for very long, while information in long-term memory stays put for a very long time (perhaps a lifetime). The capacity of short-term memory is thought to be anywhere between four and nine items, or chunks, but I'll return to this for a detailed explanation in the next chapter because it's going to play a major role in our story.

There's one other type of memory that often gets overlooked – sensory memory. This sensory memory equates to the initial point of contact, where all the information from our senses first enters the system. Information here is only going to last a few milliseconds, as most is lost or filtered out in favour of what is considered most relevant. As sophisticated as our brains are, dealing with the cacophony of multiple inputs places far too much stress on the system, and something must give. This latter point is going to play a major role in our discussion of how to make learning more effective and efficient.

The difference between these types of memory isn't only limited to time; there are also capacity limits. While we can only hold a limited amount of information in our short-term memory, it would appear that we can store a limitless amount in long-term memory. Short- and long-term memory, therefore, differ in these two fundamental ways (capacity and duration, or time), whereby short-term memory appears limited in both, long-term memory doesn't appear limited in either. But why does it seem that our memories appear to be divided in such a way? To answer this, we need to look a little more closely into the past.

Varieties of memory

In his two-volume *The Principles of Psychology*, William James describes memory as comprising primary memory and secondary memory, while it was much later that psychologists adopted the terms short and long-term memory (James, 1890). Cognitive psychologist Nelson Cowan describes short-term memory as faculties of human memory that can hold a limited amount of information in a very accessible form temporarily (Cowan, 2000). We, therefore, can't hold all that much information in our short-term memory, but we can access it quickly. The memory has been brought to mind, so to speak. It's also generally thought that in order to get new information to stay put in long-term memory, it first has to pass through short-term memory, where it's rehearsed and forwarded to a larger permanent store, where access is slower. We can then bring the information back into short-term memory where it is, again, more readily accessible. But while we can hold lots of information in long-term memory, the same isn't the case for short-term memory, so we continually bring information to mind when we require it. But the amount of information we can keep in short-term memory is limited.

Long-term memory is very different, and we only have to consider the different types of information we all hold to appreciate its complexity. During the 1970s, Canadian psychologist Endel Tulving proposed the division of long-term memory into two distinct types: declarative and non-declarative. I briefly touched on this in chapter 1, but here I want to emphasise these distinctions in relation to the division of long-term memory. Declarative memories are episodic or semantic. Episodic memory is concerned with the episodes of our life, events strung together in a rather loose and haphazard narrative. Anything we have experienced is episodic, from our first day at school, the birth of our children, or what we had for breakfast this morning. These memories are generally inaccurate, providing more of a general gist of what happened rather than a precise frame-by-frame account. Semantic memories, on the other hand, are what we might describe as general knowledge or facts. I know, for example, that Paris is the capital of France (a semantic memory), but I also recall visiting Paris (an episodic memory). I have total confidence in my assertion that Paris is the capital of France, yet I can't be as certain about the events of my visit to France because of the way episodic memories are reconstructed when recalled. I've a pretty good idea of what I got up to, such as visiting the Louvre, but I can't recall too much detail. When I do recall my visit, it comes with years of additional baggage, perhaps scenes from television shows, things I've read, or photographs I've seen, and these all get thrown into the mix and emerge

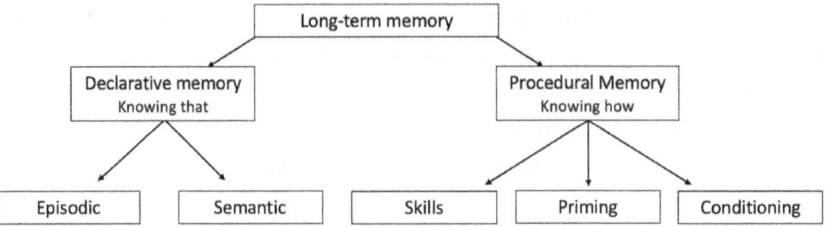

Figure 4.1 Different types of long-term memory.

as my memory of Paris. There will, undoubtedly, be gaps in my recollection and, because my mind isn't at all keen on these gaps, it will try to fill them with what seems logical and plausible. It doesn't help that I haven't been to Paris in many years, so the passing of time will have contaminated them further. This also means my memories of Paris remain frozen in time; they belong to a Paris that existed in my past. If I were to visit the city today and retrace my steps, it's unlikely I could reconcile all of what I experience in the present with what I recall from the past. If I were to ask someone who was with me, chances are many of their memories of Paris will be different from mine. For example, I recall going for a late-night walk through the streets with a friend. While I'm convinced it was perhaps 10 or 11 o'clock, they are just as convinced it was more like 2 am (Figure 4.1).

Thanks to Tulving, I also have a pretty good idea of where these different memories are in my brain. This is because Tulving injected a group of willing participants with tiny particles of radioactive gold and then asked them to recall either an episodic memory or a semantic memory (Tulving, 1989). The radioactive gold allowed him to track blood flow when he scanned their brains and identify the regions most active when people recalled the different types of memory. You might, at this point, be slightly concerned that Tulving injected volunteers with a radioactive substance, but I can assure you it was harmless. He even included himself and his wife in the study, so he must have been pretty confident. Tulving discovered that when people recalled an episodic memory, there was greater activation in the frontal lobes of the brain (the bit at the front, unsurprisingly), but when they were asked to recall a semantic memory, activation was at the back of the brain. Whether this is an accurate representation of the actual location of different types of memory is open to debate, but there is a consensus that semantic and episodic memories are different, as are implicit and explicit, or declarative and non-declarative memories. There is certainly a great deal of evidence identifying the hippocampus as vital to the storing of memories more generally, as you'll recall from the study of London taxi drivers.

We don't always know what we know

The accumulation of facts has its own peculiar quality; we may know that we know a fact, yet cannot recall it, or know the answer to a question, but have no recollection of how we came to know it. I could, for example, present you with a word list and ask you to read the list and then attempt to recall all the words on it. Say, you recalled half the words. I then give you another list of words with all the words from the word list, plus some extra ones for good measure. If I then ask you to highlight what was on the original list, chances are you'd do better than when I asked you to simply recall them (even when we take guesses into consideration). Sometimes, we just don't know what we know, while at other times, we think we know when we don't.

Declarative memory, therefore, includes memory for facts (or semantic memories) and memory for events (episodic memories). Non-declarative memories include neither. They may include skills, such as playing the piano or riding a bike, or behaviours learned through conditioning. Once we've learned to ride a bike, we don't have to think very much about what we're doing because the behaviour becomes automatic. We often describe this as motor or muscle memory. It just seems that our body knows what to do and gets on with it. Similarly, it takes a single instance of food poisoning to create a peculiar nauseous sensation when presented later with the food that made us ill. This is the same as the conditioned responses we see in rats, cats, salivating dogs, and poor Little Albert.

We can also see this difference between implicit and explicit memory when looking at people with severe memory deficits. Edouard Claparède was an early twentieth-century Swiss physician who worked extensively with patients suffering from memory disorders like Henry's. He describes his experiences with a female patient with extensive short-term memory impairments. Each day he would greet her and each day he would have to re-introduce himself because she could never recall their previous meeting. One day, he concealed a pin in his palm when he shook her hand, startling her. The following day she appeared reluctant to shake his hand again. Even though she had no explicit (or declarative) memory of the previous day's event, she appeared to have implicit awareness that shaking this man's hand elicited an unpleasant response. This is an example of non-declarative memory or implicit learning (see, for example, Claparède, 1911; Yoon et al., 2017).

When we learn something new, we may update our semantic memory or add to our store of procedural memory. It just depends on what we're learning. We may also remember the context in which we learned the information, and this can help us recall it. My memories of Paris reinforce my knowledge of Paris, even though I have no recollection of when I learned that Paris is the capital of France, or from whom I learned it. Knowing about the differences helps us to build a picture of the vast stores of knowledge that exist somewhere within the neural architecture of the brain. Understanding the relationship between these types of information can help us think about how we can learn more effectively.

You might wonder how we know memory is structured in this particular way. The inconvenient truth is that we don't; it just seems to fit with the evidence we have. Short- and long-term memory are hypothetical constructs that arose as the result of experimentation and clinical studies, resulting in a general agreement about their structure. However, there are competing views, some of which appear to fit the evidence better.

Memory and learning as information processing

The computer analogy viewed mental functions as a system of information processing, so it's hardly surprising that early theoretical models were built to look like computers. Just like a computer, theorised these early cognitive scientists, humans have input and output components and some kind of storage mechanism. This is why many of these ideas and models use terms that are also familiar to computer scientists – we process information, store information, and retrieve information. Whether the brain actually does any of these things is a topic of some debate, but the language suits our purpose, nevertheless. Even with the gradual demise of the computer metaphor, many of the terms have stuck fast, giving cognitive science an inhuman feel.

Donald Broadbent was the first cognitive psychologist to emphasise the role of information processing. His model encouraged later memory researchers, even though Broadbent's model described not memory but attention. Following on from Broadbent, Richard Atkinson and Richard Shiffrin examined the results of case studies (such as that of Henry) and experimental findings, to help build their first information processing model of memory (Atkinson & Shiffrin, 1968). It's a very simple model and perhaps looks a little too simple by today's standards, but it remains very influential and has spawned a whole new chapter on memory research. Simply put, their model (known as the multi-store or modal model) comprises three components: sensory register, where stimuli from the environment are picked up by the senses and held for a fraction of a second before some of that information is passed to a short-term store. If that information is adequately attended to, or rehearsed, it then flows into a long-term store where it should remain permanently. Now, information can travel from long-term memory back to short-term memory as well as from short-term memory to long-term memory as we bring information to mind. However, the limitations described previously also apply, so what we can hold in short-term memory at any one time remains limited (see Figure 4.2).

There are two important weaknesses of the model (at least as far as we are concerned). First, rehearsal might not be as important as the model makes out. After all, I can still remember what I had for breakfast this morning without having thought much about it all day (remember latent learning?). The second point rests on the unitary nature of the short-term store and the view that it's simply a staging post on

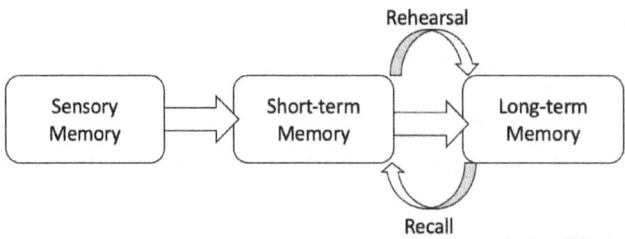

Figure 4.2 A simple stage model of memory (adapted from Atkinson & Shiffrin, 1968).

the way towards long-term memory. Henry's case implies that short-term memory is more complex than the model implies, and a multi-component short-term memory might do a better job of explaining them.

From short-term memory to working memory

Today, we continue to use the label short-term memory. However, cognitive psychologists are more likely to use the term working memory, even though the two are subtly different, as I'll explain later. Working memory is mostly associated with the working memory model developed by Alan Baddeley and Graham Hitch in the early 1970s, but the term had already been floating about for a few years. It first appeared in the literature in 1960 with an article by George Miller. In Plans and the structure of behaviour, Miller, Galanter, and Pribram write of a kind of quick access working memory, but don't really expand on the concept (Miller et al., 1960). Similarly, Atkinson and Shiffrin use the term in their 1968 paper, the article that first proposed the multi-store model of memory. But neither papers really identify short-term memory as differing from working memory.

What then is working memory, and how does it differ from run-of-the-mill short-term memory? Thankfully, definitions aren't too dissimilar. Baddeley, for example, describes it as a limited capacity system for the temporary storage and processing of information required for complex cognition. Cowan describes working memory as the ensemble of components of the mind that hold a limited amount of information temporarily in a heightened state of availability for use in ongoing information processing. Pierre Barrouillet defines working memory as the structure where mental representations are built, maintained, and modified according to our goals (Logie et al., 2021).

Robert Logie, Valérie Camos, and Nelson Cowan also offer a more comprehensive definition in their 2021 Working Memory: State of the Science. Working memory refers to our ability to keep a small amount of information readily available for our current activities, and so support decisions, guide actions, make statements, and keep track of conversations, to navigate and support creative thinking and problem solving, to remember to do things, and to update what is going on around us throughout the day. They go on to summarise working memory as an ability that we use every waking moment of our lives. It's easy to see why working memory is one of the most studied areas in cognitive psychology.

I haven't chosen these definitions at random. They represent different ways of looking at working memory with their primary proponents, Alan Baddeley and Graham Hitch, Nelson Cowan, and Pierre Barrouillet, approaching the problem from slightly different positions. There is no one single model of working memory, yet most of the influential models share similarities.

Without doubt, the working memory model of Baddeley and Hitch is the most influential of all memory models (Baddeley & Hitch, 1974). It's the one taught in psychology classes from high school to university. It's also the model most teachers interested in the learning sciences will be familiar with. The working memory model re-conceptualises the static store of Atkinson and Shiffrin into a multi-component system where things happen. It's in working memory where we keep information as we complete each stage of a task or hold the instructions of a task until the stages are complete. In working memory, we carry out mental arithmetic, hold the words in a sentence so that we can understand its meaning, and the utterances in a conversation so that we can plan and execute a response. To understand the relationship between learning and memory, it's important to have an awareness of what working memory is. While definitions may vary, there is general agreement regarding its purpose.

Here's a short demonstration of how we might use working memory. If I were to ask you to count in your mind the number of windows in your house from memory, you would need to access the information related to the task held in long-term memory and attend to it in working memory by keeping a tally of the number of windows. This is a rather complex mental task that tests our memory capacity quite highly. Not only are you having to complete each stage before moving onto the next (the tally), you also need to keep in mind the details of the task. Or what you're supposed to be doing. Working memory, then, also holds information about the details of the task and any instructions we need to complete it; otherwise, we'll start counting the windows and then forget what we're doing. People with impairments to working memory often do this – they'll start a task and then lose track of what they are doing (we all do this from time to time, of course).

As you can see with the windows example, working memory continually interacts with long-term memory. There is a flow back and forth from one to the other as you pull information about your house from the long-term store and deposit it temporarily into working memory.

Let's look at another example. Our ability to comprehend the sentence: 'Billy was frightened of the giant spider' requires the reader to make words from letters, to understand the meaning of the words and to understand the whole sentence. When we are learning to read, we hold individual letters in working memory and combine them to form words. However, in long-term memory, strings of letters are represented as words and processed semantically, that is, by their meaning. Once we can read, we don't need to sound out each letter; we just read the words unconsciously. We can't help but read them, like when we see a large advertising billboard and immediately read the slogan, even if we don't intend to. Working memory holds onto these words temporarily while we process the sentence. But we are also using long-term memory because we need to make sense of the words in relation to each other. We need to understand that Billy is the name of a person, that there is a spider involved (and a giant one at that) and that Billy is frightened of it. The sentence comprises seven words (well within the capacity of working memory) but contains 34 letters (well beyond working memory capacity). What if I gave you these words as a list and asked you to recall them? Now ask yourself what the result might be if I gave you the same words but in a different order, such as 'Spider Giant Billy Frightened Was Of The'. I'll come back to this later.

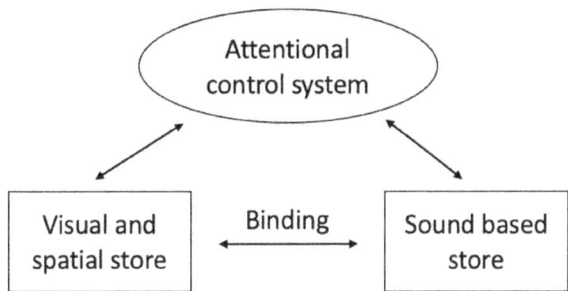

Figure 4.3 A simplified multi-component model of working memory.

The working memory model is a multi-component model, comprising a store for sound-based information (known as the phonological loop) and one for visual and spatial information (the visuospatial sketchpad). A central attention system (the central executive) allocates the necessary resources to each store, while the episodic buffer combines, or binds, this information into a continuous narrative. It's worth noting that the episodic buffer wasn't part of the original model, having been added in 2000 as an attempt to explain how we experience memories. Each component is still limited in capacity and duration and can become overloaded. You'll have noticed, for example, that your ability to concentrate on one verbal input becomes compromised if you're having to compete with a second verbal input, such as trying to read a book on the bus when the couple in the next seat is having a rather heated discussion. Importantly, sound-based inputs shouldn't interfere with visual inputs and, in many cases, can be used to enhance learning by combining modalities (pictures accompanied with text, for example), a process known as dual coding (more about this later). Figure 4.3 represents a stripped-down version of working memory.

Why do we need working memory?

While working memory is limited in its capacity and duration, it's fast. Long-term memory is slow and error-prone. Long-term memory is also much less detailed than we might think. We use the term gist memory to describe our long-term recollections because they are never an exact copy of the original event. When we read a book, for example, we don't appear to retain all the information from it, but we get a general idea of its content. If you were to ask me about Cormac McCarthy's *The Road*, I'd tell you it was about a father and son journeying through a post-apocalyptic America and that they encounter some very unsavoury characters along the way. I could tell you how it ends (don't worry, I won't), but I won't be able to go into detail about every incident in the story. What I have is the gist of the story, but not a blow-by-blow account. This notion of gist memory has been known for some time. George Stout was an early British psychologist and author of the highly influential Manual of Psychology (first published in 1898). In his manual, he describes how a student, studying Euclid for the first time, will initially attempt to learn it by heart. However, when the student has completed the work, all that will remain is the 'general method of proof' (Stout, 1901, p.454); much of the detail will have been forgotten. However, the fallibility of long-term memory can also result in important details getting stripped from our recollection or, more damaging perhaps, a memory that bears little resemblance to the one experienced.

Say I was to give you a list of medical-related words: nurse, patient, hospital, ambulance. If I included a delay between the learning element of the task (the encoding stage) and the recall stage, and then asked you to identify the words from the following list: computer, nurse, bicycle, newspaper, hospital, doctor, school, ambulance, you would be statistically more likely to include the word doctor along with nurse, patient, hospital, and ambulance. Crucially, your confidence that the doctor was part of the original list would be very high. This is a type of test (known as the DRM task after its originators, Deese, Roediger, and McDermott) often used to induce false memories – recollections of which we are very confident despite them having never taken place. Time, therefore, plays a vital role in what we remember and what we forget, but time also plays a part in how we remember. Cognitive psychologists working within the criminal justice system have long been aware that long-term memory is far too error-prone for eyewitness testimony to be even close to accurate. For decades, Elizabeth Loftus and her team at the University of Washington have gathered evidence from hundreds of studies that find people simply don't recall events in the way we think they do. Loftus has also shown again and again how simple it is to take advantage of memory fallibility by creating false memories in many of her volunteers.

Long-term memory and working memory differ not only in terms of capacity and duration but also in terms of utility. The prevailing view is that for information to take up relatively permanent residence in long-term memory, it must first pass through working memory. Similarly, for us to use that information, it must be passed back into working memory. But this might not always be the case.

Neuroscientists Tim Shallice and Elizabeth Warrington studied a patient they called KF. KF was a young man who had suffered severe brain trauma from a motorcycle accident, leading to a lesion in his left parietal-occipital region. Unlike Henry, KF had significant impairment to his short-term memory while his long-term memory remained relatively intact. He had a digit span of only one or two (so he could only hold one or two items in short-term memory). Despite severe impairment to his short-term memory, KF could still learn and retain new information over extended periods (Shallice & Warrington, 1970). If we are correct in our assumption about short-term memory, KF shouldn't have been able to learn anything. He still had problems holding onto short-term memory, but once the information had passed this stage, it could still be stored in long-term memory. KF could learn new facts, recognise words, and remember experiences, only with more difficulty and less efficiency than those with intact short-term memory.

But what he could learn might provide some insight into how he did it. He was much better at learning visual and non-verbal information than verbal information, highlighting the complex nature of short-term memory. It also poses the possibility that there might be alternative pathways or mechanisms for encoding information into long-term memory that do not rely on a fully functional short-term memory. It's likely that these alternative pathways, along with a reliance on preserved non-verbal memory systems and his use of compensatory strategies, helped him to work around his short-term memory deficits.

To add to this conundrum, a 2008 study by Jerker Rönnberg and colleagues implies that information can bypass working memory, at least in the context of auditory-visual speech perception. They concluded that certain aspects of language processing may occur without having to rely heavily on working memory, indicating the existence of direct pathways for processing information in the brain that don't involve the traditional working memory system (Rönnberg et al., 2008).

Not only is it assumed that new information must first pass through short-term memory on its journey to long-term memory, but it's also thought that the reverse is true – that information already in long-term memory flows back to working memory where we can use it. In one study from 2022, however, researchers found that information retrieved from long-term memory doesn't always need to be brought back into working memory when working memory is fully engaged (Liu et al., 2022). The researchers found neurological evidence showing that long-term memory can bypass working memory in the form of increased alpha suppression during long-term memory retrieval. This suggests that long-term memory uses a different cognitive process.

Memory and learning as depth of processing

During the 1970s, Fergus Craik and Robert Lockhart investigated the possibility that learning is more concerned with depth rather than repetition. Their claim was that memory happens as the result of processing, so memory is a by-product of thinking (Craik & Lockhart, 1972). This sounds similar to Willingham's view that memory is the residue of thought and implies a polite nod to Craik and Lockhart's levels of processing theory. The deeper we process information, the more resilient the memory, so less about memory stores, time, and capacity and more about what we do with the information during learning. Greater elaboration of the material lends itself to more effective retention. According to the theory, the human brain encodes different types of information in different ways. And at different depths or levels. The first level, structural, is the shallowest form of processing. In a typical experiment conducted by Craik and Lockhart, a volunteer might be presented with the word HOUSE and the statement, *the word is written in capital letters*. They would then need to say if the statement was true or false. We don't need to read or understand the word; simply identify the quality of its structure.

The second stage (phonetic processing) is based on how the word sounds. For example, participants would be asked if the word HOUSE rhymes with mouse. The processing of the word is slightly deeper. The deepest level of processing is called semantic processing, and participants would be asked to answer true or false to the statement, *a structure in which people live.*

The lowest level of processing would include strategies such as rote rehearsal because we don't need to know anything about the word to remember it (like Mr Jarvis's lines). But the deepest level of processing involves understanding the meaning of the word and the creation of connections and associations. There are, of course, many different incidences of 'house', such as terrace houses, detached houses, bungalows, and mansions, but they are all houses. The word house has meaning; a house is a physical structure, and our episodic memories are awash with events that have taken place in houses. A house is, therefore, more than a word written in capital letters or one that rhymes with mouse. How we think about house is more important than just thinking about it.

Depth also relates to how well-established the connections are between pieces of information. Connections can be strengthened through elaboration, the expansion of concepts in terms of why and the how (how does a plane stay up in the sky? Why doesn't it fall to the ground like other heavy objects?), but we can also strengthen the connections by linking one concept to another (a whale lives in the ocean, a whale is a mammal, a whale isn't a fish). I'll return to the way learning requires the elaboration and the assimilation of new knowledge into previous knowledge in Chapter 7.

Memory beyond boxes

Multi-component models of memory assume the flow of information from one component to another. Information can flow back and forth between short-term (or working) memory and long-term memory. A very simplistic explanation is that we manipulate information in working memory and store it permanently in long-term memory. But we also access information in long-term memory, temporarily transfer it to working memory, do something with it and then re-consolidate the slightly altered information back into long-term memory. There's an awful lot of to-ing and fro-ing, as well as some boxes and a few arrows. Of course, the boxes and arrows are part of a conceptual model – you won't find boxes and arrows in the brain, no matter how hard you search. This means it's pretty difficult to map these models onto specific brain regions, but then that's not really what the models are for. However, not all memory models are quite so boxy; indeed, contemporary accounts appear to be moving away from the box and arrow models, at least a little, while neuroscience is filling in many of the gaps, as we'll discover in Chapter 7.

Nelson Cowan is Professor of Psychological Science at the University of Missouri. His embedded processes model of memory is quite different from the usual box and arrow models, as is his greater emphasis on the role of attention. Cowan's theory can be explained a little bit like this: Imagine all the memories you have as stars in a pitch-black universe. At the moment, you're not bringing any of them to mind, so they are quite faint against the dark background. Now, imagine the faint one on the far right of the black canvas is a memory you wish to recall; as you focus your attention on it, it becomes brighter and clearer, as if you've shone a spotlight onto it. In the language of Cowan's model, what you've done is activate a portion of long-term memory, transforming it temporarily into an item in working memory. Working memory, therefore, is activated long-term memory, held in our focus of attention while we do whatever it is we need to do with it. Rather than components being discrete boxes, they are embedded within each other, hence the embedded processes model (Cowan, 1999). The flexibility of the model and the emphasis on interconnectivity also support the previously discussed study, whereby working memory may not always be necessary for the retrieval of long-term memories (Figure 4.4).

It's clear that, although most theoretical models of memory share many basic principles, they don't agree on everything. These models are certainly influential – but they are still models that attempt to explain how memory works by employing graphic representations that do not exist in the world of the living brain. Guy Claxton, drawing on earlier comments from Ulric Neisser, is critical of this *boxology*. According to Claxton, the boxes and the arrows beloved of the information processing generation look like they might be due for a trip to the dump – and that… includes long-term and short-term memory (Claxton, 2021, p.101). Claxton is right to be critical. And he's in good company. According to Cowan, practically nobody literally believes that there are boxes inside the head doing the work, even poking fun at his own model by adding, let alone boxes within boxes. Yet Cowan defends these models in terms of their ability to graphically represent processes that are often abstract, relating them to domains that are easier to think about, such as plumbing, electricity, and computer science (Logie et al., 2021, p.57).

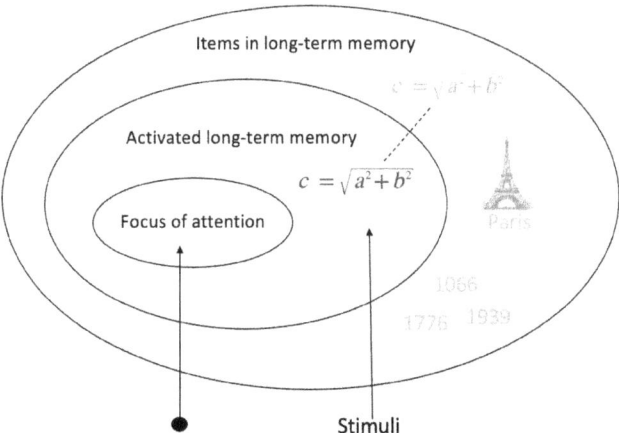

Figure 4.4 Working memory as activated long-term memory (adapted from Cowan, 1999, 2000).

If ensuring that information takes up relatively permanent residence in long-term memory is one very important aspect of learning (but one of several), we first need to work out how we can best achieve this. This isn't easy, seeing as working memory has limited resources at its disposal, and our attention can drift and we can lose focus. We also need to begin from the premise that the models we adopt have it right and, as we have seen, different models reveal many more questions. There is a general consensus that short-term memory is constrained by limited capacity, time, and attention, areas I'll return to in the following chapters.

Chapter summary

- Case studies have provided insight into how the human brain learns and the structures involved, such as the hippocampus and amygdala.

- The structure for memory is divided into sensory, short-term, and long-term memory, each with individual limits on capacity and duration. Long-term memory is further divided into declarative (episodic and semantic) and non-declarative (procedural) memory.

- Models of memory help to explain how we process, store, and retrieve information. Simple models view short-term memory as a temporary staging post, while others reconceptualise short-term memory as a dynamic working memory. Cowan's model views working memory as activated long-term memory.

- Depth of processing theory suggests memory is a by-product of processing, and deeper processing leads to more resilient memories, focusing on what we do with information rather than just memory stores and repetition.

Further reading

Firth, J., & Riazat, N. (2023). *What teachers need to know about memory.* Corwin.
McGill, R. M. (2022). *The teacher toolkit guide to memory.* Bloomsbury.

References

Atkinson, R. C., & Shiffrin, R. M. (1968). Human memory: A proposed system and its control processes. *Psychology of Learning and Motivation, 2,* 89–195. https://doi.org/10.1016/S0079-7421(08)60422-3
Baddeley, A. D., & Hitch, G. (1974). Working memory. *Psychology of Learning and Motivation, 8,* 47–89. https://doi.org/10.1016/S0079-7421(08)60452-1
Claparède, E. (1911). Reconnaissance et moitié. *Archives de Psychologic, 11,* 79–90.
Claxton, G. (2021). *The future of teaching and the myths that hold it back.* Routledge.
Collins, A. (2001). The psychology of memory. In G. C. Bunn, A. D. Lovie, & G. D. Richards (Eds.), *Psychology in Britain: Historical essays and personal reflections* (pp. 150–168). The British Psychological Society.

Cowan, N. (1999). An embedded-processes model of working memory. In A. Miyake, & P. Shah (Eds.), *Models of working memory: Mechanisms of active maintenance and executive control* (pp. 62–101). Cambridge University Press.

Cowan, N. (2000). The magical number 4 in short-term memory: A reconsideration of mental storage capacity. *Behavioral and Brain Sciences*, *24*(1), 87–185. https://doi.org/10.1017/S0140525X01003922

Craik, F. I. M., & Lockhart, R. S. (1972). Levels of processing: A framework for memory research. *Journal of Verbal Learning and Verbal Behavior*, *11*(6), 671–684. https://doi.org/10.1016/S0022-5371(72)80001-X

Hintzman, D. L. (2003). Robert Hooke's model of memory. *Psychonomic Bulletin and Review*, *10*(1), 3–14. https://doi.org/10.3758/BF03196465

James, W. (1890). *The principles of psychology* (Vol. 1). Henry Holt and Co.

Liu, B., Li, X., Theeuwes, J., & Wang, B. (2022). Long-term memory retrieval bypasses working memory. *NeuroImage*, *261*(June), 119513. https://doi.org/10.1016/j.neuroimage.2022.119513

Logie, R. H., Camos, V., & Cowan, N. (2021). *Working memory, state of the science*. Oxford University Press.

Maine de Biran. (1929). *The influence of habit on the faculty of thinking*. Williams and Wilkins.

Miller, G. A., Galanter, E., & Pribram, K. H. (1960). *Plans and the structure of behavior*. Martino Fine Books.

Murray, E. A., Wise, S. P., & Graham, K. S. (2017). *The evolution of memory systems*. Oxford University Press.

Rönnberg, J., Rudner, M., Foo, C., & Lunner, T. (2008). Cognition counts: A working memory system for ease of language understanding (ELU). *International Journal of Audiology*, *47*(Suppl. 2). https://doi.org/10.1080/14992020802301167

Shallice, T., & Warrington, E. K. (1970). Independent functioning of verbal memory stores: A neuropsychological study. *The Quarterly Journal of Experimental Psychology*, *22*(2), 261–273. https://doi.org/10.1080/00335557043000203

Squire, L. R. (2004). Memory systems of the brain: A brief history and current perspective. *Neurobiology of Learning and Memory*, *82*(3), 171–177. https://doi.org/10.1016/j.nlm.2004.06.005

Squire, L. R. (2009). The legacy of patient H.M. for neuroscience. *Neuron*, *61*(1), 6–9. https://doi.org/10.1016/j.neuron.2008.12.023

Stout, G. F. (1901). *A manual of psychology* (2nd Edition). University Tutorial Press Ltd.

Tulving, E. (1989). Memory: Performance, knowledge, and experience. *European Journal of Cognitive Psychology*, *1*(1), 3–26. https://doi.org/10.1080/09541448908403069

Willingham, D. T. (2009). *Why don't students like school?* Wiley.

Yoon, S., Duff, M., & Brown-Schmidt, S. (2017, September). Learning and using knowledge about what other people do and don't know despite amnesia. *Cortex*, *94*, 164–175. https://doi.org/10.1016/j.cortex.2017.06.020

5 Why we struggle to remember

When memory fails, learning fails. But why might memory fail? Some types of memories are more resilient than others, such as riding a bike versus remembering the events leading up to the First World War. Learning that has reached a high level of automaticity is less likely to fall foul of forgetting – if you're of a certain age, the chances are you'll still be able to recall telephone numbers from many years ago, even though you haven't used them for a long time. This is, in part, to do with the way we organise telephone numbers in our memory, but sometimes it's because things have been deliberately designed to make them more memorable (such as UK postcodes). Automating some kinds of material (such as multiplication tables or word spellings) is, therefore, very useful (as we saw in Chapter 3 with automatic behaviours). Sometimes forgetting just happens and, surprisingly, forgetting is also part of the learning process. Forgetting is natural, whether it is where we left our car keys or the content we were taught in school. Chances are, you'll have difficulty recalling what you learned when you were young, and this only gets more difficult with the passing of time. Forgetting is far from a glitch, however, and seems to be intentionally hard-wired into our neural circuitry. Often, something we think we've forgotten spontaneously reappears. At other times, no amount of nudging and prodding will do any good – the memory is gone, and it's never coming back.

If we understand how memory works, we have a much better chance of understanding why it fails. If we understand how memory fails, we have a much better chance of developing strategies to make this failure less likely. While there is some debate over why we forget, we know it involves time, capacity, interference, and attention, and these are the areas I want to focus primarily on in this chapter. As we saw previously, many of the models of learning developed over the past few decades rely heavily on the distinctions between long-term, short-term, and working memory. These models also point to the notion that information in short-term memory disappears through the passing of time (known as temporal decay), but we can prevent this by refreshing it via rehearsal. We also see evidence of this in our own experiences, for example, when we must briefly remember a phone number. This loss certainly occurs through temporal decay, but it might also occur because older information and newer information contaminate what we're trying to remember, a process known as interference. If you're trying to keep a telephone number in working memory until you find a pen and write it down, similar numbers might well disrupt this memory, altering its structure without us noticing the change. The more we rehearse information in short-term memory, the more it is likely to become a relatively permanent part of long-term memory, although, as we'll see, we may lose many of the details.

Transforming experiences into memories

What we sometimes overlook with learning is encoding. Insufficient processing at the encoding stage will lead to poor retention and, thus, inadequate learning. Context Variability Theory suggests that encoding and retrieval of information is as much dependent on the when and the where as much as the what. The implication is that retrieval of information is triggered by context, the elements of which are encoded into long-term memory at the same time as the to-be-learned information. These contextual elements act as cues, enhancing our retrieval ability. The more cues, the greater the likelihood we'll successfully recall the information. If the appropriate cues cannot be located, retrieval fails (so-called context-dependent forgetting).

Duncan Godden and Alan Baddeley tested this phenomenon in a rather imaginative way, using 18 participants from the University of Stirling's scuba diving club (Godden & Baddeley, 1975). They were interested in how the environment in which we learn something influences our ability to remember it later. They had some participants learn a list of words underwater and then tested them on their recall ability, also underwater. Others learned the words on land and were then tested on land. Finally, some learned the words on land but were tested underwater. Results were pretty striking. Divers who learned and were tested in the same environment recalled significantly more than those where the environment differed between the learning and recall phase, implying that we are better at remembering items when the learning context matches the recall context.

Similarly, Donald Overton asked participants to learn material when they were either drunk or sober. The drunk participants found it difficult to recall the material when sober, but easier when drunk (Overton, 1972). The same was true with the sober participants. In another study, Charles Darley (Darley et al., 1974) had participants hide money while they were high on marijuana and discovered they found it easier to locate the cash when they were again high, but not when they weren't.

Studies have also looked at context-dependent memory in different settings. Harry Grant and colleagues from Iowa State University, for example, discovered that students who learn material in a noisy environment do better when tested in a similar environment (and the same was true for a silent environment) than when the environment differed between noisy and silent (Grant et al., 1998).

We forget for different reasons – temporal decay, interference with other stimuli, and loss of contextual cues. But how long can information last? We might assume that if information has entered long-term memory via short-term memory, this information is going to stay put. After all, long-term memory is assumed to potentially last a lifetime. If I, for example, memorised a series of historical dates today and made sure I could recite them from memory, then I should still be able to remember them tomorrow. Of course, it isn't that straightforward.

Is time the enemy of memory?

Research into memory began well before the advent of cognitive psychology, with the pioneering work of nineteenth-century German experimental psychologists who began investigating memory as early as 1879. It was in Germany, towards the end of the nineteenth century, that Wilhelm Wundt established the world's first experimental psychology laboratory at the University of Leipzig. His lab provided all that was necessary at the time, including a series of well-equipped rooms and a steady supply of doctoral students. Wundt will forever remain one of the most important figures in the history of psychology but, despite his reputation and obvious influence, this brief paragraph is going to be the only time I mention him. That's because I want to focus on another German psychologist of the time: Hermann Ebbinghaus.

Ebbinghaus's early career was very different from that of Wundt. After obtaining his doctorate from the University of Bonn in 1873, he would cultivate his interest in human memory, an area for which he is best known. In 1880, he obtained an unsalaried position at the University of Berlin, where he could continue his research. Rather than a purpose-built laboratory and an army of eager young students, Ebbinghaus worked alone, attempting to counter the prevailing view of the time that higher mental functions, such as memory, couldn't be studied scientifically. This was clearly going to be a difficult task, not least because an experimental psychologist needs volunteers, and Ebbinghaus had none. He, therefore, opted to use the only person available – himself, a decision that would cause ripples of criticism throughout time, but one he had little other option but to take. Having decided to use himself as his only participant, he set about trying to design his experiment. First, he needed something he could learn and test himself on, but he had to choose carefully because he couldn't know in advance what he was going to learn. Also, he needed a stimulus that carried no association. Word lists were the obvious option, but words carry meaning, and he wanted to eliminate any possibility of using what he already knew to help him remember the material. The word milk, for example, can be associated with the word cow, and he could use this association as a memory cue.

In the end, Ebbinghaus opted for nonsense syllables, comprising a consonant followed by a vowel and ending with another consonant. These syllables have become known as consonant-vowel-consonant trigrams and are still used today.

He needed to be able to sound them out but take care they didn't sound like actual words. We don't know all the words he used but can assume they might have included the likes of DAX, BOK, and YAT. After generating over 2,300 of these trigrams, Ebbinghaus printed each one on a separate card and placed the cards in a box. He would then draw them out at random, look at them for a fraction of a second, pause for 15 seconds and go through the list again. He repeated the procedure until he could recite a series of syllables at speed. By varying the lengths of exposure and learning intervals, Ebbinghaus detected a pattern of learning and forgetting emerging. He also found he could remember meaningful material, such as a poem, ten times more easily than he could the trigrams (an important factor that I'll come back to later). However, with repeated exposure to the trigrams, he could remember the lists for longer. But it was the first few repetitions that seemed the most important.

If he repeated the syllables immediately after exposure, recall was better than if there was a longer interval, but the most rapid memory loss was within the first hour, followed by a slightly lower loss of recall after nine hours, where the loss was about 60 percent, rising to around 66 percent after 24 hours. If we were to plot these results on a graph, we would see an initial sharp decline followed by a gentler, shallower curve, describing the way forgetting forms a curve. We now recognise this graph as the forgetting curve, and it's what Ebbinghaus is best remembered for (and it confirms what Robert Hooke proposed two centuries earlier, as noted in Chapter 4). But he also discovered some other interesting facets of memory. Syllables at the beginning and end of the list tended to be recalled more often than those in the middle, the so-called primacy and recency effects, and the timing of repeated exposure to the material made a big impact on later recall, a phenomenon known as the spacing effect (more on these later).

There is little doubt that these findings were of paramount importance to later research into memory and learning, not least because Ebbinghaus eventually overturned the belief that certain mental functions couldn't be studied empirically. However, there's much more to his studies than meets the eye. First, there was a genuine attempt to reduce confounding variables that might bias the data. For example, Ebbinghaus tested himself at the same time every day and made sure his immediate environment was kept constant, even to the extent of remaining mindful of not varying his daily activities in the hour or so before the tests. He kept the time consistent by using a metronome, thus ensuring that he spent exactly the same time on each syllable and said each syllable with the same voice inflection. This attention to detail and the care and skill with which he conducted his experiments are just as important as his experimental findings. In his seminal publication, Über das Gedächtnis (published in English as Memory: A Contribution to Experimental Psychology) in 1885, Ebbinghaus details 20 studies that took place over a number of years (Ebbinghaus, 1885). This attention to detail made it much easier for others to replicate his findings. For example, Austrian psychologist Adolf Jost memorised sets of 12 syllables, all of which were repeated 24 times every other day but in different distributions. He discovered he was better able to remember on the second day than on the first and on the third day better than on the second, leading to what became known as Jost's Law of Forgetting (Alin, 1997). In another series of experiments conducted between 1911 and 1912 at the University of Michigan, Nellie Perkins confirmed both men's findings (Perkins, 1914).

What then are we to take from this? We know memory decays over time (the forgetting curve). The memory decays because we don't return to the information often enough. We can retain the memory for longer if we revisit it often. But at some point, the memory will become permanent and refreshing won't make much difference. Learning, then, begins as a classic forgetting curve, but we reduce the curve each time we revisit the material. Each time we refresh, we forget less. Learning, then, can be thought of as spaced or distributed, because we are spreading out learning across a longer time period rather than expecting to remember everything all at once.

Capacity limits

You'll recall that the two major differences between short- and long-term memory are concerned with capacity and duration. Capacity is often measured via a procedure known as immediate digit span, that is, the number of single digits a person can retain in short-term memory before they disappear. When discussing digit span, we usually refer to George Miller's 1956 study (it remains one of the most cited papers in the history of psychology), yet it was a relative unknown, Joseph Jacobs, who first investigated the capacity of memory back in 1887. Jacobs initially asked his participants (students from North London Collegiate College) to repeat back nonsense syllables (a technique already used by Ebbinghaus) but found they varied too greatly in relative difficulty of pronunciation and relative facility to rhythm. He, therefore, abandoned this idea and instead chose letters (except for W) and numbers (except for seven). These omissions were necessary to ensure equal length and speed of vocalisation. He found that, on average, participants could successfully repeat back around seven letters and nine numbers (Jacobs, 1887). In the same year, Francis Galton carried out similar studies into what was then described as prehension by investigating the memory capacity of a group of patients at the 'Earlsworm Asylum for Idiots' (Galton, 1887). It's worth noting here that both Galton and American psychologist William James had, by this time, hypothesised that memory has both short and long-term components; primary memory, suggested James, represents the small amount of information held at the trailing edge of the conscious present, while secondary memory is the vast body of knowledge stored over a lifetime (James, 1890).

It wasn't until 1956 that Miller found, on average, people could hold between five and nine pieces of information in short-term memory at any one time, or more precisely, 7 ± 2 chunks (sometimes referred to as Miller's magic number). According to Miller, the capacity of verbal short-term memory is determined by the number of chunks, or pieces of information, we can store, and not the number of items or the amount of information (Miller, 1956). More recently, Nelson Cowan has suggested that the capacity of short-term memory is closer to four items, although he used focus of attention to calculate capacity rather than the number of digits held (Cowan, 2000). Cowan's is probably a closer estimate, but the two men used different methods to reach their conclusions, and their theoretical base also differed. While Miller's estimates are based on chunks of information, Cowan limited chunking in his experiments, focusing instead on discrete items. He also emphasised the role played by a person's focus of attention. It's therefore difficult to directly compare the two studies.

The capacity of short-term memory is therefore somewhere between four and nine, depending on how we measure it. But short-term memory is certainly limited, and violation of these capacity rules can lead to forgetting because we might attempt to hold too much information. If you were attempting to learn, say, 15 random digits in order, it's highly unlikely you'd be able to recall them all. However, there is a great deal of flexibility because of a technique known as chunking, or the grouping together of pieces of information into meaningful groups. As we'll see later, chunking allows us to increase our digit span significantly and learn certain types of information faster by considering short-term memory limitations and long-term memory structures.

What happens when we disrupt rehearsal?

Husband and wife team Lloyd and Margaret Peterson were interested in two interrelated aspects of short-term memory: how long information remains in short-term memory before it decays (its duration), and the consequences of limiting our ability to rehearse the information. To investigate this, they presented volunteers with lists of trigrams one at a time and had them recall them after intervals of 3, 6, 9, 12, 15, or 18 seconds. In addition, they asked them to count backwards in threes or fours from a specified random number until they saw a red light appear. The counting was to prevent rehearsal of the trigrams, a technique developed a year earlier by Lloyd Peterson and John Brown and known as the Brown-Peterson technique. Not surprisingly, perhaps, the volunteer's ability to recall the trigrams was associated with the length of the delay, ranging from 80 percent correct after three seconds to less than 10 percent after 18 seconds. The Petersons concluded that short-term memory has a limited duration and that when rehearsal is prevented, information will decay after about 18–30 seconds (Peterson & Peterson, 1959).

In addition to these seminal studies in memory, researchers have identified other aspects of the way we recall and fail to recall information, even if this information is little more than lists of numbers and letters. Alan Baddeley, for example, discovered that people can remember more short words than long words, a phenomenon known as the word length effect (Baddeley et al., 1975). But why would this be the case? The most obvious explanation is that longer words take longer to vocalise internally, increasing the time to process them. In line with Ebbinghaus's forgetting curve, studies like Baddeley's imply that memory is subject to time-based decay – increased processing time increases the likelihood that items in short-term memory will be irretrievably lost.

Another interesting finding concluded that people have a tendency to remember the first and last words in a list, but forget those in the middle, indicating that the earlier words have entered long-term memory while the later ones are still resident in short-term memory. Words in the middle, however, have fallen into a dark hole whence they shall never return. This phenomenon has been called the primacy and recency effect and was first observed by Ebbinghaus. In 1966, Murray Glanzer and Anita Cunitz found that if they presented volunteers with a list of words to recall but then prevented rehearsal, they still had a tendency to remember the first few words (the primacy effect) but have difficulty recalling those at the end of the list, the assumption being that the first few words have already entered long-term memory but, because of the rehearsal prevention task, they have disappeared from short-term memory (Glanzer & Cunitz, 1966).

Overloading the system

At face value, it might appear that the main reason we forget is through the passing of time – not much of an earth-shattering revelation. But if we dig a little deeper, an interesting pattern emerges. If we suppose that all new information must enter short-term memory and pass into long-term memory before it can take up relatively permanent residence in our minds, it logically follows that any failure to do so must take place in the early stages of acquiring new information. Short-term and working memory operate within certain limitations (such as duration and capacity), and it would make sense that, if we exceed these limitations, something is bound to give. This view represents the basic tenets of what's known as cognitive load.

One of the earliest references to cognitive load (also referred to as mental workload, especially in earlier literature) was in a 1966 paper on auditory vigilance. Jerrold Levine describes it as the amount of information that the observer is required to store in memory and later retrieve (Levine, 1966). Oskar Palinko defines cognitive load as the relationship between cognitive demands placed on the user by a task and the user's cognitive resources (Palinko et al., 2010).

Cognitive load, therefore, is about the mental resources we have available to complete any given task. As the demands of the task increase, the more difficult the task becomes, something we know through experience. This is because, as we have seen, working memory operates within certain limitations. It's not all about memory, however, because memory and attention work in unison. More about this later.

Palinko investigated the cognitive demands placed on drivers. Driving any vehicle can be a cognitively demanding task, with lapses in focus and concentration potentially leading to devastating consequences. The driver's attention splits in multiple ways, from the mechanisms of driving to the behaviour of passengers, pedestrians, and other road users. While many of these processes become automated with time, requiring little conscious effort, there are moments when drivers need to focus more effort on the task and avoid distractions (such as negotiating unfamiliar urban systems or dealing quickly with incidents as they arise). Driving increases cognitive load by demanding more of our limited cognitive resources. Learner drivers experience higher demands and, therefore, higher load, just like anyone learning a new task. The premise here is that as our skills at driving increase, many of the tasks required become automatic or unconscious. Automatic actions require less mental effort, thus reducing the immediate demands on the driver.

Palinko and his co-researchers observed volunteers on a driving simulator and used eye-tracking technology to assess cognitive demands. Eye-tracking measures several variables, including pupil diameter variations and gaze shifts, which are potentially useful signs of cognitive load. In their study, an increase in cognitive load affected driving performance, with higher levels resulting in changes in gaze behaviour, longer fixation durations, more frequent gaze shifts, and differences in visual attention distributions (Palinko et al., 2010). Cognitive load is, therefore, concerned with two important mental functions: memory and attention.

Because of the limitations of the cognitive processing system, a bottleneck forms if the demands of the task outweigh cognitive limits. This bottleneck results in the flow of new information slowing down, limiting the amount of information we can process at any one time. Pierre Barrouillet of the University of Geneva approaches cognitive load through the lens of his Time-Based Resource Sharing model of working memory. He defines cognitive load as the proportion of time during which processing occupies the bottleneck and impedes the memory task (Barrouillet et al., 2007)

According to Barrouillet's framework, when people carry out a task, the cognitive system rapidly switches between processing the information and storing it, so our focus of attention continually flips between carrying out the task and refreshing the memory trace. Storage and processing can't take place at the same time, and this results in a bottleneck where both functions compete for resources. When the focus of attention is on processing, memory suffers; when the focus of attention is on storage, processing suffers. Crucially, when cognitive load is low, there is more time to refresh the memory trace, but when cognitive load is too high, more resources are directed towards processing, thus negatively impacting retention. Because working memory span decreases as cognitive load increases, there is always going to be a processing/storage trade-off. Recall performance, therefore, isn't dependent on the duration of the task or the number of digits to be recalled but on the ratio between the amount of work to be done and the time allowed to do it.

Cognitive load in teaching and learning

Cognitive load appears strongly implicated in everyday cognitive functioning; the fewer resources we have available, the greater the likelihood our thinking is going to be adversely affected as the complexity of the task increases. So how does cognitive load impact learning? Cognitive load theory (CLT), developed by John Sweller of the University of New South Wales, approaches cognitive load from a teaching and learning perspective. CLT has become popular among teachers over the last decade or so, despite Sweller's initial theory dating back to the late 1980s. Like all models, CLT is under continual development, but its basic premise remains relatively stable.

While cognitive load is generally described in the singular, CLT divides load into three separate mechanisms: intrinsic load, extraneous load, and germane load. Intrinsic load refers to the mental effort required to process the information. As the material increases in complexity, the load also increases. Intrinsic cognitive load varies, dependent upon the learners' prior knowledge and understanding. If we think again about learning to drive a car, the complexity of the task depends on how familiar we are with driving. Similarly, for a student learning algebra for the first time, understanding how to solve quadratic equations involves the processing of several interrelated concepts, such as variables, exponents, and coefficients. If studying a foreign language, a student must simultaneously learn vocabulary, grammar rules, and pronunciation. They must then integrate all these components into the construction of sentences.

Extraneous load refers to the mental effort imposed on learners by the way information is presented to them, rather than the complexity of the content. Any information that is deemed unnecessary or unhelpful is viewed as a hindrance to learning. This might include superfluous animations as part of a PowerPoint presentation or information that doesn't directly relate to the learning task. If a student is learning about the water cycle and the textbook contains lots of irrelevant information, complex, hard-to-interpret diagrams, and a cluttered, difficult-to-follow design, this is going to create unnecessary extraneous load. Similarly, if a teacher is using overly complex or technical language, the students may end up expending more cognitive effort on understanding the jargon than on grasping the key details of the topic.

Germane cognitive load is the mental work involved in understanding the to-be-learned material and integrating this new information with existing knowledge. Germane load was thought to be essential to the assimilation of new information into schemas (covered in the following chapter). When teaching and learning strategies are effective, germane load operates by encouraging deep processing and helps learners in understanding and organising material.

While germane load is still often referred to in the literature, it's no longer a major component of the model. According to Sweller, because working memory resources that need to be devoted to learning are determined by intrinsic and extraneous cognitive load, no instructional consequences of germane cognitive load have been identified, and so germane cognitive load is no longer considered an independent source of load, and the term is less commonly used (Sweller, 2023).

CLT, therefore, can provide a useful framework from which to design learning protocols, but it's not without its critics. Cognitive psychologist and educationalist

Guy Claxton, for example, has described it as just plain obvious: basic common sense dressed up in quasi-scientific clothes. (Claxton, 2021). Dylan Wiliam, on the other hand, claims CLT is the single most important thing for teachers to know (quoted in Claxton, 2021).

Many factors can increase load, including the difficulty or novelty of the task, emotional states such as anxiety (see Chapter 11) and sleep quality. Perhaps you're chatting with a friend, and something comes on the radio that sounds interesting or important; you can either listen to the radio or carry on with the conversation, but rarely can you do both. Similarly, attempting to complete a complex mathematical equation in a noisy environment is going to force us to lose focus because there are simply too many stimuli to process. This means that cognitive load is related to attention, being able to maintain our focus on the task at hand. Skills such as learning to drive place immense pressure on cognitive resources, which is why learner and new drivers need to concentrate much harder than experienced ones. With practice and experience, many actions become automatic, and cognitive load decreases.

In learning environments, overly complex instructions, poorly designed resources, and difficult-to-understand language will add to the strain placed on learners as they attempt to complete a task. There are ways to mitigate these negative factors, as well as strategies that can help to optimise cognitive load (to find that sweet spot between where load is high enough to adequately challenge, yet not so high that it prevents learning and I'll discuss many of these in Chapter 13.

Cognitive limitations represent a major barrier to effective learning. Maintaining load at an optimal level is, therefore, an important factor when thinking about how to improve our ability to retain information and use that information effectively. Now that we know a little about what's going on when we learn, we can consider ways to circumvent some of these limitations. Put simply, how can we prevent learners from forgetting what they've learned? Recall is important, but so is encoding – if learning events have failed to encode properly, they either won't be able to be recalled or will only be remembered as fragments of semi-comprehended concepts. But are we missing something?

Attention: the missing variable?

Many years ago, I found myself sitting in a room at Durham University, headphones piping words into my brain. As the words were uttered, I was repeating them aloud, just as I'd been instructed. After I'd completed the task, I was asked if I could detect any difference between the words being said in my right ear and those in my left. I recall feeling a little perplexed by the question, as I'd assumed both ears were hearing the same information from the headphones. My answer was, therefore, no, I hadn't noticed any difference. To my surprise, it turned out that the words spoken in my right ear were in English, but in my left ear, the same words had been spoken in French.

The activity with the headphones was all to do with attention, more specifically, selective attention. The reason I hadn't noticed any difference between the two inputs was because my brain had selected the information that was easily understood and filtered out the information that, to me at least, was far more difficult to comprehend. Attention is important for successful learning because it plays a key role in memory and the mechanisms that ensure successful retention. Often, however, we overlook the role of attention in favour of working memory, yet we can't appreciate the role played by either of these without including attention. In Cowan's Embedded Processes Model, working memory is viewed as that bit of our long-term memory that has become the focus of attention. From Cowan's perspective, working memory is activated long-term memory. It was studies into attention that ultimately led to the first models of memory, so we need to look at how attention works and how we can improve it if we are to make the most of the tools we have.

Are you paying attention?

My own schooldays were characterised by moments of attention and, more often, inattention. Those who are prone to daydreaming often find it difficult to focus on the external world and, instead, retreat to their private internal one. Others become easily distracted by what their classmates are up to or by events unfolding on the other side of the window. Teachers can mitigate this by ensuring they keep potential distractions to a minimum, but people tend to focus more on areas of study that interest them, or by educators they find engaging. As we'll see, the ability to remain focused certainly improves with age – keeping the attention of a class of six-year-olds is not the same for 18-year-olds.

Our ability to remain focused, therefore, follows a developmental trajectory. As certain areas of the brain involved in higher-order functions develop, we become better at filtering out distractions, both from the environment and within our heads (I'll discuss this more in Chapter 13). Some might argue that it's the school environment, particular subjects or teachers that result in pupils' inattention, but that's not always the case. It's certainly harder to focus on something you find uninteresting, no matter how engaging the teacher tries to make it sound. As adults, we have developed the ability to hold our attention for longer, although we might still start scrolling through our phones during a work meeting. Boredom and daydreaming certainly aren't inherently bad, and can often fuel curiosity and creativity, but they can also derail our learning. All definitions of attention highlight selecting relevant information and minimising irrelevant information, just like the way my brain selected English over French. The experiment I was part of at Durham used a method called dichotic listening that investigates the role of this selection process, what gets selected and what gets rejected. But what is attention? And what is it to pay attention?

Air traffic controllers and cocktail parties

During the 1950s, electronic engineer-turned cognitive scientist, Colin Cherry, was investigating the problems faced by air-traffic controllers. The controllers were having to deal with multiple messages: those from the pilots, loudspeakers, and the control tower. Messages would become intermingled and make their task increasingly difficult. This led Cherry to coin the term *the cocktail party problem*: how is it that, finding ourselves at a social event where there are many conversations taking place at once, are we able to exclude those we find uninteresting or personally irrelevant and focus on what remains? To help answer this question, Cherry adapted and refined the dichotic listening test, originally designed by cognitive psychologist Donald Broadbent. This was the test I took part in at Durham. However, Cherry also had participants repeat out loud only one message, a technique known as shadowing. These shadowing experiments revealed that very little information can be extracted from the non-attended message (Cherry, 1953).

Say, for example, I played you two different songs, one in your right ear and one in your left, and then asked you to sing along with the song you heard in your right ear. This might be a little difficult at first, but once you've locked into the song, chances are, you'll have little recollection of the song playing in your left ear. You'll still detect certain physical properties of the unattended song, such as the tone or how loud the sound is, so some information is getting through even when you're attending to something else.

Donald Broadbent was the first to propose a systematic explanation for this phenomenon. While we choose certain information to attend to based on physical properties, such as pitch or loudness, the rest (the unattended information) gets filtered out because our cognitive system simply can't cope with multiple inputs. Only the attended information, therefore, gets selected for higher or deeper processing. This is what we describe as selective attention. We can concentrate on one thing and ignore (or filter out) all the other information, so much so that (according to the Broadbent model) we have little or no recollection of the unattended stimuli (Broadbent, 1966). However, this might not be entirely accurate. Some processing of the unattended information seems to take place, and not all experimental findings can be explained using this filter model.

But what if the inputs are different? Broadbent used auditorily presented messages and words, but what if the shadowing task combined an auditory presentation with pictures? Here, both pictures and words are recalled more thoroughly, indicating that if inputs are dissimilar, they are both processed. This finding is strikingly like the working memory model (developed much later), adding weight to the proposal that memory and attention are so closely related that separating them is highly problematic. Does this then mean that similar information is selectively processed, and that unattended information is lost? This is the implication of Broadbent's model, but there are some problems with this notion.

When Broadbent carried out a study whereby volunteers listened to three digits presented one after the other in one ear and (at the same time) another three different digits in the other, participants recalled the digits ear by ear, rather than pair by pair. So, if the left ear heard 247 and the right ear heard 318, participants would recall 247,318 and not 234,178. However, in their classic 1960 study, Gray and Wedderburn took a slightly different approach by using a mixture of digits and words. For example, participants were presented with *Who, 6, there*, in one ear and *4, goes, 1* in the other. Recall was not ear by ear, but by meaning, with most participants recalling, *who goes there* and *4, 6, 1* (Gray & Wedderburn, 1960). Meaning and context are vital to understanding, and we unconsciously create meaning from chaos (a point I'll return to in the next chapter). This seems to be true of memory and attention certainly, but also perception, which is perhaps why we often see faces in slices of burnt toast and random household objects, a phenomenon known as pareidolia – the brain is attempting to find patterns, to create meaning where there is none.

We already know that we can learn without being aware of it, such as with latent learning, but can we also detect this type of learning through selective attention? In one study, researchers gave participants two auditory lists of words and told them to shadow one while ignoring the other. Some words had already been paired with a mild electric shock on the unattended list (because psychologists love the combination of willing volunteers and electricity). They measured the galvanic skin response (a measure of anxiety) of the participants as they were presented with the conditioned words on the unattended list and (sometimes) discovered a physical reaction. That is, they had associated the word with the electric shock, even though they were told to ignore that particular list (Von Wright et al., 1975). When they saw the word, it triggered an association with the pain of electricity. The same response was found with similar-sounding words or words with similar meaning. The implication here is that selection doesn't appear to occur as early as the Broadbent model implies. Anne Treisman, another British cognitive psychologist, concluded that unattended information is reduced (or attenuated) rather than being entirely filtered out (Treisman, 1964).

Attention and cognitive load

The research also implies that attentional resources are limited and may suffer overload (just like working memory). Again, working memory models attempt to explain this in similar terms to those of attention models, including the notion that different types of information are more readily processed simultaneously (pictures and words, for example). More recent notions of attention link it directly to working memory limitations. Klaus Oberauer, professor of cognitive psychology at the University of Zurich, suggests that attention represents a collection of mechanisms that allows us to focus in on chunks of information, either as a broad focus of attention representing the upper capacity of around four chunks, or narrow focus of attention where one chunk is selected at a time (Oberauer & Hein, 2012). A person might, therefore, attempt a mathematical equation requiring several stages by holding the parts of the problem in working memory (broad focus) but select only one chunk to complete a specific stage (narrow focus). It's easy to see how this relates to Cowan's Embedded Processes model and the view that working memory is a kind of activated long-term memory.

So, attention isn't only necessary for carrying out tasks, it's also vital for ensuring that learning has a much better chance of staying put. Information that isn't fully attended to isn't processed deeply and is likely to decay quickly. This isn't always the case, of course, and there is a possibility that some information will end up in long-term memory with no conscious awareness (such as with latent learning). Attention is also about maintaining focus over time, and this time is also limited. Attention follows a developmental trajectory, meaning that young children are much less adept at focusing their attention than older ones. Primary school children will, therefore, succumb to distractions more easily than teenagers, and older adults are more skilled at focusing on a specific task. Certain individual differences may limit this, including anxiety, depression, and conditions such as ADHD and Autistic Spectrum Disorder. However, other biological and physiological conditions also play a role, including quality of sleep and certain medications.

Identifying an average attention span is, therefore, difficult. Some studies have found that the attention span of undergraduate students is around 10–15 minutes, after which they become increasingly distracted and switch off (Bradbury, 2016). However, these studies are most often carried out in lecture theatres, so generalising the findings to other environments isn't possible. It could be that attention is also related to how relevant, important, or interesting the information is. After all, teenagers can often maintain intense focus when playing video games or engaging in activities unrelated to formal learning. Attention also influences motivation, which relates to other factors, including rewards, the perceived value of the task and whether the activity serves a wider goal (see Chapter 12).

Nelson Cowan views attention as crucial to working memory function, so much so that his findings showing that working memory capacity is around four pieces of information is often compared to Miller's magic number 7. However, as we've seen, Miller and Cowan measured capacity in different ways. Just as there are individual differences in working memory, so there are also differences in a person's ability to select relevant information and ignore irrelevant information. People who perform better on working memory tasks are better at choosing what to encode into long-term memory (Cowan et al., 2011).

External distractions

Our lives are full of distractions, perhaps more so today with our smartphones and social media feeds. Studies have found mobile phones to be a distraction even when they're turned off and in our bags (Thornton et al., 2014). Indeed, mobile phones have borne the brunt of much of the discussion around a hypothesised shrinking of attention spans. But there are many other candidates, including the way educators manage and even decorate classrooms.

You'd be hard pushed to find a classroom that doesn't have some kind of display. Sometimes, every spare centimetre of space is taken up with examples of student's work, posters, and many other kinds of subject and non-subject related decoration. But do displays act as an unwanted distraction, or do they serve a useful purpose? Early research discovered that putting up students' work can increase self-esteem, so it might have an indirect impact on achievement. However, this relationship is complex (Maxwell & Chmielewski, 2008). More recently, the emphasis has shifted towards exploring the possibility that over-decorated classroom might put added pressure on learners' limited attentional resources. This potential cognitive overload might lead to increased off-task behaviour.

In one study, researchers explored the impact of visual displays on 24 typically developing children with an average age of five years. They systematically manipulated the amount of visual displays in an artificial classroom over the course of six brief science mini-lessons. The classroom displays varied between heavily decorated and no displays. Lessons were video recorded, and behaviour coded in terms of visual engagement (on-task – looking at the teachers or at books; off-task – looking at peers or at the walls).

There was far less off-task behaviour recorded in the no displays condition, although the children were still distracted by their peers. Children also scored lower on learning tasks in the heavily decorated condition (Fisher et al., 2014). However, this was a tiny study of only 24 young children, so drawing any firm conclusions from a single small study is difficult. We also have to bear in mind that this wasn't a real classroom, and there is a high probability that the children were distracted more by the novel environment than the displays. Furthermore, the study used eye-gaze analysis to measure the levels of distraction. This method might not be as accurate as eye-tracking technology.

In another study, Peter Barrett and colleagues from the University of Salford, UK looked at several physical characteristics of 153 classrooms in 27 UK primary schools (total number of children 3,766), including complexity and colour (which would include displays). They concluded that physical characteristics accounted for 16 percent of the variance in academic progression over the course of one year but discovered a curvilinear relationship. This indicates that too much and too little physical complexity were predictive of poorer academic progress. Barrett cautiously concluded that the complexity of the classroom could interact with a child's ability to focus attention, which may then impact potential learning (Barrett et al., 2015). It's worth noting that Barrett didn't manipulate the level of classroom visual distraction, so we can't be certain that the visual displays had a direct impact on learning.

A more recent addition to the literature looked at the impact of classroom displays on both typically developing children and children with autistic spectrum disorder (Hanley et al., 2017). A total of 89 children were recruited – 37 with ASD between the ages of 7 and 10, and 52 typically developing children between 5 and 13 years old. The children were presented with a video lesson where a teacher stood in front of a screen that was either decorated with a display taken from an actual classroom or a blank screen. The children were then assessed using a worksheet and eye-tracking equipment. Researchers found all children spent more time looking at the display in the visual display condition and less time looking at the teacher than those in the no display condition. ASD children spent the most time looking at the display. Those who spent more time looking at the display scored lower on the assessment.

This study provides useful information on how displays may have a greater negative impact on those children with already impaired attentional abilities. However, the artificial nature of the study is certainly a weak point. First of all, this was a video and not a real classroom setting. Also, it might not be typical for a teacher to stand in front of a display and would more likely be standing in front of a board of some kind. This makes it difficult to determine if these findings could be replicated in a real-world classroom. These studies provide snapshots of artificial lessons which may have resulted in less attentive students. What would happen if we ran a study in a real classroom over several days, weeks, or months? Would the participants pay less attention to the displays over time? It's clear that more research is needed before we can reach any definitive conclusions.

Working memory and attention

Working memory is distinguished from short-term memory by attentional processes. Cowan views working memory as including short-term memory and other processing mechanisms that help make use of short-term memory (Logie et al., 2021), while Engle describes working memory as only referring to the attentional-related aspects of short-term memory (Engle, 2002). This seems like a fair distinction to make and allows us to zero in on the attention aspects of learning. Referring to the multi-component model of Baddeley and Hitch, we can say that the phonological loop and visuospatial sketchpad represent short-term memory, but it's the inclusion of the central executive that makes it a truly working memory. This, then, is how I intend to distinguish between the two.

This chapter has focused on the role of cognitive limitations as an explanation of forgetting, the premise being that unsuccessful encoding and consolidation have reduced the strength of learned information in long-term memory, while stress placed on our attentional capacity will lead to greater cognitive load. We can view these limitations through the lens of CLT or more generalised notions of cognitive load, including attention. In the next chapter, I want to focus on how we process information so that it is meaningful.

Chapter summary

- Forgetting is a natural and important part of learning, with several contributing factors. Memory failure occurs due to time (temporal decay in short-term memory), interference from other information, insufficient processing during encoding, and the loss of contextual cues that aid retrieval.

- Short-term and working memory have limitations in both capacity and duration, which can lead to forgetting and influence learning.

- Short-term memory has a limited capacity, often cited as around 7 ± 2 chunks of information, and a limited duration, with information decaying after about 18–30 seconds if rehearsal is prevented. Exceeding these limitations can result in forgetting.

- Cognitive load, the mental resources required for a task, plays a significant role in learning. High cognitive load, whether due to the complexity of the material (intrinsic load) or the way information is presented (extraneous load), can hinder learning by exceeding the capacity of working memory. Effective learning strategies aim to manage cognitive load to optimise information processing and retention.

- Attention is crucial for successful memory and learning as it enables the selection and deeper processing of information. Attention is necessary for information to be effectively encoded into memory, and limitations in attentional resources can lead to information being missed or quickly forgotten.

- Selective attention allows us to focus on relevant information and filter out distractions, but this process has its limits and can be influenced by several factors.

- The learning environment, particularly visual distractions, can impact attention and learning outcomes. Overly complex or cluttered visual displays in classrooms may exceed learners' attentional resources, potentially leading to increased off-task behaviour and lower learning task scores, especially for young children and those with attentional difficulties like ASD. However, more research is needed to draw definitive conclusions in real-world classroom settings.

References

Alin, L. (1997). The memory laws of Jost. *Göteborg Psychological Reports*, *27*(1), 1–21.

Baddeley, A. D., Thomson, N., & Buchanan, M. (1975). Word length and the structure of working memory. *Journal of Verbal Learning and Verbal Behavior*, *14*(6), 575–589. https://pdfs.semanticscholar.org/b470/cbb6c7c235f670bb63601da7c9d853219718.pdf

Barrett, P., Davies, F., Zhang, Y., & Barrett, L. (2015). The impact of classroom design on pupils' learning: Final results of a holistic, multi-level analysis. *Building and Environment*, *89*(February), 118–133. https://doi.org/10.1016/j.buildenv.2015.02.013

Barrouillet, P., Bernardin, S., Portrat, S., Vergauwe, E., & Camos, V. (2007). Time and cognitive load in working memory. *Journal of Experimental Psychology: Learning Memory and Cognition*, *33*(3), 570–585. https://doi.org/10.1037/0278-7393.33.3.570

Bradbury, N. A. (2016). Attention span during lectures: 8 Seconds, 10 minutes, or more? *Advances in Physiology Education*, *40*(4), 509–513. https://doi.org/10.1152/advan.00109.2016

Broadbent, D. E. (1966). Perception and communication. *Education + training*, *8*(6). https://doi.org/10.1108/eb015727

Cherry, E. C. (1953). Some experiments on the recognition of speech, with one and with two ears. *The Journal of the Acoustical Society of America*, *25*(5), 975–979.

Claxton, G. (2021). *The future of teaching and the myths that hold it back*. Routledge.

Cowan, N. (2000). The magical number 4 in short-term memory: A reconsideration of mental storage capacity. *Behavioral and Brain Sciences*, *24*(1), 87–185. https://doi.org/10.1017/S0140525X01003922

Cowan, N., Aubuchon, A. M., Gilchrist, A. L., Ricker, T. J., & Saults, J. S. (2011). Age differences in visual working memory capacity: Not based on encoding limitations. *Developmental Science*, *14*(5), 1066–1074. https://doi.org/10.1111/j.1467-7687.2011.01060.x

Darley, C. F., Tinklenberg, J. R., Roth, W. T. et al. (1974). The nature of storage deficits and state-dependent retrieval under marihuana. *Psychopharmacologia*, *37*, 139–149. https://doi.org/10.1007/BF00437420

Ebbinghaus, H. (1885). *Memory: A contribution to experimental psychology*. Teachers College.

Engle, R. W. (2002). Working memory capacity as executive attention. *Current Directions in Psychological Science*, *11*(1), 19–23. https://doi.org/10.1111/1467-8721.00160

Fisher, A. V., Godwin, K. E., & Seltman, H. (2014). Visual environment, attention allocation, and learning in young children: When too much of a good thing may be bad. *Psychological Science*, *25*(7), 1362–1370. https://doi.org/10.1177/0956797614533801

Galton, F. (1887). Supplementary notes on "prehension" in idiots. *Mind*, *12*(45), 79–82. https://doi.org/10.1093/mind/os-12.45.79

Glanzer, M., & Cunitz, A. R. (1966). Two storage mechanisms in free recall. *Journal of Verbal Learning and Verbal Behavior*, *5*(4), 351–360. https://doi.org/10.1016/S0022-5371(66)80044-0

Godden, D. R., & Baddeley, A. D. (1975). Context-dependent memory in two natural environments: On land and underwater. *British Journal of Psychology*, *66*(3), 325–331. https://doi.org/10.1111/j.2044-8295.1975.tb01468.x

Grant, H. M., Bredahl, L. C., Clay, J., Ferrie, J., Groves, J. E., McDorman, T. A., & Dark, V. J. (1998). Context-dependent memory for meaningful material: Information for students. *Applied Cognitive Psychology*, *12*(6), 617–623.

Gray, J. A., & Wedderburn, A. A. I. (1960). Grouping strategies with simultaneous stimuli. *Quarterly Journal of Experimental Psychology*, *12*(3), 180–184. https://doi.org/10.1080/17470216008416722

Hanley, M., Khairat, M., Taylor, K., Wilson, R., Cole-Fletcher, R., & Riby, D. M. (2017). Classroom displays—Attraction or distraction? Evidence of impact on attention and learning from children with and without autism. *Developmental Psychology*, *53*(7), 1265–1275. https://doi.org/10.1037/dev0000271

Jacobs, J. (1887). Experiments on "prehension." *Mind, os-12*(45), 75–79. https://doi.org/10.1093/mind/os-12.45.75

James, W. (1890). *The principles of psychology* (Vol. 1). Henry Holt and Co.

Levine, J. M. (1966). The effects of values and costs on the detection and identification of signals in auditory vigilance. *Human Factors: The Journal of Human Factors and Ergonomics Society, 8*(6), 525–537. https://doi.org/10.1177/001872086600800607

Logie, R. H., Camos, V., & Cowan, N (2021). *Working memory.* State of the Science Oxford University Press.

Maxwell, L. E., & Chmielewski, E. J. (2008). Environmental personalization and elementary school children's self-esteem. *Journal of Environmental Psychology, 28*(2), 143–153. https://doi.org/10.1016/j.jenvp.2007.10.009

Miller, G. A. (1956). The magical number seven, plus or minus two: Some limits on our capacity for processing information. *Psychological Review, 63*(2), 81–97. https://doi.org/10.1037/h0043158

Oberauer, K., & Hein, L. (2012). Attention to information in working memory. *Current Directions in Psychological Science, 21*(3), 164–169. https://doi.org/10.1177/0963721412444727

Overton, D. A. (1972). State-dependent learning produced by alcohol and its relevance to alcoholism. In B. Kissin, & H. Begleiter (Eds.), *The biology of alcoholism.* Springer. https://doi.org/10.1007/978-1-4684-0895-9_8

Palinko, O., Kun, A. L., Shyrokov, A., & Heeman, P. (2010). Estimating cognitive load using remote eye tracking in a driving simulator. *Eye Tracking Research and Applications Symposium (ETRA),* 141–144. https://doi.org/10.1145/1743666.1743701

Perkins, N. L. (1914). The value of distributed repetitions in rote learning. *British Journal of Psychology, 1904–1920, 7*(2), 253–261. https://doi.org/10.1111/j.2044-8295.1914.tb00113.x

Peterson, L., & Peterson, M. J. (1959). Short-term retention of individual verbal items. *Journal of Experimental Psychology, 58*(3), 193–198. https://doi.org/10.1037/h0049234

Sweller, J. (2023). The development of cognitive load theory: Replication crises and incorporation of other theories can lead to theory expansion. *Educational Psychology Review, 35*(4), 1–20. https://doi.org/10.1007/s10648-023-09817-2

Thornton, B., Faires, A., Robbins, M., & Rollins, E. (2014). The mere presence of a cell phone may be distracting implications for attention and task performance. *Social Psychology, 45*(6), 479–488. https://doi.org/10.1027/1864-9335/a000216

Treisman, A. (1964). Monitoring and storage of irrelevant messages in selective attention. *Journal of Verbal Learning and Verbal Behavior, 3*(6), 449–459. https://doi.org/10.1016/S0022-5371(64)80015-3

Von Wright, J. M., Anderson, K., & Stenman, U. (1975). Generalisation of conditioned G.S.R.s in dichotic listening, 135–153 In P. M. A. Rabbitt, & S. Dornic (Eds.), *Attention and performance* (Vol. V). Academic Press.

6 Context matters

Remember Ebbinghaus? His forgetting curve is used to explain why rehearsal is essential for long-term retention. But how useful is it, really? A single study cannot tell us very much about what that study set out to investigate. Studies must be evaluated in light of the wider research community, replicated and analysed. Replication is the backbone of research, but if replication fails, it's not necessarily the end of the world, although it might require adjustments to theories and models. Many theories, such as Sweller's Cognitive Load Theory, have been built around failed replications – as the evidence changes, so does the model.

As for Ebbinghaus, his findings (and those of Jost and Perkins) certainly highlight the fact that time is a major factor in forgetting and that by refreshing the memory we can increase the likelihood that it'll become a relatively permanent fixture of long-term memory. Refreshing simply means returning to the information, so if we are learning a list of words, we memorise them over hours, days, or weeks. There is more to learning than memorisation, but these insights alone prove useful as they indicate how we might learn more efficiently, certainly in terms of memorisation. The question of how long my memory is going to last and how much information will be lost after how many days, however, is largely irrelevant, seeing as people forget things at different rates and for different reasons. Just knowing that information will be lost over time is quite enough. I do, however, have some reservations when it comes to the forgetting curve as laid out by Ebbinghaus, because it doesn't really consider the reality of what, why, and how we learn. But my first criticism is about methodology, in that Ebbinghaus used only one participant to test his claim, and that one participant was himself. Today, this very fact would have invalidated his research for obvious reasons, but his study has been replicated many times using a more scientific sample, and the results are always the same, or at least very similar. This means his findings are broadly supported. But replication isn't everything.

The problem with Ebbinghaus

Replication is concerned with the degree to which we can repeat a study and obtain the same results. Many studies in cognitive psychology can be replicated, in part because they take place in laboratory-style settings where researchers can control environmental variables. If, for example, I gave you a list of words to learn and then asked you to recall them in any order (known as free recall), I could pretty much guarantee that you'd recall more words from the beginning of the list (the primacy effect) and the end of the list (the recency effect), creating a rather pleasing U shape when plotted on a graph (the so-called, serial position curve). Now, if immediately after learning the words and before asking you to recall them, I gave you a distraction task, let's say I ask you to count backwards from 100 in threes for 30 seconds, I can guarantee you'd still be able to recall the words from the beginning of the list, but be less successful with the ones at the end of the list. If we then plotted these results on a graph, our neat U would have become a rather gloomy downward slope. But the words I use will also matter, and I'd have to match them for word length, because we know people can remember more short words than long words (the word length effect). So far, so good. Any replication needs to be a copy of the original experiment (or as near to it as possible), although we can carry out partial replications. However, a more pressing matter concerns ecological validity – the extent to which the experiment corresponds to what happens in the real world. When was the last time you were asked to learn a series of nonsense words? Unless you've been a participant in a psychology experiment, I suspect your answer is *never*. Words have meaning, and different memory systems operate in unison to help provide context and understanding (the essence of learning). The method Ebbinghaus chose bears little resemblance to what people actually learn in the real world. I'm not alone in my criticism of Ebbinghaus.

Tom Pear (pronounced Peer) was professor of psychology at the University of Manchester, UK, and was appointed Britain's first full-time professor of psychology in 1919. In his book, Remembering and Forgetting, he expresses doubts about the value of nonsense syllables in studies of memory and learning. Such investigations have resulted in valuable knowledge concerning the laws governing the economy and the training of the memory for relatively meaningless material, he wrote (Pear, 1922, p.135). Such laws, he believed, simply weren't up to the task of offering anything worthy to memory research. After all, memory is more complex than this and laden with meaning and experience. Pear would go on to take a different approach, drawing mainly from Sigmund Freud's ideas about repression.

Perhaps the most vehement critic of the Ebbinghaus method was another British psychologist, Frederic Bartlett. Bartlett (like Pear) rejected the Ebbinghaus method because it avoided the complexity of meaning. Bartlett argued that Ebbinghaus had thrown out the baby with the bathwater by eliminating meaning from his experiments (Baddeley, 2019). Remembering something we have learned involves an interaction between short-term working memory, semantic long-term memory, and episodic long-term memory. Past learning influences future learning because when we remember something, we access memories we stored previously. Not only that, but we use cues to recall this information, and many of these will be episodic. When people recall information, they are often also recalling the time and place where they initially encountered the information, as in the Godden and Baddeley study with the divers (context-dependent retrieval), and even their internal biological state (state-dependent retrieval).

Bartlett's approach couldn't have been more different from Ebbinghaus's. He would present participants with complex material (his most influential study from 1932, dubbed the War of the Ghosts, used a story from Native American folklore) and then ask them to recall it at different time points. Bartlett found that the unusual use of language and cultural specificity of the story led participants to recall it in a way that made sense to them. All his participants were British, and they found it hard to retell the story because it didn't match their own cultural experiences. Not only did the volunteers shorten the story, but they also reconstructed it based on their own knowledge. They left out parts they didn't understand and simplified other parts, which is most likely why the reproduced stories were shorter. They would also replace words such as canoe with boat because it was more familiar (Bartlett, 1932). Unlike Ebbinghaus, Bartlett was less interested in the amount of information recalled and more in what they remembered.

New information is integrated with existing knowledge, leading to both enhanced recall and errors based on effort after meaning, that is, people create the meaning only after reading the story. According to Bartlett, the organisation of such knowledge results in the formation of schemas, or structured mental representations. Unfortunately, the notion of schemas was thought to be too vague at the time and wouldn't be fully explored until the advent of cognitive psychology in the 1950s (and neuroscientists wouldn't catch on until much later), yet they have now become a vital addition to the learning sciences and are going to play an important role throughout the following chapters.

But how valid are Bartlett's findings? Since the original study, several studies have attempted partial replications to confirm what Bartlett discovered. All failed, with many of the researchers suggesting that replication was impossible. There are perhaps many reasons these replications failed that might not relate to a terminally flawed theory. If we look at Ebbinghaus's study, which has undergone successful replication many times, we notice his emphasis on detail along with the simplicity of his experiments. While we don't have a record of the exact words he used, we know everything there is to know in order to replicate it fully. Bartlett's War of the Ghosts study, on the other hand, suffers because of its complexity and, dare I say, woolly nature. It's a much trickier study to understand and, therefore, replicate. It wasn't until 1999 that Erik Bergman and Henry Roediger attempted a near-full replication of Bartlett's study. Bergman and Roediger found participants forgot the story over time but introduced rationalisation and distortion into their accounts, with increases in the proportion of material distorted as the retention interval increased. They also imported new propositions at longer delays, adding further support for Bartlett's findings and conclusions (Bergman & Roediger, 1999).

Memory and meaning

As Bartlett noted, recalling something isn't just about remembering a meaningless string of letters – we mustn't neglect meaning. We can view information as the raw material necessary for creating knowledge, and we apply certain operations to do this. When we apply these operations to the information, we are, in cognitive science parlance, engaging in information processing. But it's more difficult to process information if it makes no sense, and all we can do with the information is hold it in memory because we have no way of slotting it into the knowledge we already have; there is nothing we can do to transform trigrams from an input (or raw information) into something that we can think of as knowledge. Our memory systems exist to process information, not meaningless three-letter nonsense words, so we cannot process them at a level deep enough to lead to stable retention; they are meaningless and will always remain meaningless. Using nonsense trigrams is certainly useful to some degree because it provides information about how people learn things that they have never encountered, and that this kind of information will fade over time. Yet they tell us little about how memory and learning interact on a daily basis. Episodic and semantic memory operate in parallel, the things we already know, helping us to learn new things, and this interrelation creates knowledge.

Let's look at a simple example. I give you a list of words to learn. Let's say apple, bicycle, house, flower, telephone, horse, computer, table, kitchen, chips, train. I then ask you to recall them immediately afterwards, in any order. How well do you think you'd do? There are 11 items in the list, and they are of different lengths, so you should struggle to remember them because the list exceeds your short-term capacity of between five and nine items and, following the word length effect, the longer words should be more difficult to remember than the shorter ones. But because they are familiar words, the chances are you might very well recall them all. In addition, if you can see your phone right now or you're sitting at your computer, these longer words might come easily because you can associate them with an item you can currently see. But you have previously formed a mental representation of all the items, and you have knowledge of the words that go far beyond their physical structure. This deeper knowledge may help you make meaningful connections between them; a bicycle and a train are forms of transport; you cook chips in a kitchen. In the previous chapter, I introduced you to cued recall, so I could present the words as pairs: bicycle – train, kitchen – table, and so on. In fact, you could probably recall many more words this way because the pairing of the items creates associations that make recalling them easier. Pairing words like this is very common in language learning, such as father – Vater – father, mother – Mutter, sister – Schwester, brother – Bruder. You would then be asked for the German word for father or the English translation of Mutter. Also, most people can visualise these items and apply meaning to them (flowers grow in gardens, they have petals and attract bees).

You'll recall that the working memory model of Baddeley and Hitch includes both a sound-based component (the phonological loop) and a component dedicated to visual and spatial information (the visuospatial sketchpad). It then follows that the image and corresponding word are processed in different ways by separate mechanisms, optimising the stress (or load) placed on our limited resources. Furthermore, we can further exploit our natural tendency to place items into categories by presenting items with category labels. An early study by Endel Tulving and Zena Perlstone illustrates this nicely.

In their classic study conducted in 1966, Tulving and Pearlstone gave participants a written list of 48 words to learn, organised into 12 categories of four words each. In one condition, the words were given a category label, such as *animals* or *fruit,* and volunteers were told they would be tested on their recall of the words *but not the category labels*. Meanwhile, in a second condition, only the list of words was presented, that is, without the category label. The group given the category labels recalled significantly more words than the group given the lists only, suggesting that the labels acted as contextual cues that were used to access the words (Tulving & Pearlstone, 1966). Perhaps the memory had just decayed, and the cues were irrelevant? To address the possibility, Tulving presented participants with, yet again, a list of words before asking them to write down as many as they could in any order. Later, and without having seen the list again or the previous answers, participants were asked to recall them once more. This was then repeated a third time. Some participants recalled a word on the third trial but failed to recall it on trials one and two; decay theory wouldn't have predicted this because a memory trace can't decay and then be miraculously reinstated. Retrieval failure, on the other hand, can offer a plausible explanation by arguing that different retrieval cues were involved in the three trials (Tulving & Osler, 1968). According to the theory of cued forgetting, therefore, certain factors that were present at the time of memory encoding (when the memory was stored in the long-term system) become aids to recall later on.

Similarly, consider the following extract taken from a study by John Bransford and Marcia Johnson:

> The procedure is actually quite simple. First, you arrange things into different groups. Of course, one pile may be sufficient depending on how much there is to do. If you have to go somewhere else due to lack of facilities that is the next step, otherwise you are pretty well set. It is important not to overdo things. That is, it is better to do too few things at once than too many. In the short run this may not seem important but complications can easily arise. A mistake can be expensive as well. At first the whole procedure will seem complicated.
> (Bransford & Johnson, 1972)

Understanding the paragraph is problematic because it's presented without context. In their study, Bransford and Johnson found that volunteers were less likely to remember the paragraph than those volunteers given its title. When the paragraph is presented with the title *Instructions for Washing Clothes*, it makes sense, even if you've never actually washed any clothes. Context is important, certainly in terms of comprehension. Many jokes rely on the recipient understanding their contents and context, as well as how the comedian might attempt to play with the words they use. Take, for example, the joke *I asked my yoga teacher if they could teach me to do the splits. They said, 'how flexible are you?' I said, 'I can't do Tuesdays and Thursdays.'* Understanding the joke (not the same as finding it funny, by the way) requires us to understand the context and the way the comedian has manipulated our expectations. We need to have knowledge of the word *flexible* and understand that we can apply it in different ways and in different contexts.

We can also see this in what are known as garden path sentences. Garden path sentences are structured in such ways as to unintentionally invite misinterpretation, or they lead the reader up the garden path. One common example used in research is *the old man the boats*. The initial assumption is that *old* is an adjective and *man* is the noun, as in *the old man,* and the rest of the sentence makes little sense. However, the sentence is describing that the old are the people who man the boats, *man* is a verb, not a noun, as in to *man the boat*. Not only do garden path sentences disrupt our assumptions regarding context, but they also place greater pressure on working memory. Like the joke about doing the splits, they lead us in one direction, only to turn at the last moment, leaving us either amused or confused.

This need for context is an everyday occurrence, from understanding a joke to engaging in conversation or reading a novel (or educational material) with annoying, ambiguous wording. Reading science fiction or fantasy novels, for example, requires the reader to engage with often unknown concepts and worlds for which they have no point of reference. Take, for example, the novels of George R. R. Martin, author of the amazingly successful *Game of Thrones* series. To begin with, the reader must work hard to understand the lay of the land; there are new countries, cultures, and customs to encounter, as well as an alternative history. As the reader begins to understand the geography of Westeros, its regions, and how they relate to each other, the story becomes easier to understand. By the time the reader finishes the last novel, they have accumulated a wealth of knowledge about this imaginary world and can draw on this knowledge to aid comprehension. Knowing how the different families interact, their allies and their enemies, the Machiavellian tendencies of the many (many) characters, the culture of Dothraki, and the history of the Unsullied, allows us to make a deeper sense of the narrative, even though there are many surprises along the way. The knowledge we've accumulated helps us to understand the twists in the narrative. If you're unfamiliar with Game of Thrones, many of the terms I've just used will mean nothing to you, and this is entirely the point.

Take, however, a slightly different book (and the television series). *The Man in the High Castle* by Philip K. Dick is an alternative history novel, the premise of which lies with Germany victorious in the Second World War and the United States under German and Japanese occupation. The reader has some understanding of genuine history, such as Germany's alliance with Japan against the United Kingdom, the United States, and their allies, but the outcomes are different in the fictional account. We then need to shift our internal contextual thinking to understand the storyline. What we know helps us to make sense of what we don't. The same is, of course, true for any activity or topic of learning. The rules of football might appear unfathomable to begin with, but with experience, the player or supporter is better able to anticipate the outcome and comprehend the game. We hold this information in our memories and access it as necessary. Without this stored knowledge, we would be like Henry, adrift in a world we only half understand and can barely comprehend.

Knowledge is, therefore, about more than single concepts or hierarchical structures. Our long-term memories are awash with all sorts of information, from memories related to our own lives to current affairs, theoretical concepts, and partially understood ideas. We hold information within our memories that is more complex in its conceptual organisation than lists and facts. Furthermore, concepts don't exist in isolation; they are related to each other, both in their temporal and causal structure and their relationship to the real world. We can think of memory as relational, and this relational processing can aid learning in powerful ways. Take a simple and common example. You and a group of friends decide to go to a restaurant one evening. Already there are concepts you all understand, even in some rudimentary way, such as the idea of a restaurant, your relationship and shared histories with your friends, even the very concept of friendship. And what about getting to the restaurant? You're route through the streets, from one place to another? What time are you meeting? The very concept of time itself? This list can go on and on, but these are things we need not concern ourselves with too much. They are deeply understood because of the manner in which our brain deals with information.

Let's skip ahead to the restaurant. You approach a member of staff and tell them you have a table booked. A staff member shows you to your table, and you order drinks (perhaps you ask for a wine list). Your party is given menus from which you order your food. At the end of the night, you ask for the bill and pay (perhaps you leave a tip). Now, imagine the same experience, only this time you have no idea what you are supposed to do when arriving at the restaurant. Do you just see a table and sit down? How do you order your food or ask for drinks? How do you know who or how much to pay at the end of the night? We know what to do when we go for a meal at a restaurant, even if we have never been to a particular restaurant, because we have a kind of blueprint stored in our long-term memory. It's a very useful blueprint because it allows us to expend less cognitive energy on attempting to work out what we're meant to do. It's also adaptable, so we can add to it if this new restaurant does things slightly differently from the other ones we have visited (so we don't embarrass ourselves by asking for the wine list when going to a fast-food outlet for a burger). These blueprints are Bartlett's schemas (or schemata). They provide useful cognitive shortcuts because the human brain works more efficiently when limited resources are considered.

Schemas can be both declarative (knowing that) and procedural (knowing how), so as well as the restaurant schema, we also have a riding a bike schema and a driving a car schema. But these mental representations don't stop there. I know what a dog is because I've seen many in my lifetime. When I try to visualise a dog, I'll picture in my mind an animal with four legs, covered in fur, perhaps with its tongue dangling from its mouth and panting. When I was very young, my family had a Springer Spaniel, but we also had a Golden Labrador and a Great Dane. Now, these three breeds of dogs weren't identical, but I still recognise them all as dogs. My dog schema can store a general mental representation of all dogs (four legs, fur, and so on), but I can also subclassify these into different breeds. When I encounter a breed I haven't seen before, I don't scream 'what on Earth is that strange creature?', I simply recognise it as a dog, note the not-encountered-before elements and update my dog schema. But schemas allow me to deal with even more complexity. I, therefore, know that a fox is in the same family as the Springer Spaniel my parents had when I was a child. However, a fox has very little in common with a domesticated dog. I recognise a fox as a dog-like animal, but I also know that it is not a dog.

Schema theory isn't associated with a particular individual; it's an integration between several ideas and studies developed over many decades. The Swiss developmental psychologist Jean Piaget used the term to describe how young children acquired knowledge and understanding, but it was Frederic Bartlett's use of the term in 1932 that is most relevant to the current topic. His ideas centred on procedural memory, even though the distinction between procedural and declarative memory wouldn't come about until years later. Like Tolman, Bartlett is now considered a cognitive psychologist, while at the time the fledgling discipline was more concerned with behaviourist views of human action (even though Bartlett considered himself to be a social psychologist, with interests ranging from psychology to anthropology and sociology, so he was a cognitive scientist even before anyone knew what one was). Of particular interest to learning, Bartlett viewed behaviour as more than simple stimulus-response associations, insisting that people don't reproduce an exact copy of a previous moment. Nor do they create something entirely new, as described previously in his War of the Ghosts study. Prior experiences help people make sense of new experiences by supplying expectations and frameworks for action.

Jean Piaget was the first to suggest that we add (or assimilate) new information into current existing schemas, an action that created cognitive dissonance because this new information doesn't integrate easily. Schemas are, therefore, forced to change or to accommodate these new experiences. Schemas fuel cognitive development through biological stages, but also via interaction with the world of nature and objects and interaction with others. But schemas also aid many types of learning because they provide background, meaning, and context in the present. Their flexible nature, however, means that when we learn something new related to a current schema, we assimilate the new information and update our schema.

Rather than use the term schema, Roger Schank and Robert Abelson suggest that humans develop a grammar for procedural knowledge in the form of scripts for all common life events (Schank & Abelson, 1977). Schank, an artificial intelligence theorist and cognitive scientist, developed a computer program capable of answering questions about events in a restaurant based on scripts of what typically happens. Later, Schank and Abelson expanded on their script theory by indicating the existence of deeper levels of organisation. For example, many scripts share certain attributions, such as waiting in line at a post office and waiting in line at a restaurant. Similarly, William Brewer and James Treyens found that when people were shown a scene of an office and then later asked to recall the items they saw, they included both those things they genuinely did see and also items that fit the office schema (such as a stapler) but weren't actually there. The scene had triggered the appropriate schema and may have been used as a memory aid (Brewer & Treyens, 1981). This study not only highlights the workings of schemas but also how they can work against us. This is particularly relevant to learning, as well as other areas of concern, such as the accuracy of eyewitness testimony.

Educational psychologist Richard Anderson first applied schema theory to education in the late 1970s. His research into comprehension found that memory and learning depend on the continuous flow of new and already known knowledge (Anderson, 1978). The new information is then assimilated into the current schema. To fully comprehend something, it's necessary to have some understanding of it. Schemas, therefore, help us make sense of situations and allow writers, readers, speakers, and listeners to make assumptions about what the reader or listener already knows. If, for example, I give a talk at an education event attended by teachers, I know there are certain contexts I can describe in less detail because I understand my audience has the pre-requisite schemas available to access; I don't need to explain what a classroom is, or a curriculum; I can use anecdotes and assume my audience will understand them. At the same time, I can convey new information from cognitive psychology on how to structure lessons differently, and this information can then be assimilated into the relevant schema. If, however, I am giving a talk to a group of people without knowledge of how schools operate, I'll need to plan accordingly in order to match their level of prior knowledge.

Schemas spare up much-needed resources and allow people to get on with the job at hand. If we view them in this way, it becomes easier to see how they can enhance learning. Working memory is both limited and resource-intensive, and the more load we place on it, the more likely it will feel the strain. However, a problem sometimes arises because of schema theory being an amalgamation of several yet interrelated ideas, so the term might be used slightly differently depending on the context. For example, a social psychologist might refer to Bartlett's version of schema, while a developmental psychologist might rely on Piaget's notion of schema. In the next chapter, we'll look at schemas from a neuroscience perspective.

The problem with schemas

The way the human brain organises information into schemas helps us learn new things faster and more efficiently. But there's also a downside. Schemas rely on general principles to understand much of what we experience in the world. This, in turn, has a part to play in stereotyping, prejudice, and discrimination. The powerful have, for centuries, used what we now understand as schemas to set one group against another based on these internal knowledge structures. Unscrupulous politicians may well paint a particular group of people as lazy or violent and dangerous by tapping into certain cultural stereotypes, viewing individuals only as part of a group and that group as one we should avoid at all costs. Unfortunately, it doesn't always take a would-be despot to manipulate us, and often we are pretty good at warping reality based entirely on what we believe, even if our beliefs bear little resemblance to the objective facts.

Jason Coronel and his co-researchers from Ohio State University set out to test how schemas can lead people to misremember factual information. They were interested in how people recalled numerical information if the data ran counter to their own internal schemas. The researchers presented participants with short written descriptions of four societal issues involving numerical information. On two of the issues, they ran a pre-test to discover the relationship between the issue and the participants' understanding of it. For example, they presented volunteers with information that most Americans supported same-sex marriage than opposed it, and participants agreed that this was, indeed, the case. In other words, the data was schema consistent. But they also presented volunteers with data that were schema-inconsistent. For example, most people in the United States (according to polls) believe that Mexican immigration into the country increased between 2007 and 2014 when, in fact, it declined from 12.8 million to 11.7 million (their belief ran counter to objective facts). After being presented with the statements, participants were given a surprise recall test (they were not told in advance to remember the information).

Participants were pretty accurate in their recall of the data; however, on the schema-inconsistent information, there was a tendency to reverse the numbers. Rather than remembering that Mexican immigration fell from 12.8 million to 11.7 million, they recalled it had risen from 11.7 million to 12.8 million. Maybe they simply weren't paying attention when they read the information? Information that violates people's schemas should attract greater attention than information that is schema-consistent, so we should be more accurate with schema-inconsistent information. To investigate this, the researchers used eye-tracking technology to see if participants were focusing more on the information that ran counter to their schema. Sure enough, the volunteers spent more time reading the schema-inconsistent information, their eyes continually flicking from one section to another, presumably to reconcile the contradictory data. However, despite greater attention, their ability to remember the information correctly remained compromised (Coronel & Sweitzer, 2018). This would indicate that the errors were less to do with attention and more to do with misremembering. Participants were recalling the gist of the information, but to maintain consistency with their own mental models (their schemas), they misremembered the position of the data. Their desire for consistency was more powerful than the desire to be accurate. Schemas, therefore, can also lead us to misremember.

Schemas and the development of expertise

The Dutch psychologist Adriaan de Groot doesn't always get the same recognition as other cognitive psychologists; his name is often restricted to a paragraph or two in psychology textbooks or a brief citation in the work of others, such as Anders Ericsson and Alan Baddeley. Nevertheless, De Groot has been described as 'the pioneer of cognitive psychology' and was proclaimed the most influential Dutch psychologist ever by an independent panel that included Ericsson (De Groot died in 2006 at the age of 91). In his lifetime, he'd worked as a high school teacher and an industrial psychologist for a railway company, but it's his studies of chess players that he's most known for. He was, himself, a passionate and highly skilled player (see Gobet, 2018)

De Groot's combined interests in chess and psychology converged when he began interviewing other players about the strategies they employed during their games, beginning his investigations in the 1930s when still a student. He showed chess players a sample board and asked them to talk through their strategies as they decided on their next move. He assumed that expert players were more skilled at carrying out mental calculations, working out possible moves and their consequences. What his interviews revealed, however, was that skill at chess seemed to be more about memory and how players used it. Chess is a highly complex game, especially at the expert and grand master level. It's estimated that there are around 10 to the power of 20 (or 1 followed by 20 zeros) potential games of chess and that human players (as opposed to computers) will consider tens, if not hundreds, of positions before selecting a move. Only rarely will they think through to a win, lose, or stalemate situation.

De Groot compared the performance of five grand masters and five expert players in choosing a move from a particular board position. He then asked them to think aloud and determine the types and number of moves they would consider. Surprisingly, perhaps, grand masters didn't consider more alternative moves than experts, but they took less time to make their move. Independent observers also judged the final moves of the masters to be superior to those of the experts. Then, when participants were given a five-second presentation of board positions from actual games and asked to reconstruct them from memory, grand masters were correct 91 percent of the time compared to 41 percent for experts. Crucially, however, when pieces were randomly arranged without any appreciation of chess rules, both groups performed equally poorly (de Groot, 2008). What appears to be happening is that the players are sifting through their memory of previous games and using their prior knowledge to plan their next move. Rather than creating solutions from scratch for every game, they are making use of the information they already have. It's probable that these previous games are stored as schemas, the positions on the board acting as cognitive cues that provide rapid access to them. But this is only effective if the board positions represent actual games. This rapid cue-based access also places less strain on limited cognitive resources, enabling the player to cope with the current positions in a cognitively economical manner. Experts, therefore, don't necessarily have better memories or think faster than novices, but they can employ strategies that place less strain on working memory, while their problem-solving strategies depend on the knowledge already available as schemas.

Experts differ from novices both in the structure of domain-related knowledge (what they know about chess) and the ability to retrieve episodic domain-related information (recalling a previous chess encounter and board setup). We assume that this information is accessed and rapidly transferred to short-term working memory, but Ericsson suggested that they may actually be utilising long-term working memory (Ericsson & Kintsch, 1995). Long-term working memory represents a unitary model of memory with no reference to different modalities (as in, for example, the components of Baddeley and Hitch's working memory model). This means that all information is part of a schema, and the individual elements are defined by an activation level that declines over time (following the temporal decay hypothesis) but is slower for information for which people are experts. This means that experts can hold more information for longer and with fewer cognitive costs than novices. Experts exhibit superior episodic memory for domain-typical information, possibly because of their ability to access long-term memory directly to rapidly and reliably encode and retrieve the information instead of maintaining it in short-term memory alone.

There is, however, a downside. Experts' superior recognition is often exaggerated for information related to the central goals within the domain. Experienced drivers, for example, use information stored in long-term memory to drive their car and arrive safely at their destination (their goal), but rarely recall much of the actual journey (unless something out of the ordinary occurs). One study, for example, found that computer programmers asked to complete a coding task had worse incidental recall (information they weren't required to recall) than novices for details of code. The experts paid greater attention to the goal structure (the end result) than to the actual detail of the code (Adelson, 1984). Another study found that recall of patient information following a medical diagnosis task varied non-monotonically with the level of expertise, creating an inverted U. Participants with an intermediate level of expertise recalled more information about the patient than either those with more or less expertise. The poorer recall was attributed to selective attention and abstraction, consistent with the use of schemas (Schmidt & Boshuizen, 1993).

One of the most significant implications, however, is probably the role schemas play in people's ability to process information rapidly. Furthermore, if schemas are activated directly in long-term memory via long-term working memory, there should be less load placed on short-term working memory, with its resource limitations (capacity and duration). This process then poses a potential dilemma because it has always been assumed that working memory acts as a 'front-end', that information must first pass through a short-term or working memory store before it can take up relatively permanent residence in long-term memory (Forsberg et al., 2021). Both theories of long-term working memory and Cowan's Embedded Processes Model refer to direct activation of long-term memory via focus of attention (they are both generally considered unitary models, although Cowan's model embeds processes within others). This would rule out the possibility that some information is encoded directly into long-term memory, bypassing working memory altogether.

Regardless of the role of working memory, the development of expertise appears to involve the construction of these knowledge schemas; the more we have at our disposal, the faster we can assimilate new information and recall what we already know. This also makes intuitive sense and seems to fit with our lived experience. Take, for example, birth rate data. If you look at a graph displaying the number of births in the United Kingdom from 1930 to the present, there are several peaks and troughs. There is a definite fall at the beginning of the 1940s, but it then rises again until about 1950, falls again and then rises significantly into the 1960s. Some of these peaks and troughs are complex, but even if we have only a rudimentary understanding of twentieth-century history, we can draw some conclusions from these figures. The most obvious is that the birth rate fell around 1940–1946, or thereabouts. This, of course, coincides with the Second World War, when most men were abroad and having children was probably far from people's thoughts. I recall discussing this with a class of 16- and 17-year-olds, and was quite surprised by how few made the connection. Those who could were drawing on their knowledge of history to answer a question related to sociology.

Learning, as we have discovered, isn't only about remembering new information; it's also concerned with linking this new information to existing knowledge. Learning is generative; in that learners generate understanding by connecting new information to what they already know. Learners, therefore, attend to the relevant information and organise the material in working memory. They then integrate this information (as schemas) within long-term memory. A vital component of successful learning, therefore, is the meaning and context attributed to the material. If we cannot relate the new material to what we already know, we can only process this information at a shallow level (consistent with Craik and Lockhart's Levels of Processing theory). On the other hand, if the material has meaning (and we create meaning from what we already know), we have a much better chance of successfully integrating this information into long-term memory, representing a deeper level of processing.

This is why memorisation doesn't result in deep learning. This is true for Mr Jarvis's infamous lines, but it's even more so for Ebbinghaus's trigrams. There is no way of organising nonsense syllables into deeper cognitive structures because they are meaningless. We can select them and organise them, but never integrate them. They are the most shallow of constructs, barely representative of learning at all. The more complex the information, the deeper the processing; the deeper the processing, the more effective the learning. I now want to illustrate this point from a slightly different perspective. Element interactivity is a concept within Cognitive Load Theory, pertaining to the amount of information (or how many elements of information) a learner must process at the same time in order to understand a concept or perform a task. Some tasks can be viewed as having low element interactivity, while others have high element interactivity.

Take, as an example, the memorisation of isolated words, such as a list of foreign vocabulary. Each word is an independent element, with no need for the learner to relate the words to any other element. The task represents low element interactivity. Similarly, a basic maths problem, such as $2 + 2 = 4$, doesn't involve many interacting elements – you just apply a straightforward rule to the two numbers. However, the equation $2x + 3 = 7$ involves several elements that require manipulation in stages. The equation has high element interactivity. This would also apply to writing an essay, where we would have to consider multiple elements at once, such as structure, grammar, coherence of arguments, relevance of supporting evidence, and flow of ideas (see, for example, Ashman et al., 2020).

From a Levels of Processing perspective, low element interactivity represents shallow processing and would therefore be less likely to be retained in long-term memory. That said, low element interactivity would also result in lower cognitive load. Conversely, high element interactivity would lead to deeper processing and better retention but would require more effort due to higher cognitive load. This might, on the surface, create somewhat of a dilemma, because CLT seems to suggest that lower cognitive load is better for learners.

We began this chapter with a re-evaluation of the classic forgetting curve experiment. The criticisms directed at Ebbinghaus in no way dismiss or minimise the remarkable contribution these early experiments afforded psychology and cognitive science. Ebbinghaus's achievements retain a vital role in what was to follow. The criticisms arguably relate to what is useful, considering what we now know. As Henry Roediger points out, Ebbinghaus cannot be faulted for not anticipating every method, finding, or theory in the field, nor even for the scope of his techniques (Roediger, 1985). However, as Claxton notes, almost no research on education since around 1970 has made use of nonsense syllables, precisely because they place peculiar demands on memory that are unrelated to those in the classroom.

Ebbinghaus's research does not apply, except when we are made to learn complete nonsense (Claxton, 2021, p.99).

Learning requires context and meaning, as well as the use of previous learning to enhance current learning. Learning is generated through, not just what we learn, but what we already know. Context and meaning are vital, and in this regard, Claxton is on point. This continual interplay between new information and what we already know is at the heart of the new science of learning.

Chapter summary

- While influential, Ebbinghaus' forgetting curve may not be very useful for learners and educators because the methodology used lacks real-world application, particularly in regard to meaning and context.

- Prior knowledge and the ability to make meaningful connections are essential for effective learning and retention. Meaning allows information to be processed at a deeper level and integrated with existing knowledge.

- Schemas are structured mental representations that organise our knowledge and understanding of the world and are essential for integrating newly learned information into what we already know. However, they can also lead to errors in knowledge and understanding.

- Deep learning involves actively connecting new information to existing knowledge, going beyond mere memorisation.

References

Adelson, B. (1984). When novices surpass experts: The difficulty of a task may increase with expertise. *Journal of Experimental Psychology: Learning, Memory, and Cognition*, *10*(3), 483–495. https://doi.org/10.1037/0278-7393.10.3.483

Anderson, R. C. (1978). Schema-directed processes in language comprehension. *Cognitive Psychology and Instruction*, *I*, 67–82. https://doi.org/10.1007/978-1-4684-2535-2_8

Ashman, G., Kalyuga, S., & Sweller, J. (2020). Problem-solving or explicit instruction: Which should go first when element interactivity is high? *Educational Psychology Review*, *32*, 229–247. https://doi.org/10.1007/s10648-019-09500-5

Baddeley, A. (2019). *Working memories: Postmen, divers and the cognitive revolution*. Routledge.

Bartlett, F. C. (1932). *Remembering: A study in experimental and social psychology*. Cambridge University Press.

Bergman, E. T., & Roediger, H. L. (1999). Can Bartlett's repeated reproduction experiments be replicated? *Memory and Cognition*, *27*(6). https://doi.org/10.3758/BF03201224

Bransford, J. D., & Johnson, M. K. (1972). Contextual prerequisites for understanding: Some investigations of comprehension and recall. *Journal of Verbal Learning and Verbal Behavior*, *11*(6), 717–726. https://doi.org/10.1016/S0022-5371(72)80006-9

Brewer, W. F., & Treyens, J. C. (1981). Role of schemata in memory for places. *Cognitive Psychology*, *13*(2), 207–230. https://doi.org/10.1016/0010-0285(81)90008-6

Claxton, G. (2021). *The future of teaching and the myths that hold it back*. Routledge.

Coronel, J. C., & Sweitzer, M. D. (2018). Remembering political messages in dynamic information environments: Insights from eye movements. *Human Communication Research*, *44*(4), 374–398. https://doi.org/10.1093/hcr/hqy006

de Groot, A. D. (2008). *Thought and choice in chess*. Amsterdam University Press.

Ericsson, K. A., & Kintsch, W. (1995). Long-term working memory. *Psychological Review*, *102*(2), 211–245. https://doi.org/10.1037/0033-295X.102.2.211

Forsberg, A., Adams, E. J., & Cowan, N. (2021). The role of working memory in long-term learning: Implications for childhood development. In *The psychology of learning and motivation* (1st Edition). Elsevier Inc. https://doi.org/10.1016/bs.plm.2021.02.001

Gobet, F. (2018). Adriaan De Groot: Marriage of two passions. *ICGA Journal*, *29*(4), 236–243. https://doi.org/10.3233/icg-2006-29421

Pear, T. H. (1922). *Remembering and forgetting*. Methuen.

Roediger, H. L. (1985). Remembering ebbinghaus. *Contemporary Psychology: A Journal of Reviews*, *30*(7), 519–523. https://doi.org/10.1037/023895

Schank, R. C., & Abelson, R. P. (1977). *Scripts, plans, goals and understanding: An inquiry into human knowledge structures*. Lawrence Erlbaum.

Schmidt, H. G., & Boshuizen, H. P. A. (1993). On the origin of intermediate effects in clinical case recall. *Memory & Cognition*, *21*(3), 338–351. https://doi.org/10.3758/BF03208266

Tulving, E., & Osler, S. (1968). Effectiveness of retrieval cues in memory for words. *Journal of Experimental Psychology*, *77*(4), 593–601. https://doi.org/10.1037/h0026069

Tulving, E., & Pearlstone, Z. (1966). Availability versus accessibility of information in memory for words. *Journal of Verbal Learning and Verbal Behavior*, *5*(4), 381–391. https://doi.org/10.1016/S0022-5371(66)80048-8

How the brain constructs knowledge

Cognitive psychology and neuroscience have a rather interesting relationship that can be both illuminating and frustrating. We can't always map models of learning and memory onto brain regions, yet neuroscientists do often refer to these models when explaining neurological processes. What this means is that, while we might refer to the working memory model of Baddeley and Hitch, with its separate components, we can't necessarily point to a physical brain or brain scan and say, *that's where the phonological loop is*, or *see that? That's the central executive*.

Whether there is a specific part of the brain that specialises in certain memory functions is a topic of some debate. The localised theory of memory suggests that specific memories (or types of memory) are located in discrete, identifiable brain regions. For example, Maguire's study of London taxi drivers found increased volume in the cabbies' hippocampi. Henry's brain showed damage to localised regions, implying that damage to these areas is responsible for specific memory impairments. According to this view, memories are contained within engrams and localised circuits. An engram, first proposed by Richard Semon in 1904, is believed to be a basic unit of memory, the activation of which induces memory retrieval (Schacter et al., 1978). Recent research using a technique called optogenetics has identified potential specific neurons and circuits that appear to be involved in storing particular memories, but the search for the elusive engram still occupies the time of many neuroscientists.

But not all neuroscientists subscribe to this view. The distributed theory of memory posits that memories are spread across networks and involve multiple brain regions. Karl Lashley conducted a series of studies on rats in the mid-twentieth century in an attempt to find where in the brain memories are situated. Despite his best efforts, he found no area of the brain specific to memory. From this, Lashley concluded memories were a product of mass action, relying not on a single region but the overall functioning of the brain (Eichenbaum, 2016). Connectionist models based on artificial neural networks also assume memories are stored as patterns of connections. In this respect, the loss of a single neuron won't lead to the loss of any memory. Current AI models also adopt a connectionist view.

The prevailing wisdom, however, adopts a hybrid approach, with local circuits contained within distributed networks. This means that while specific aspects of memory might be processed and stored in localised circuits, such as the hippocampus forming new memories while the amygdala stores emotional memories, the complete memory is distributed across a network of regions. For example, sensory details of a memory could be stored in sensory cortices, while emotional content is stored in the amygdala. Overall coherence of the memory is then managed by the hippocampus. In Maguire's taxi driver study, we see evidence of localisation, in that the brain region associated with spatial navigation and memory is significantly larger. However, procedural aspects of navigation, such as driving skills, likely involve other regions, such as the basal ganglia and the motor cortex. We can then interpret these findings at a localised, distributed, and hybrid level. This may also be the case for different types of memory, such as episodic and procedural, and different stages, such as encoding and retrieval. For example, encoding might involve more localised processing in the hippocampus, while long-term storage could be distributed across the cortex.

There are an awful lot of *mights* and *coulds* here, highlighting the ongoing scientific journey towards understanding the human brain. It's worth noting, however, that cognitive psychology and cognitive neuroscience aren't entirely separate entities, and there is always overlap. In time, the emphasis may well shift from a computer to a brain-based metaphor. What has become particularly interesting over the past few years is neuroscience's approach to schemas and how they emerge as a by-product of encoding and consolidation. In addition, scientists are now better equipped to investigate all aspects of learning (including memory and forgetting) in terms of what the brain is doing, whereas much of what we understand about memory has relied on laboratory studies, the interpretation of research findings, and the creation of box-and-arrow models. Nevertheless, neuroscience is still in its infancy, despite already providing a wealth of information about memory and learning.

Working memory and the brain

We've already explored models of working memory devised from experimental and case studies. But what is the position from a neuroscience perspective? If we accept the view that working memory is essential for transferring new information into a more-or-less permanent state stored in long-term memory (as well as thinking in the present), then there must be a physical component within the brain that allows this process to occur. Baddeley and Hitch propose a theoretical model composed of a central executive that controls resources, a store for dealing with phonological information, and one for visual and spatial information. While this model is theoretical, the components appear to map quite well with specific brain regions. A functional area known as the dorsolateral prefrontal cortex is thought to be implicated in working memory and decision making, including the maintenance, manipulation, and retrieval of information. It also potentially has a role to play in dealing with cognitive limitations, such as capacity limits (cognitive load). A region of the brain called the anterior cingulate cortex operates as an attentional controller (equivalent to the central executive), while the parietal cortex acts as a workspace for sensory or perceptual processing. Theoretical models do, then, somewhat explain what's happening in the brain, even though our understanding of brain functionality remains far from complete.

The memory cycle

Let's look a little more deeply at another aspect of memory – the process of encoding. I've already discussed encoding as an important stage in getting information into long-term memory, but I now want to return to it from a neuroscientific perspective, including the formation of schemas.

Cognitive models of memory are useful for providing a theoretical description of how memory works based on experimental and clinical findings. But we can also investigate these systems by looking at brain regions that are more active when this process occurs (as in the taxi driver and translator studies described previously). Encoding is the first stage in what neuroscientists have dubbed the memory cycle. It's often overlooked because it's a rather complex process we don't fully understand. Generally, we think of encoding as the stage where the external world is changed into a form we can store and recall (or how information is represented in the mind). From a physiological perspective, encoding relates to how this information is presented by the brain's neural system, how it relates to brain structure, firing neurons, and the formation of connections between them. It's thought that new information is encoded into memory via the hippocampus, as well as regions of the medial temporal lobe (MTL). As we've seen, the hippocampus plays an important role in memory processes and is thought to connect different parts of what make up a specific episode, a process referred to as binding. You may recall from Chapter 4 that binding is handled by the episodic buffer in Baddeley and Hitch's model.

Every experience, including specific learning episodes, involves several elements. There is a specific thing we are learning and the components that make up this experience. But there are other elements involved, such as time, place, people, and so on. It's the hippocampus that collects all these pieces together and arranges them in a specific way. This means that, after encoding, the memory is what we describe as episodically detailed. This information is then consolidated (the second stage of the memory cycle) either during sleep or during wakeful rest. Consolidation in this context refers to the process by which memories become stable and long-lasting after their initial acquisition. This process involves the transformation of short-term memories into more enduring long-term memories. This consolidation process is important for building schemas.

Prior to consolidation, the memory is temporary and easily altered, but consolidation transforms the memory into something more stable. However, during this process, the episodic details of the event (such as time and place) fade away, leaving only the most important details. Because of this stripping away of details, many of our recollections appear more as vague resemblances than accurate memories. This might, at least on the surface, seem like a bad thing, but in terms of learning, it allows the memory to take on a more general form, which is useful for transferring a concept used in one situation and applying it to another similar one.

But Charles Brainerd and Valerie Reyna think it's a little more complicated than that (Brainerd & Reyna, 2019). They suggest memory traces are the product of two different processes: gist memory and verbatim memory, and they both exist simultaneously for the same event. Fuzzy trace theory (sometimes referred to as dual trace theory) explains how false memories might arise and how this impacts the criminal justice system in terms of eyewitness testimony. But it can also provide some insights into how what we believe we've learned can be, not only inaccurate, but also way off the mark. I'll illustrate these two types of memory with a very simple example.

As I'm sitting here typing, I've just remembered that I've left a drink and a snack in the kitchen (when I'm working, I'm generally fuelled by tea, coffee, and a plentiful supply of biscuits). This description, that I've left my drink and snack in the kitchen, is gist memory, devoid of any specific detail. Nevertheless, there are more details I could divulge; my drink is tea (and Yorkshire Tea at that), and the snack biscuits are Jammie Dodgers. The first description involves non-recollection retrieval and focuses on the semantic details rather than the surface details, while the second is recollective memory, where I've mentally reinstated the contextual features of my memory with all the details attached; the Yorkshire tea in my favourite Doctor Who mug that yells exterminate when I pick it up, and there's a plate with four Jammie Dodgers.

According to fuzzy trace theory, both this gist and verbatim memories form simultaneously, but we can store the gist memory after only processing a fraction of their details (Draine & Greenwald, 1998). We then have access to two records of the same experience – the detailed verbatim one (the actual event), and the more superficial gist one (the meaning of the event). Recounting my memory will always contain a mixture of verbatim and gist retrieval, so sometimes I'll say I've left my tea and biscuits in the kitchen, that is, I've reconstructed the event from gist. At other times (although much less likely), I'll describe the event in more detail, down to the type of biscuits and the Doctor Who mug. The problem is that, because gist becomes mixed up with verbatim, I may well misremember, creating a false memory. My gist memory will certainly contain some genuine memories, but it'll also involve the false ones. The gist memory merely reminds me I've left my drink and a snack in the kitchen, so I might recall coffee instead of tea or Oreos instead of Jammie Dodgers. I'm assuming the tea is in my Doctor Who mug, but it might not be. All or some of these recollections might be wrong. Or all of them might be accurate. If you were to escort me into a darkened room, shine a light directly into my face, and interrogate me about what I left in the kitchen, the questions you ask, and how you ask them, are going to influence what I genuinely remember, what I've forgotten and what I truly believe to be correct, but isn't. Your questions might act as cues that nudge my memory, but they might also lead me astray: *Did you make your coffee in the Doctor Who mug?* Well, I made a drink in it, but now I'm not sure if it was tea or coffee because you seem pretty confident it was the latter. However, my verbatim memory may well fight back: *No, I know it was tea because I remember putting the bags in the pot* (yes, I'm old enough to still have a teapot). My responses will also depend on which of the traces are stronger and the time elapsed since the event and the interrogation. But over time, the verbatim memory will fade more rapidly than the gist memory (Kintsch & Mangalath, 2011). If I had recalled making a cup of coffee rather than tea, this would represent a false memory (and false memories are much more common than you might think).

A more obvious example might be our memories of the books we've read of the films we've watched. While reading a novel, we often become invested in the characters and travel with them, enthusiastic onlooker, picking out every detail of their lives as it relates to the narrative. If it's a really good book, we might feel a pang of disappointment when we reach the last page and have to say farewell to the characters we've grown to know. But after a couple of days, the details will have started to fade, and if we're asked about the story, we'll most likely only be able to give a brief description of what it was about. What was only a day or so ago a story that engrossed us has been stripped of its detail and nuance, leaving behind only the gist. However, when we begin to explain the story to our friend, we may well find that a more detailed memory arises and one recollection nudges another, with widely varying degrees of accuracy.

How verbatim and gist memory interact depends, in part, on our age. Both systems improve between childhood and adulthood; in early development, there's an asymmetrical relationship, in that gist memory evolves more gradually than verbatim memory. However, in late adulthood, verbatim memory declines while gist memory remains largely intact. It also appears that some people are more susceptible to the creation of false memories through verbatim-gist memory interaction. This is particularly the case for people with clinical conditions such as PTSD, but it would also appear that adults displaying lower levels of intelligence are also susceptible, as are elderly adults. Interestingly, although not surprisingly, adults who hold beliefs that violate established scientific facts (such as conspiracy theorists) are also more likely to fall victim to false memories, and you'll recall from Chapter 6 that schemas play a role in how accurately we remember something. Contrary to early descriptions of false memories that considered them as somewhat vague and less vivid than real memories (for example, Conway et al., 1996), more recent accounts have found them to be virtually indistinguishable (Lampinen et al., 1999). According to the phantom recollection principle, false memories are often vivid. Jason Arndt suggests that when people remember by re-constructively processing gist, they can recover realistic contextualised details that make false memories seem real (Arndt, 2012). Fuzzy trace theory might also explain why we only have a vague idea, or what we learned at school, because verbatim memory is going to fade much quicker than gist memory – all you're left with is a vague recollection of what you, for a while, seemed to know in detail.

Retrieval in the brain

Once our new memory is encoded and consolidated, we should be able to retrieve it. We don't always retrieve memories in the same way (it often depends on the type of memory), and the memory we retrieve is rarely the same as the one we encoded. Furthermore, they alter over time beyond our conscious awareness. This is why I describe recalled memories as reconstructed memories because we alter them slightly each time we recall them, even though we never realise we're doing it. This often occurs because we don't always recall an episode with the same cues, so recalling details in an exam hall won't necessarily employ the same retrieval cues as recalling the same information at the pub during quiz night. One might have been, for example, stripped of episodic details (the where and when), while the other might include a more detailed description of where we learned it, who we were with, and so on.

This ultimately means that retrieval will again alter the features of the memory, with the potential of both creating false memories and correcting these errors. After retrieval, the memory will probably go through a process of reconsolidation. Retrieval, or reactivation, places the memory trace into a fragile state where it must undergo a process of stabilisation (Kiley & Parks, 2022). We can use this stage to correct errors and weed out false information, but we can just as easily add errors to it. This cycle might only happen once, but for some memories, it could very well last for weeks, months or even years, continually altering the memory in subtle ways.

Schemas in the brain

The by-product of this memory cycle is the gradual build-up of schemas, and schemas are useful tools when it comes to attempting to explain how knowledge is represented in our minds. While schemas have traditionally been the purview of cognitive psychologists, they have over the past decade or so begun to interest neuroscientists. The first neuroscientific study to engage with schemas on any concrete level was published in 2007 but didn't involve humans.

Dorothy Tse of the University of Edinburgh and her team found rats were better at encoding and consolidating new information if it fitted with a previously stored spatial schema, adding to the notion that the more you know, the quicker you learn (Tse et al., 2007). Since then, neuroscientists have become quite enthusiastic about an area of research that once only attracted cognitive psychologists. This combining of neuroscience and cognitive psychology into cognitive neuroscience is bound to allow us to explore fresh developments in learning science and perhaps rid schema theory of some of its fuzzier elements. Neuroscientists generally agree with cognitive psychologists about the nature of schemas, but approach them from a physical position, or how they can be represented within the brain's systems. As they pertain to the memory cycle, it's been proposed that schemas are continually adjusted to optimise understanding of the world and to predict future occurrences. How the brain actually constructs, uses, and adapts schemas still isn't fully understood from a neuroscience perspective, but there have been some suggestions.

One particularly interesting proposal is known as the schema-linked interactions between medial prefrontal and medial temporal regions framework (thankfully, referred to as the SLIMM framework). The SLIMM framework proposes that the medial prefrontal cortex (mPFC) detects resonance from an activated schema and attempts to integrate the newly learned information into it (Van Kesteren et al., 2012). This usually happens during offline processing (sleep or wakeful rest). This process is different from both encoding and retrieval and is part of the consolidation stage. The hippocampus and the mPFC then determine the level of detail stored as part of the memory, and how weak or strong the connections are to an existing schema. The strength is probably determined by how closely related the items are. For example, a cat and a dog are both domesticated animals kept as pets, but a Great Dane and a Pug are both types of dogs, so the connection between the cat and the dog will be weaker than the connection between the Great Dane and the Pug.

Why might the brain organise information into schemas?

We know that learning and memory are crucial to survival, and yet it's not always useful to remember only unique episodic events. It's certainly helpful to remember where you found that recent haul of juicy berries and nuts, but it's perhaps even more useful to be able to use this information to predict where they usually grow. If our ancient ancestor picked the berry bushes clean, it wouldn't be much use returning to the same bush next time, hoping to be able to collect some more. But if we could also note the characteristics of where the bushes grew and when they were abundant with berries, we could use this information to find alternative sources of food. Our brains then become prediction machines (or engage in predictive coding) because we have evolved to think about what might happen next. The world can be dependable; the sun rises every morning and sets every night; winter is colder than summer, and food (at least in ancient times) was scarcer at certain times of the year.

But the world is also ever-changing, and humans and non-human animals will need to adapt to certain events, such as climate change. Schemas, therefore, provide a clear and consistent internal model of the external world and do this by creating generalised memories. Not only that, but they can also generate prediction errors. If, for example, our ancestor predicted that a certain similar bush produced berries that looked the same, only to discover they were inedible, the error in the schema could be corrected and re-consolidated. This doesn't always work, however, and sometimes it's difficult to assimilate new information into a well-developed schema. Plus, there's also some danger that this process can produce false memories.

Memories stored as schemas are, therefore, flexible, and this is what we need if we're going to become effective learners. Because schemas are generalised memories, we can apply them to many other circumstances, creating what cognitive psychologists call cognitive flexibility or flexible learning. This cognitive flexibility is a major component of executive function, which I'll discuss in detail later in Chapter 12.

The schema paradox

If we consider the brain to be a prediction machine, what happens when these predictions are wrong? From what we've learned so far, we are much better at remembering information if we can easily incorporate it into a current schema – what we already know helps with learning more. Paradoxically, however, recall is also better when we encounter information that is unexpected or doesn't fit with our expectations. Take, for example, a 2024 study by Aimee Stahl and Lisa Feigenson.

Stahl and Feigenson recruited 335 children with an average age of 36 months. They divided the children into two groups and showed them a gumball-type machine, only they filled the machine with toys rather than gumballs. In the first condition, the researchers had filled the machine with a mix of pink and purple toys, but in the second condition, they had filled it with only purple toys. They gave each child a coin to put in the slot and retrieve a toy. They then told them the toy was called 'Blick' (a made-up word to avoid any pre-existing knowledge that might help them recall the name).

Now, because psychologists are just plain devious, they had rigged the second condition so that the child might receive a pink toy, even though the machine only contained purple toys. In condition 1, the chance of receiving a pink toy was probable; in condition 2, it was impossible. Later, the researchers asked the children the name of the toy. Those in the second condition (the impossible one) were more likely to remember the name than those children in condition 1 (Stahl & Feigenson, 2024)

What can this study tell us about how the brain reacts to these expectation violations? Let's look at a slightly different example. Consider the following list of fruits.

APPLE, PEAR, ORANGE, tomato, BANANA

When asked to learn such lists and recall them later, participants overwhelmingly recall tomato better than the others. This is what Hedwig von Restorff termed the isolation effect (von Restorff, 1933). The isolation effect posits that an item that is distinct from other items on a list is better recalled. Stephen Schmidt distinguishes between two types of distinctiveness: Primary distinctiveness describes an item that differs perceptually or conceptually from other items close by (tomato, rather than TOMATO in the list above). And secondary distinctiveness, where an item appears unusual according to general knowledge (Schmidt, 2008). For example, the duck-billed platypus is a mammal that lays eggs, making it distinct among most other mammals (the echidna is the only other mammal to lay eggs).

Events that violate our expectations can be contrasted with those that conform to them. The latter event allows for the incorporation of new information into existing knowledge as schemas. So, if schemas are so important for learning, why does information that doesn't conform to expectations still lead to enhanced recall? This paradox is often posed in terms of congruency (the event conforms to our expectations) and incongruency (it violates these expectations). In studies, both high congruency and high incongruency lead to superior retention.

Let's look at another example, one presented by Andrea Greve, a researcher at the MRC Cognition and Brain Sciences Unit at the University of Cambridge (Greve et al., 2019).

Consider the following statement:

The blue handbag contained a tomato.

Now, I know what you're wondering – why would someone keep a tomato in their handbag? The suggestion that a handbag contains a tomato doesn't fit with our handbag schema. If the blue handbag contained a hairbrush, there wouldn't be any violation of our expectations. We don't generally find tomatoes in handbags. In studies, participants would be more likely to recall the tomato than other items in the handbag. How about the statement:

The blue bag contained a tomato.

This statement is neither highly congruent nor highly incongruent. The nature of the bag isn't specified, so it could be a shopping bag rather than a handbag – it doesn't violate our expectations (or appear inconsistent with our handbag schema). Let's, then, examine the following three statements:

The blue handbag contained a tomato.

The blue bag contained a tomato.

The blue bag contained a hairbrush.

The first statement violates our expectation, while the second is neutral. The third conforms to expectations. If I were to ask a group of volunteers to learn all three statements and then ask them about the contents of the bag, the results would likely form a very pleasing U shape. In other words, my volunteers would recall the contents of the bag better in the first and third statements. Conforming to our pre-stored schema is helping us remember the third statement and drawing attention to the violation of the schemas in the first.

Greve and her colleagues believe our brains are processing congruent information and incongruent information differently, drawing on the SLIMM framework to explain it. Information that is consistent with our handbag schema leads to activation of the mPFC, selecting information that is only relevant to the active schema. This leads to the selective encoding of schema-relevant information to the exclusion of irrelevant details. However, when we encounter information that violates our handbag schema (the tomato), a prediction error occurs. This error then triggers the MTL system (including the hippocampus) to encode a more detailed memory of the surprising event than if the event were schema-consistent. Suppression of irrelevant information likely takes place after encoding, probably when the information is recalled and reconsolidated. It's unlikely, however, that our handbag schema would be updated because handbags don't usually contain tomatoes.

Schemas play a vital role in learning. They could be a simple by-product of the memory cycle, yet they are certainly relevant to our quest to identify how we can learn more effectively. Forgetting what we've learned is, at least in part, related to how well we can assimilate new information into an existing schema. This is then part and parcel of what we can describe as elaborative or deep learning. Rather than simply memorising facts, we actively identify meaning and context. Then, we associate the new information with what we already know and use this to further build connections through internal schemas. There will be errors, but hopefully the internal error-correction system will take care of many of them. We may, therefore, assimilate a spider (an arachnid) into our insect schema or a tomato into our vegetable schema, but through interrogation, we correct this error and reconsolidate the information during the memory cycle. However, another important aspect of schemas (alongside cognitive flexibility) is that they make learning more efficient, releasing much-needed resources for other cognitive operations.

What, then, can all this tell us about effective learning? The most important takeaway is related to the act of knowledge construction and generative learning. Being able to recall facts and figures is useful, but without elaboration, this usefulness is limited. To enhance their utility, we need to link new information to older information, whereby the information becomes knowledge, something that has more far-reaching consequences. This knowledge forms through the emergence of schemas, and our ability to access these schemas tells us something about what we have learned and what we know and don't know. But we also need to activate the appropriate knowledge at the right time. Gist is useful, as is familiarity, but the emergence of multiple interlocking schemas allows one piece of information to be used in multiple ways and in different contexts.

Chapter summary

- While models of memory and attention are useful, mapping them onto brain structures can be complex.

- The memory cycle posits that information is encoded, consolidated, retrieved, and re-consolidated, often several times. Consolidation, occurring during sleep or wakeful rest, stabilises memories and contributes to schema building by retaining important details while episodic details fade. Retrieval is a reconstructive process that can alter memories and is followed by potential re-consolidation.

- Fuzzy trace theory (or dual trace theory) proposes that both gist memory (semantic details) and verbatim memory (surface details) are formed simultaneously for the same event. This theory explains how false memories can arise from the interaction and potential confusion between these two types of memory traces. Verbatim memory tends to fade faster than gist memory over time.

- The SLIMM framework is a neuroscientific proposal for how the mPFC integrates new information into existing schemas during consolidation, with the hippocampus and mPFC determining the level of detail stored. The framework offers a neuroscientific explanation for the formation of schemas.

- The schema paradox states that while information congruent with existing schemas is well-remembered, information that violates expectations (incongruent information) also leads to enhanced recall.

References

Arndt, J. (2012). False recollection: Empirical findings and their theoretical implications. In B. H. Ross (Ed.), *The psychology of learning and motivation* (Vol. 56, pp. 81–124). Academic Press. https://doi.org/10.1016/B978-0-12-394393-4.00003-0

Brainerd, C. J., & Reyna, V. F. (2019). Fuzzy-trace theory, false memory, and the law. *Policy Insights from the Behavioral and Brain Sciences*, 6(1), 79–86. https://doi.org/10.1177/2372732218797143

Conway, M. A., Collins, A. F., Gathercole, S. E., & Anderson, S. J. (1996). Recollections of true and false autobiographical memories. *Journal of Experimental Psychology: General*, 125(1), 69–95. https://doi.org/10.1037/0096-3445.125.1.69

Draine, S. C., & Greenwald, A. G. (1998). Replicable unconscious semantic priming. *Journal of Experimental Psychology: General*, 127(3), 286–303. https://doi.org/10.1037/0096-3445.127.3.286

Eichenbaum, H. (2016). Still searching for the engram. *Learning and Behavior*, 44(3), 209–222. https://doi.org/10.3758/s13420-016-0218-1

Greve, A., Cooper, E., Tibon, R., & Henson, R. N. (2019). Knowledge is power: Prior knowledge aids memory for both congruent and incongruent events, but in different ways. *Journal of Experimental Psychology: General*, 148(2), 325–341. https://doi.org/10.1037/xge0000498

Kiley, C., & Parks, C. M. (2022). Mechanisms of memory updating: State dependency vs. reconsolidation. *Journal of Cognition*, 5(1), 1–13. https://doi.org/10.5334/joc.198

Kintsch, W., & Mangalath, P. (2011). The construction of meaning. *Topics in Cognitive Science*, 3(2), 346–370. https://doi.org/10.1111/j.1756-8765.2010.01107.x

Lampinen, J. M., Neuschatz, J. S., & Payne, D. G. (1999). Source attributions and false memories: A test of the demand characteristics account. *Psychonomic Bulletin & Review*, 6(1), 130–135. https://doi.org/10.3758/BF03210820

Schacter, D. L., Eich, J. E., & Tulving, E. (1978). Richard Semon's theory of memory. *Journal of Verbal Learning and Verbal Behavior, 17*(6), 721–743. https://doi.org/10.1016/S0022-5371(78)90443-7

Schmidt, S. R. (2008). Distinctiveness and memory: A theoretical and empirical review. In J. H. Byrne (Ed.), *Learning and memory: A comprehensive reference* (pp. 125–144). Elsevier. https://doi.org/10.1016/B978-012370509-9.00143-1

Stahl, A. E., & Feigenson, L. (2024). Young children distinguish the impossible from the merely improbable. *Proceedings of the National Academy of Sciences of the United States of America, 121*(46). https://doi.org/10.1073/pnas.2411297121

Tse, D., Langston, R. F., Kakeyama, M., Bethus, I., Spooner, P. A., Wood, E. R., Witter, M. P., & Morris, R. G. M. (2007). Schemas and memory consolidation. *Science, 316*(5821), 76–82. https://doi.org/10.1126/science.1135935

Van Kesteren, M. T. R., Ruiter, D. J., Fernández, G., & Henson, R. N. (2012). How schema and novelty augment memory formation. *Trends in Neurosciences, 35*(4), 211–219. https://doi.org/10.1016/j.tins.2012.02.001

von Restorff, H. (1933). Über die Wirkung von Bereichsbildungen im Spurenfeld. *Psychologische Forschung, 18*(1), 299–342. https://doi.org/10.1007/BF02409636

Knowledge is power (just not always)

Schemas allow us to quickly access stores of learned information that we have grouped in such a way as to make them transferable from one situation to another. They are also flexible enough to be updated in response to new incoming information. It then stands to reason that prior knowledge will impact heavily on current and future learning. But as we've seen, this advantage can arise through both schema consistency (when current learning matches the contents of stored schemas) and schema inconsistency (when current learning violates the contents of a schema). While schemas were once considered theoretical, evidence from neuroscience appears to support the idea that the brain organises information into schema-like constructs.

What we already know is going to impact how effectively and efficiently we learn new information. However, the information will have to be consolidated adequately enough to not only become long-lasting but also connect to the knowledge already present as schemas. This view reinforces the notion made over 50 years ago by the American educational psychologist David Ausubel that the most important single factor influencing learning is what the learner already knows (Ausubel, 1968). To paraphrase Ausubel, once we know that, we can then teach (and learn) accordingly. According to Hambrick and Engle, this view is one of the most influential ideas to emerge in cognitive psychology in the past 25 years (Hambrick et al., 2019, p.340). The research literature often refers to this view as the Knowledge is Power hypothesis (for example, Simonsmeier et al., 2022). But there remains a naïve assumption that relevant prior knowledge will always facilitate learning, even though this proposition is rarely expressed in the literature. As Garvin Brod points out, Ausubel didn't claim that prior knowledge was always helpful, just that it is a strong determinant of what a student will learn in a lesson (Brod, 2021). And as we'll see in this chapter, prior learning can also negatively impact learning, even though its gains far outweigh its losses.

Learning is far from a passive activity. As we've seen throughout the preceding chapters, effective learning arises through effort and a combination of dynamic processes. Learning is generative. According to Logan Fiorella and Richard Mayer, learning involves actively constructing meaning from to-be-learned information by mentally reorganising it and integrating it with existing knowledge (Fiorella & Mayer, 2015).

This view is consistent with what we understand about how schemas aid learning, and one that Fiorella and Mayer have incorporated into their SOI (select-organise-integrate) model of generative learning, which I'll discuss in Chapter 13.

Why do starting points matter?

Recent research supports the notion proposed by Robert Merton that those individuals who start out with an advantage not only maintain it but also extend it (Merton, 1968). This phenomenon has been dubbed the Matthew effect. While Merton observed eminent scientists received disproportionate credit for their contributions compared to their lesser-known colleagues, the Matthew effect has since been extended to include its impact on learning and wider social and educational outcomes. Students from privileged backgrounds, for example, often have access to better educational resources than their less privileged peers. They also often begin formal education with a better grasp of reading and writing, as well as being more verbally confident. These students are more likely to do well in school, attend university and have a potential for higher earnings once they enter the labour market. The prevailing view is that children who begin school with lower competencies in skills such as reading and maths remain behind for the duration of their schooling, with the gap between the most and least advantaged increasing over time.

Thorsten Schneider and Tobias Linberg, for example, found that primary school children in Germany who had above-average language skills at age 5 tended to have even higher language competency at 9. Those with lower language skills at 5, however, made less progress, implying that even though they received the same education, the gap between the two groups was maintained (Schneider & Linberg, 2022). Interestingly, the researchers also noted that verbal development correlated with the mother's level of education. As the mothers' level of education increased, their children made more progress. On the flip side, Sonja Herrmann and her colleagues found that primary school children (again, in Germany) with lower initial scores in mathematics displayed greater learning gains than middle range and higher achievers. Importantly, however, the attainment gap never fully closed. Herrmann suggests that the German system, with its emphasis on foundational maths education, probably helped to mitigate the achievement gap (Herrmann et al., 2022). But why did the higher achievers still do better? The most likely explanation is that these children benefited more from help outside school, perhaps through additional resources or family support.

How prior knowledge helps (and hinders) learning

Prior knowledge can help us learn more efficiently, and there are several reasons for this. However, there are also ways in which it's detrimental to learning. Many of these mediators of prior learning have been discussed in earlier chapters, but it's worth re-visiting them within a prior knowledge context.

Positive mediators

Attention

I discussed attention in Chapter 5, and it might not seem all that surprising that our ability to stay focused and on task plays multiple roles in learning. Research finds that people with higher levels of prior learning in a particular area pay more attention to the important features of new to-be-learned information (for example, Tanaka et al., 2008; Yu et al., 2012). If, for example, we know a little about the Norman conquest of England, we are more able to zero in on new content because we will access what we already know to help make sense of the new content. It's much easier to focus on episode 4 of a television show if you've already watched episodes 1–3. And we all know how hard it is to concentrate on a film if we've missed the first half.

You'll recall from Chapter 5 that our attention selects features that are familiar during dichotic listening tests. This is one reason, as a study participant, my attention was selected for the audio in the English language while filtering out the French input. This also explains why experienced chess players can rapidly identify key pieces and positions on a chessboard, while novices often cannot identify the strategic significance. In a classroom environment, students with greater prior knowledge of a topic are more likely to focus on new, related information. This makes intuitive sense because the material fits within their existing knowledge framework. One of the main criticisms of the Ebbinghaus method is that the stimulus material excludes meaning and context. Because of this, participants cannot rely on prior knowledge to assist with recall. But in real-world settings, it's rare for us not to apply what we already know to make sense of new situations.

Encoding and interpretation

Prior knowledge helps us understand and remember new information. For example, readers with background knowledge can better grasp and recall the context of a given text (van Kesteren et al., 2014). Learners are employing knowledge from prior learning to make sense of new learning, and as we've seen, the creation of these connections results in more resilient retention and better comprehension. We saw this with the washing clothes study from Bransford and Johnson in Chapter 6 in terms of context. It's easy to see how good foundational knowledge in mathematics, for example, would help students learn more efficiently later. This is clear from the study of the mathematical ability of German children mentioned previously.

Binding of new information into chunks

You'll recall from the previous chapters that binding is the process whereby parts that make up a specific episode are connected. Binding allows for more efficient memorisation, processing, and retrieval because all the parts are in the same space, with their connections to each other stored as one, rather than many, items. Chunking as a method of overcoming capacity limitations has been the mainstay of memory research since Miller's digit-span experiments. You'll recall that Miller discovered the capacity of short-term memory to be between five and nine pieces, or chunks, of information (our immediate digit span, although it doesn't only apply to digits). Miller wasn't particularly specific about what he meant by the term chunk, and, even today, it has an ambiguous quality. Often, we mistake grouping for chunking or use the terms synonymously, but they are different processes and are used for different purposes. Perhaps the easiest way to get around this ambiguity is to explain how chunking can help us remember and how it relates to prior knowledge.

People attempt to make connections between items, and often they're not even fully aware of it. One very interesting way to improve our digit span is through chunking. Nelson Cowan defines a chunk as groups of items that have strong, pre-existing associations to other items (Cowan, 2000), so we can immediately see the relationship between chunking and prior learning. Even though the digit span technique measures the capacity of short-term memory, chunking links these short-term memory items with information already contained in long-term memory. But how does chunking work in the real world? People certainly tend to group digits together so they can more easily memorise them. Telephone numbers are the most obvious example. For example, UK phone numbers have two parts: a dialling code that represents the area (usually comprising five digits and beginning 01, and then an eight-digit number, giving a total of 11 digits, which is beyond the span of most people. Despite their length, however, people still remember their phone numbers, although perhaps not as many as in the past because of the rise of the smartphone and landline telephones that store telephone numbers by name.

Nevertheless, most people of a certain age may recall several phone numbers, including those of friends and family, besides their own. The reason we can remember them so well is certainly down to repetition, but it's also down to grouping. The dialling code represents one group of five digits followed by six digits that many people split into two sets of 3. This means that, as far as our memory is concerned, there are three pieces of information and not 11 digits; we've tricked our working memory into holding more information than it should. This is an example of grouping, but not chunking.

Chunking differs from grouping in the way items are represented in long-term memory. You may well be able to link a phone number to prior knowledge, but this isn't usually how we remember them. Let's take the following group of numbers: 10661914191819391945. There are 20 digits in the list, while the capacity of short-term memory lies somewhere between five and nine – there's no way we should be able to keep hold of all these numbers. We could try to group them, for example, 106 619 141 and so on, but the effectiveness of this method is low. A much better way would be to chunk them like this: 1066 1914 1918 1939 1945. Twenty digits now become four chunks, but each chunk represents something already stored in long-term memory: the dates of the Battle of Hastings, the start and end of the First World War and the start and end of the Second World War. Of course, I've already picked the relevant numbers to illustrate how chunking works, but all of us can link strings of digits to things relevant to us. You may, for example, set a bank card PIN to a number that applies to you, such as a birthday or anniversary. We are using prior learning to expand our working memory capacity.

In a paper from 1980, Anders Ericsson and Bill Chase describe the participant 'SF' (later revealed to be Steve Faloon), an avid runner, who extensively used his knowledge of running times to recall up to 79 digits. Interestingly, however, he could not increase the number of consonants he could recall, probably because he couldn't associate them with pre-stored long-term information (Ericsson et al., 1980). Over the course of their research, Chase and Ericsson worked with other digit span experts, many of whom found their own methods to relate groups of numbers with long-term memories, what they described as retrieval structures.

We can, therefore, chunk numbers, but what about letters? Take, for example, FBICIATV. We could chunk them like this: FB ICI ATV, or like this: FBI CIA TV. Chances are the second option is represented in most people's long-term memory, while the first may or may not be, depending on whether you're young enough to make Facebook out of FB, know that ICI is a chemical company or are old enough to make Associated Television out of ATV (or adventurous enough to have an All-Terrain Vehicle). We, therefore, need the knowledge of these pieces of information already in our long-term memory; otherwise they remain meaningless, or, in Cowan's words, they do not have strong, pre-existing associations to each other – they're just a string of random letters. Our ability to chunk successfully is therefore related to what we already know (information already held in long-term memory). This also fits with the widely held notion that learning is cumulative – the more you learn, the more you can learn. Learning also becomes quicker and more efficient because we are optimising the load by keeping our mental effort at a level that doesn't overstress it. This deeper understanding of chunking can then be used to better implement learning strategies that take advantage of the way we can link pre-stored information to newly acquired information.

Strategy development

If we already have knowledge about how we can best learn (perhaps by reading this book), we are better equipped to employ strategies and solutions that make learning more efficient and effective. Similarly, prior knowledge about the effectiveness and efficiency of problem-solving strategies can facilitate exploration, goal-directed behaviour, and the construction of more advanced new strategies. Strategy development broadly falls under the umbrella of metacognition (Chapter 12) and concerns the ability to think about our learning, plan, set goals and monitor our successes and setbacks.

Research finds that those with prior knowledge of problem-solving approaches can more efficiently explore solutions and create new strategies. This applies to all domains, but is more so in domains like mathematics, where understanding basic concepts helps in tackling more complex problems (Schneider et al., 2011).

Source evaluation

Perhaps more than ever, the ability to validate the credibility of information sources is a vital skill that is often overlooked. Prior learning can help evaluate the plausibility of new information, operating akin to a personal fact-checker. For example, if we have deep prior knowledge of climate change, we are more likely to be sceptical of claims denying its existence (Lombardi et al., 2016).

Negative mediators

There are, therefore, many positive mediators of prior learning. However, what we already know can also hinder present and future learning in several ways.

Misconceptions and incomplete knowledge

Learning doesn't always go the way we planned. Sometimes we remember some of what we learned about a topic, while at other times we get the wrong end of the stick. This can then result in us reaching incorrect conclusions. For example, believing the Earth is flat (a misconception) can interfere with our understanding about related concepts like planetary motion and gravity (Vosniadou & Brewer, 1992). Identifying and correcting these errors as they arise is, therefore, crucial if we are to update erroneous schemas.

Perceptual biases and inflexible learning

Past experiences with a particular problem can sometimes make it harder to find simpler solutions, even if they are more efficient, due to a perceptual bias called the Einstellung effect. This has been understood for some time, at least since the 1940s. Abraham Luchins, working within the Gestalt tradition outlined in Chapter 3, was one of the first to demonstrate the phenomenon using the water jug problem. He gave participants three water jugs of different capacities (for example, 21, 127, and 3 units) before asking them to measure out a specific amount (for example, 100 units). However, for the first few problems, the volunteers were instructed to solve the problem in a very specific and often overly complex way. This might involve filling the 127-unit jug and then using it to fill the 21-unit jug one and the three-unit jug twice. While later problems could have been solved easier using a simpler method, most participants continued to use the more complex method. Luchins suggested this was because the earlier problems had established mental sets (or Einstellung) which guided later problem-solving. Those participants who used the initial complex method struggled to find easier ways of completing the task (Luchins, 1942). Similarly, Heather Sheridan and Eyal Reingold found that expert and novice chess players given familiar but suboptimal moves (dubbed the Einstellung move) continued to use those moves even though better options were available (Sheridan & Reingold, 2013).

How might this look in the classroom? Take, for example, a biology class examining plant growth factors. Students place plants in different light sources and measure their growth over a predetermined time. They discover that plants placed in direct sunlight grow faster than those placed in shade. The teacher then gives them a new experiment to complete, again looking at plant growth. They placed one plant in full sunlight, the second in partial shade, and the third near an artificial light source with carefully controlled nutrients. Students might assume the plant in full sunlight will do better based on the findings of the previous experiment. Yet, they fail to consider other variables, such as soil quality, water availability, and the nutritional content of the soil. Here, their previous knowledge (that more sunlight equals better growth) prevents them from taking other factors into consideration.

Automatisation and inflexibility

We tend to think of automatisation, the process by which skills and knowledge become automatic with repeated practice, as a good thing in learning. Automatisation results in increased efficiency because once skills and knowledge become automatic, we can direct cognitive resources towards more complex tasks. For example, automatic word recognition in reading allows us to focus on comprehension. It also reduces cognitive load, freeing up working memory, and speeds up retrieval. However, it's not all positive.

Highly automated responses can lead to rigidity, making it difficult to adapt to novel problems (Lemaire et al., 1999). So can an over-reliance on heuristics (mental short-cuts, or rules of thumb). When decision-making is too automatic, we might ignore alternative strategies or fail to critically evaluate new information. Similarly, automatisation can lead to inflexibility, preventing adaptation to novel problems and stifling transfer. Take, for example, the following conundrum (given to participants in a study conducted by Pamela Ansburg and Roger Dominowski):

Throw a Ping-pong ball so that it will go a short distance, come to a complete stop and then reverse itself. You can't bounce it against a wall, or any other object and you can't attach anything to it.

Let's start by examining what we know about Ping-pong balls. They are used for playing table tennis (or Ping-pong), where opponents use small bats to hit the balls over a low net attached to a table. Our image of the Ping-pong ball is of players hitting it back and forth horizontally. Throwing it against a wall will violate the rules, as will pushing it up against any other object. There is a very simple solution, but what's stopping most of us from reaching it is bound up in our stored knowledge of Ping-pong balls. Would it make any difference if I swapped the Ping-pong ball for a basketball? It might help some of you, but not all. The problem with a Ping-pong ball is that our experience is of it travelling on a horizontal trajectory, that is, back and forth from one player to another, but a basketball is more likely to travel vertically, or up and down. What if I throw the Ping-pong ball up into the air? It will travel a short distance vertically, stop, and then drop back down into my hand. The solution is simple, but your prior knowledge might prevent you from considering other possibilities. For some people, introducing the basketball primes them to think of other possibilities (Ansburg & Dominowski, 2000).

We can see this in the real world as well. People who have been employed in the same job for many years find it difficult to adapt to changing working practices. Similarly, musicians who have practiced a piece for years in a specific way may find it difficult to adapt to a different tempo or style, leading to inflexible behaviour. In a maths class, a student may have learned to solve multiplication problems by automatically applying the standard algorithm (stacking numbers and carrying over). However, when faced with a word problem that requires multiplication in a different format, such as *If each table seats 8 people, how many tables do we need to sit 72 people?*, they struggle because they rigidly apply their automated procedure without understanding the underlying concept.

Increased possibility of interference

By having an extensive knowledge in a particular field, related concepts may interfere with each other, leading to confusion. Interference is also an important factor in forgetting, so we might remember a concept as relating to a particular topic when it actually relates to another. The likelihood is that some of this information has disappeared from memory entirely. A 2007 study by Alan Castel highlights how prior knowledge can interfere with current learning (Castel et al., 2007). Castel and his team recruited 40 undergraduates between the ages of 18 and 23. They gave participants two lists of words to learn. The critical list comprised 11 animal names that were also the names of American football teams, for example, dolphins, falcons, and colts. The second list comprised body parts. After learning the lists, volunteers were given a filler task so that they couldn't mentally rehearse the list but could create a delay between the learning session and the recall test. After the recall test, all volunteers were asked to complete a series of multiple-choice questions aimed at assessing their knowledge of football. They were then allocated to either a high-knowledge group, or a low-knowledge group.

The researchers found that participants with higher prior knowledge of football recalled more words from the list. However, they were also more likely to recall words that didn't appear on the original list. Most notably, eagles, panthers, and cardinals – all NFL football teams. So what's going on here?

As we've seen, the brain organises items in categories, so we group similar items together within schemas. This can then result in enhanced recall and more efficient learning. But we can also end up triggering information that might apply to the category, but isn't part of the learned information, resulting in memory errors. Memory errors are a product of associative activation – we associate certain items with other items within the same or overlapping categories. Retrieving relevant information is as much about the retrieval process as it is the encoding process, and we also reconstruct memories when we recall them. Let's look at how these errors might occur in relation to the study above.

People with a deep knowledge of American football will have well-organised schemas. This may include the names of teams and the links between them, as well as more general knowledge about the sport. When football experts recall a concept within their domain of expertise, that concept activates related concepts in their schema. This activation spreads through the network of connected ideas. If we were to show a football expert the word 'bears', for example, they would trigger the 'bear' concept held in their animal schema. However, they may also trigger their football schema and recall the Chicago Bears. This can then lead to memory errors. If the list includes the animal names falcons, colts, and rams, participants may also activate eagles (an animal that was not on the list).

Using knowledge beyond its original context

Cognitive psychologist Walter Kintsch suggests this knowledge is connected through a series of nodes and links. Nodes are concepts, or important units of knowledge connected by links, forming extensive networks of related information (Kintsch, 1991). Let's take two concepts as an example: crime and animals. The links between different animals are stronger than those that link animals to crime. However, there is a link between cat and burglar. In this way, links spread out through the network, every concept connecting to another. The word heart is connected to the concept of biology or blood flow, but also symbolically to love. We might even link heart to memory, as in learning something by heart (a leftover phrase from when people believed the seat of consciousness was the heart). The link between heart and love might be weaker than heart and blood flow unless it's approaching Valentine's Day and we're looking for a gift for our nearest and dearest. The more frequently we use these links, the stronger the connection is, and these links become bridges between existing knowledge and new information.

Having the knowledge of something and being able to retrieve that knowledge indicates learning, but there's more to it than that. Learning often involves similarities between different types of information or the acquisition of general rules that we can apply to other problems or situations. This learning outcome is referred to as transfer, or transfer of learning, and it's without doubt one of the most important aspects of knowledge acquisition. But it's also one of the most difficult to get right.

Transfer is generally defined as the productive application of prior learning and experiences in novel situations. By novel situations, we mean a context in which the original material differed from the current application. We might, therefore, learn a formula in a mathematics lesson and then apply it to a physics problem or a research methods class. Or we might take something learned in the classroom and use it within a real-world context. But we might also apply transfer when our goals change or when what we have learned is being assessed differently from the way it was originally. We might, therefore, use what we have learned in a physics class to design a model aircraft or knowledge about human behaviour in one culture and apply it to a different one or the same culture in a different context.

The theory of transfer has a long history, at least as far as the early days of psychology. At the turn of the twentieth century, behaviourist Edward Thorndike found that the courses high school students took had very little influence on their problem-solving skills. They may have gained knowledge from their studies in mathematics, physics, chemistry, and Latin, but couldn't apply this to real-world problems (Thorndike & Woodworth, 1901). Because of his findings, Thorndike became an advocate of a more active type of learning, having concluded that the traditional teacher-led approach to education wasn't able to prepare young people for the challenges they would ultimately face later.

Not all types of transfer are the same. As an experienced car driver, I could, no doubt, successfully drive other types of vehicles (such as a van or truck) even though I never have. The task is different, but the habitual experience, such as working the clutch and changing gears, as well as obeying the rules of the road, is very similar. This type of transfer is what David Perkins and Gavriel Salamon call low road transfer (Perkins & Salomon, 1992). There are many features of driving a vehicle that are shared with other types of vehicles. I learned to drive a car with a standard gearbox and eventually became accustomed to the way I would need to step on the clutch every time I shifted from one gear to another, but many years later I bought a car with an automatic gearbox and the transition from one to the other was barely noticeable. However, if I were to learn computer coding and then have my proficiency assessed by having to write a game program, simply knowing how to code won't guarantee I'll successfully complete the task. To develop a working game, I'm going to have to search for connections between what I know and how I need to apply it. This is high road transfer. High road transfer is more demanding, requiring exploration, discovery, and the flexible adaptation of skills. It, therefore, represents a deeper form of processing, as the skills we need to apply in order to achieve transfer require elaboration.

According to Perkins and Salamon, transfer also results in two broad instructional strategies: hugging and bridging. Hugging is a low road strategy that directly guides and engages the learner in a particular desired performance. Teachers, therefore, might encourage students to revise for exams by completing mock exam papers. We might also prepare people for job interviews by having them engage in a practice interview, rather than providing them with general advice. In this way, the learning task 'hugs' the target of assessment – we teach to the test, if you like. Bridging, on the other hand, encourages intentional abstraction of the general rules by searching for connections among our many varied experiences and applying these examples to new situations. For example, a teacher might suggest to students that they adapt an exam strategy based on their previous experience. This, then, creates an opportunity to analyse and reflect on the strengths and weaknesses of the strategy and create a general strategic plan for future exams. Bridging would suggest that instructional design should include the creation of generic skills to be used in different situations.

Cognitive theories of transfer generally refer to the application of abstraction and analogy. According to the late Richard Skemp, an important figure in mathematics education, abstraction is an activity by which we become aware of similarities among our experiences (Skemp, 2012). In a biology class, for example, we may be taught about the pioneering work of Gregor Mendel, who, in the nineteenth century, uncovered the genetic laws behind multiple generations of pea plants. Mendel's discoveries gave rise to the modern discipline of genetics. What we learn from Mendel's work goes beyond pea plants, so we would need to generate a general law from his findings to use within different contexts. A learner, therefore, needs to understand that what they learn about pea plants can then be applied to other species and the science of genetics more generally. The same would be the case in physics lesson about the conservation of energy. Mathematics and science progress through the use of these deep conceptual principles. On the surface, they may look dissimilar, but they are defined in terms of the same categories or models.

Analogies, metaphors, and prior learning

Analogies and metaphors are powerful tools for bridging the gap between prior knowledge and new concepts. Metaphors shape not just language but how we think and learn, influencing our understanding of complex concepts (Lakoff & Johnson, 1980). They work by mapping similarities between familiar and unfamiliar ideas, making abstract or complex information easier to understand. However, their effectiveness depends on how well the prior knowledge aligns with the new content.

Analogies function by drawing structural similarities between two domains— one well-understood (the base) and one unfamiliar (the target). We might, therefore, compare electrical current to water flowing through pipes to help learners understand voltage and resistance. I've already discussed the brain as a computer comparison, and this is perhaps a good way to explain the subtle difference between analogies and metaphors, even though they both rely on prior learning and, from this perspective, operate in the same way.

If I said the brain is a computer, I'm employing a metaphor because I'm making a direct conceptual comparison. That doesn't mean the brain is literally a computer, only that we can think of it as one because many of the things it does, computers also do. But what if I claimed the brain was like a computer? Here, I'm employing analogy by explicitly comparing relationships between two things – the brain is like a computer: it processes information, stores memories in different locations, and retrieves them when needed.

Analogies, therefore, leverage prior knowledge to help us understand and explain new information. Like other aspects of prior knowledge, they can reduce cognitive load and help us construct new schemas or adapt current ones more efficiently. This then leads to deeper learning by highlighting structural rather than superficial similarities, encourages active participation, and builds active comparisons. But not all comparisons are useful, for example, describing the brain as a muscle. While this analogy may be useful in promoting the notion of cognitive effort and growth, it can lead to incorrect assumptions about how learning works. While it has its limitations, the brain as a computer analogy is more appropriate than the brain as a muscle.

Why can't we just Google it?

The relationship between past, current, and future learning means that what we already know helps us learn more efficiently. But it also highlights the gradual nature of deep learning. Deep learning takes time, while shallow learning (such as rote memorisation) can be achieved quickly but fails to imbed effectively. Memory prefers to snack rather than gorge. This means there's a threshold to initial learning. I can't simply read the Wikipedia entry on quantum physics and claim that I know about quantum physics. Chances are, I'll forget it quickly, and even if I manage to retain some of it, I'm unlikely to be able to apply this information to different scenarios.

Since the growth of the Internet, there has arisen a view in some circles that learning is less necessary than it once was because we can always Google it. When once we might have learned about a new area of interest by focusing intently on a book or completing a course, the tendency today is geared towards browsing and skimming. This often results in a shallow type of learning, and shallow learning reduces understanding. As we've seen, the accumulation of knowledge requires deep, elaborative processing and consolidation into networks of previous learning, and for this to take place, we need more than a simple, quick flick across a Wikipedia entry or a quick scan over the latest AI chatbot output. This is, of course, before we even think about the accuracy of what we're reading. What we then end up with is a loose collection of semi-recalled facts, often isolated from other related learning. In addition, inaccuracies will creep in and be consolidated, creating false memories and, unless these errors are corrected via re-consolidating processes, it becomes impossible to distinguish errors from accurate accounts of the information. For obvious reasons, this makes transfer unlikely because we're unable to recognise general rules and similarities that exist between sets of information.

The proliferation of technology and media can indeed challenge our capacity to concentrate, but there are also signs that these changes are adding to our fluid intelligence, that is, our ability to find meaning in confusion and solve new problems, independent of acquired knowledge. It's perhaps too early to tell how rapid technological change is going to impact learning, understanding, and the accumulation of knowledge.

Using prior knowledge isn't as straightforward as we might think (or hope). It certainly helps more than hinders, but one of its key advantages is that it tells us what learners know and what they don't. Assessing prior knowledge before beginning a new topic or area of study can also provide the opportunity to correct errors and misconceptions. One important thing our discussion on prior knowledge has also emphasised in that deep learning takes time. Previously, I introduced you to the illusion of explanatory depth, the notion that we think we know things in greater detail than we actually do. This may, in part, arise from a lack of processing depth caused by our naïve assumptions about how quickly we can learn things enough to explain them to someone else or fully answer questions about them.

You'll recall my earlier discussion of the memory cycle, that new information proceeds through several stages, including consolidation where the neurological system imbeds and connects this newly learned information to what we already know. Re-consolidation then alters this information again and can also operate as an error correction mechanism. Even then, repeated exposure to the newly learned information will strengthen connections between neurons and, over time, schemas emerge and go through a process of updating as new information is assimilated. This process may take hours, days, or weeks, depending on the complexity of the new learning. It will be some time before we can transfer this learning to different situations because we really need to know it well before we can achieve this. But it's not only about time, but about how we use our time. Revisiting what we've learned by re-reading, for example, constitutes passive learning, whereas deliberate practice and elaboration are active, and active learning is always better than passive learning. Transfer of learning is also an active process with no one-shot test because we have to consider how current learning affects subsequent learning. We also need to seek feedback to ensure that we haven't misunderstood what we've learned. This is important regarding schema formation because, if errors are assimilated into the pool of related information, we won't be able to distinguish the error from what we initially learned.

Chapter summary

- Prior knowledge significantly impacts both the effectiveness and efficiency of learning new information.

- Prior knowledge helps learning through various positive mediators. These include directing attention to important features of new information, aiding encoding and interpretation of new material by connecting it to existing knowledge, facilitating the binding of new information into chunks for more efficient memorisation, supporting strategy development for more effective learning and problem-solving, and assisting in source evaluation by acting as a personal fact-checker.

- Prior knowledge can also hinder learning through negative mediators. These include existing misconceptions and incomplete knowledge that can interfere with understanding new concepts, perceptual biases like the Einstellung effect that can make it difficult to find simpler solutions, automatisation leading to rigidity and inflexibility in applying knowledge, and an increased possibility of interference where related concepts confuse each other, leading to memory errors.

- Transfer of learning, the productive application of prior learning in novel situations, is a crucial aspect of knowledge acquisition but can be challenging.

- Deep learning, which involves elaborative processing and consolidation, is essential for the effective use of prior knowledge and transfer, contrasting with shallow learning often associated with simply accessing information online.

References

Ansburg, P. I., & Dominowski, R. L. (2000). Promoting insightful problem solving. *Journal of Creative Behavior*, *34*(1), 30–60. https://doi.org/10.1002/j.2162-6057.2000.tb01201.x

Ausubel, D. P. (1968). *Educational psychology: A cognitive view*. Holt, Rinehart and Winston.

Brod, G. (2021). Toward an understanding of when prior knowledge helps or hinders learning. *NPJ Science of Learning*, *6*(1), 2–4. https://doi.org/10.1038/s41539-021-00103-w

Castel, A. D., McCabe, D. P., Roediger, H. L., & Heitman, J. L. (2007). The dark side of expertise. *Psychological Science*, *18*(1), 3–5. https://doi.org/10.1111/j.1467-9280.2007.01838.x

Cowan, N. (2000). The magical number 4 in short-term memory: A reconsideration of mental storage capacity. *Behavioral and Brain Sciences*, *24*(1), 87–185. https://doi.org/10.1017/S0140525X01003922

Ericsson, K. A., Chase, W. G., & Faloon, S. (1980). Acquisition of a memory skill. *Science*, *208*(4448), 1181–1182. https://doi.org/10.1126/science.7375930

Fiorella, L., & Mayer, R. E. (2015). *Learning as a generative activity*. Cambridge University Press. https://doi.org/10.1017/CBO9781107707085

Hambrick, D. Z., Burgoyne, A. P., & Oswald, F. L. (2019). The role of interests in the development of expertise. *Vocational Interests in the Workplace* (May), 280–299. https://doi.org/10.4324/9781315678924-14

Herrmann, S., Meissner, C., Nussbaumer, M., & Ditton, H. (2022). Matthew or compensatory effects? Factors that influence the math literacy of primary-school children in Germany. *British Journal of Educational Psychology*, *92*(2). https://doi.org/10.1111/bjep.12462

Kintsch, W. (1991). The role of knowledge in discourse comprehension: A construction-integration model. *Advances in Psychology*, *79*(C), 107–153. https://doi.org/10.1016/S0166-4115(08)61551-4

Lakoff, G., & Johnson, M. (1980). *Metaphors we live by*. University of Chicago Press.

Lemaire, P., Reder, L., Ashcraft, M., Campbell, J., Carr, J., Dixon, J., Geary, D., & Zbrodoff-for, J. (1999). What affects strategy selection in arithmetic? The example of parity and five effects on product verification. *Memory & Cognition, 27*(2), 364–382.

Lombardi, D., Nussbaum, E. M., & Sinatra, G. M. (2016). Plausibility judgments in conceptual change and epistemic cognition. *Educational Psychologist, 51*(1), 35–56. https://doi.org/10.1080/00461520.2015.1113134

Luchins, A. S. (1942). Mechanization in problem solving: The effect of Einstellung. *Psychological Monographs, 54*(6), i–95. https://doi.org/10.1037/h0093502

Merton, R. K. (1968). The Matthew effect in science. *Science, 159*(3810), 56–63. https://doi.org/10.1126/science.159.3810.56

Perkins, D. N., & Salomon, G. (1992). Transfer of learning. In T. Husén, & T. N. Postlethwaite (Eds.), *The international encyclopedia of education* (2nd Edition, pp. 425–441). Pergamon.

Schneider, M., Rittle-Johnson, B., & Star, J. R. (2011). Relations among conceptual knowledge, procedural knowledge, and procedural flexibility in two samples differing in prior knowledge. *Developmental Psychology, 47*(6), 1525–1538. https://doi.org/10.1037/a0024997

Schneider, T., & Linberg, T. (2022). Development of socio-economic gaps in children's language skills in Germany. *Longitudinal and Life Course Studies, 13*(1), 87–120. https://doi.org/10.1332/175795921X16233448663756

Sheridan, H., & Reingold, E. M. (2013). The mechanisms and boundary conditions of the einstellung effect in chess: Evidence from eye movements. *PLoS One, 8*(10). https://doi.org/10.1371/journal.pone.0075796

Simonsmeier, B. A., Flaig, M., Deiglmayr, A., Schalk, L., & Schneider, M. (2022). Domain-specific prior knowledge and learning: A meta-analysis. *Educational Psychologist, 57*(1), 31–54. https://doi.org/10.1080/00461520.2021.1939700

Skemp, R. R. (2012). *The psychology of learning mathematics*. Routledge. https://doi.org/10.4324/9780203396391

Tanaka, D., Kiyokawa, S., Yamada, A., Dienes, Z., & Shigemasu, K. (2008). Role of selective attention in artificial grammar learning. *Psychonomic Bulletin and Review, 15*(6), 1154–1159. https://doi.org/10.3758/PBR.15.6.1154

Thorndike, E. L., & Woodworth, R. S. (1901). The influence of improvement in one mental function upon the efficiency of other functions. II. The estimation of magnitudes. *Psychological Review, 8*(4), 384–395. https://doi.org/10.1037/h0071280

van Kesteren, M. T. R., Rijpkema, M., Ruiter, D. J., Morris, R. G. M., & Fernández, G. (2014). Building on prior knowledge: Schema-dependent encoding processes relate to academic performance. *Journal of Cognitive Neuroscience, 26*(10), 2250–2261. https://doi.org/10.1162/jocn_a_00630

Vosniadou, S., & Brewer, W. F. (1992). Mental models of the earth: A study of conceptual change in childhood. *Cognitive Psychology, 24*(4), 535–585. https://doi.org/10.1016/0010-0285(92)90018-W

Yu, C., Zhong, Y., & Fricker, D. (2012, June). Selective attention in cross-situational statistical learning: Evidence from eye tracking. *Frontiers in Psychology, 3*. https://doi.org/10.3389/fpsyg.2012.00148

Why learning should be hard (but not too hard)

During the 1970s, psychologists at the MRC Applied Psychology Unit (now the MRC Cognition and Brain Sciences Unit) at the University of Cambridge were working in partnership with the British Post Office. Their most successful collaboration was the design of the UK postcode system (considered the most memorable in the world), but British psychologists from the unit also helped to design training programmes.

By the 1970s, the Post Office was undergoing a rapid process of modernisation, including automated letter sorting. A problem arose, however, because the system at the time couldn't decipher handwriting, forcing them to consider employing skilled typists to do the job. The Post Office had two options. Either they could hire an army of typists, or they could train postal workers to type. Today, of course, many people have developed at least a limited typing proficiency, but 40 years ago, it was standard practice to send hand-written documents to the 'typing pool' where professional typists would do it for you. In the end, the Post Office decided to train the workers they had, finding itself in the position of having to teach some 10,000 postal workers to type.

Alan Baddeley (he of the working memory model) saw this as an opportunity to examine the most effective ways to teach people a new skill, drawing on Ebbinghaus's discovery of the spacing effect. The spacing effect posits that for any material, information is better remembered if there is a larger rather than a small interval between the first time it is studied and the second (Smith & Firth, 2018, p.17). There's a vast research literature pertaining to the effect, some of which I'll discuss later, but for now, I want to stay with Baddeley and his work with the Post Office.

By the time the British Post Office had begun to mechanise, experimental psychologists, like Baddeley, were turning their attention to practical, real-world problems, rather than sticking with the laboratory-based experiments that mainly involved having volunteers learn lists of words (so-called verbal learning experiments). Baddeley, therefore, set about designing training schedules that could test the most appropriate time scales to teach people to type. What makes Baddeley's study useful is that it demonstrates the links between academic learning and skills learning and how we can draw upon findings from cognitive psychology to enhance both. Baddeley decided on four training methods, the results of which he could compare for effectiveness. He gave one group one training session of one hour per day, a second two sessions of one hour a day, the third one session of two hours per day, and the last group, two sessions of two hours per day (Baddeley & Longman, 1978).

He found the most efficient schedule to be one session of one hour per day, while the least efficient was the two-hour sessions. When the sessions were distributed over time, the participants learned more effectively than when the sessions were blocked. Distributed learning, therefore, was more effective than blocked learning. In addition, Baddeley asked participants to complete a questionnaire on how satisfied they had been with the sessions. Those in the one session, one hour per day group were the most dissatisfied, believing they were learning more slowly despite being the most efficient group in the long-term (in technical terms, they suffered from faulty metacognitive awareness). This point is interesting for several reasons, not least because it implies that distributed practice leads to fewer short-term but greater long-term gains, and people may not see progress over a shorter time scale. This emphasises people's desire to see quick and efficient results, but as we've seen, slow and steady is usually the best option for learning. With an education system based on fast gains and quick turnaround, we may be encouraging a way of learning that isn't sustainable over the long term (remember, our memory prefers to snack, not gorge).

Let's look at this as a slightly different example, one that involves my habit of binge-watching television shows on streaming platforms like Netflix. Over the past couple of years, I've noticed a curious phenomenon. Initially, I put it down to the inevitable slow decline of my cognitive functions as I age, but being the curious person I am (and not being entirely comfortable with the *I'm just getting old* explanation), I wanted to investigate the alternatives. It all has to do with the way I (and perhaps many of us) watch television. I'm more likely now to catch up on TV programmes and to binge-watch all episodes over a short period. The problem I seem to have is that I can't always remember what I've watched and really have to make an effort to recall what the programme was about – I've even started watching something before realising that I've already sat through all ten episodes. Curiously, I recall more about TV shows I watched when I was younger, so I assumed I was just getting a bit confused in my old age, or I was fooling myself into thinking that I recalled them. I can't recall every episode of *Blake's 7* or *The Six Million Dollar Man*, but I can still conjure up images of the main characters in my mind, and I have the gist of the storyline, yet I struggle to recall anything about the shows I've binged-watched, even after only a few days.

Luckily, researchers at the University of Melbourne investigated this very phenomenon back in 2017. Jared Horvath and his colleagues had volunteers watch the BBC Cold War drama *The Game*. They split their participants into three groups, with one group watching all six episodes in succession (the binge-watching group), one group watching daily, and the third weekly. Participants were then asked to complete a questionnaire at intervals of 24 hours, 1 week, and 140 days. Results revealed two very interesting factors. First, the binge-watching group consistently rated *The Game* as less enjoyable than the other two groups. Second, the binge-watchers showed the sharpest decline in memory recognition 140 days following the final episode (Horvath et al., 2017).

Now, I know what you might be thinking. What does binge-watching TV shows have to do with learning? Watching each episode of a TV show one after another is a good example of blocking, just like how we might learn an entire topic in short, sustained periods before moving to the next. Watching one episode a day (or even once a week) activates the spacing effect, resulting in better memory retention and comprehension of the material. This is most likely because memories take time to embed, and we often have to forget some of the information for memory to operate effectively (more on this later). If the next episode has a re-cap (the *previously on…* type of thing), this gently reminds us of what happened in the previous episode – it's like a teacher recapping the previous lesson before introducing new material.

There's probably an added factor here as well. The anticipation of waiting for the next episode creates an emotional cue. As the time and day get closer, we look forward to the next instalment. We might also talk about the programme to friends, family, and work colleagues, and this reinforces the memory and adds to the emotional energy – the *I can't wait to see what happens response*.

We can, therefore, see the spacing effect in skills training and our daily activities. But how might it operate in the classroom? While there is plenty of research from verbal learning experiments, the same can't be said for more naturalistic classroom-based studies. Many studies also tend to be of shorter duration than we might see in real learning environments, reducing the findings' ecological validity (or the ability to generalise findings to the real world where variables are less controllable).

Studies on the effect often concern themselves with identifying an optimal inter-study interval (ISI). The effectiveness of the interval can then be assessed by testing participants on the learned content sometime after the final presentation of the material, known as the retention interval (RI), or how long you need to remember the information. We, therefore, consider the time span between the final learning session and, say, an end-of-stage test (Figure 9.1). How, for example, will

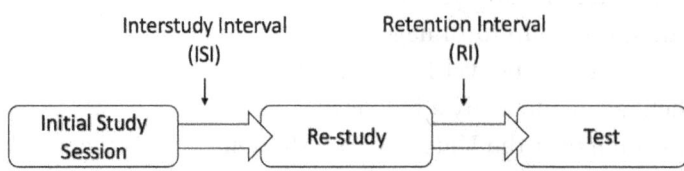

Figure 9.1 Interstudy and retention intervals in the spacing effect.

teaching and learning look if we test the to-be-learned information tomorrow, next week, or in several months' time?

Let's look at a study by Nicholas Cepeda and colleagues published in 2008. The researchers had 1,354 participants learn 32 obscure trivia facts, such as *snow golf was invented by Rudyard Kipling*, or *What European nation consumes the most spicy Mexican food? Answer: Norway*. The facts were obscure to minimise the possibility that volunteers could access prior knowledge to help them recall the facts later. As we've seen, prior knowledge is a cornerstone of learning, so it's one variable we need to control for carefully. The study used 26 ISI and RI combinations – the researchers manipulated the gap between the first and second presentation of the fact, along with the gap between the final presentation and the test (Cepeda et al., 2008).

While, in general, distributed learning fared better than blocked learning, there are important factors to consider. First, the ISI matters: excessively spaced learning, for example, is no different from blocked learning – both prove detrimental. Increasing the ISI leads to better retention, but only up to a point, after which further increases either have no effect or decrease retention. Another important point to remember is that optimal ISI increases as desired RI increases. This means that if you want to remember something for a few minutes, opt for a short ISI (less than one minute). If you want retention to last much longer (weeks, months, and even years), a longer ISI is going to be more beneficial. For long-term learning, you ideally need to be spacing out the content over multiple days.

This is fine, but how can we gauge the optimal ISI? According to Cepeda, a 1 day ISI is optimal for a 7 day RI, but a 21 day ISI is optimal for a 350 day RI, concluding that a 5–10 percent delay is optimal. Rohrer and Pashler suggest that the gap between studying and restudying should be between 10 and 30 percent of the time between the first presentation of the material and the time in which the material is to be needed, such as a test or exam (Rohrer & Pashler, 2007).

In an enlightening study from 2014, Carolina Küpper-Tetzel, Melody Wiseheart, and Irina Kapler had participants (210 undergraduate and graduate students) learn 28 word pairs using 56 concrete and familiar nouns, ensuring there was no semantic relationship between the words in the pair. They designed learning schedules over three levels, representing expanding, contracting, and equal inter-study. In the expanding schedule, intervals increased (one day, then five days); in the contracting schedule, intervals decreased (five days, then one day); in the equal schedule, intervals were kept constant at three days and three days. They divided retention intervals into 15 minutes, 1 day, 7 days, and 35 days (Küpper-Tetzel et al., 2014).

Results confirmed that the optimal schedule depended on the retention interval. For shorter RIs of one to seven days, a contracting learning schedule (that is, decreasing intervals between learning sessions) resulted in the best free recall performance on the final test. For longer RIs of up to 35 days, an equal or expanding learning schedule (constant or increasing intervals) resulted in better performance compared to a contracting schedule. Surprisingly, there was no difference between equal and expanding schedules across any RI. This might suggest that the interval between the last two learning sessions is more critical for the final memory performance than the interval between the first and the second session.

How, then, can we explain these findings? One explanation has to do with context-dependent retrieval (a theory we met in Chapter 5). For shorter retention intervals, learners experience a greater overlap between the last two learning sessions and the final test. You'll recall that Contextual Variability Theory posits that memories are encoded along with contextual cues, so if you study the material in the same room and at the same time of day, that information will be encoded along with the learned information. However, this means that as the time between study sessions increases, the context also changes, providing fewer cues and making it harder to retrieve the memory. A shorter retention interval favours contracting schedules because they take advantage of the contextual similarity between the final study session and the test. Longer retention intervals favour equal or expanding schedules because they promote the encoding of a wider variety of contextual cues.

From spacing to interleaving

Nate Kornell and Robert Bjork set out to investigate the extent to which distributed practice proves detrimental to induction learning. You might recall from chapter 1 that inductive learning involves learners making sense of the world by observing and drawing inferences from examples. Induction learning contrasts with memorisation and direct instruction via the emphasis on developing a general understanding of concepts and categories that we can apply to new instances (transfer). Kornell and Bjork began by considering a suggestion presented to them by Austrian-American educational psychologist Ernst Rothkopf that *spacing in the friend of recall, but the enemy of induction.* Massed practice, he argued, allows us to notice the similarities between successive episodes or examples. Say we were teaching a lesson about different animals. By presenting learners with examples of mammals, amphibians, and reptiles at the same time, they could immediately draw out the similarities and differences between them. Spacing out the lesson, for example, teaching mammals on day 1, amphibians on day 2, and reptiles on day 3, would increase the chance that characteristics of each animal will be forgotten between successive presentations (see Figure 9.2). But is this the case in practice? This is what Kornell and Bjork wanted to find out and, in the process, discovered something rather intriguing (Kornell & Bjork, 2008).

In their study, Kornell and Bjork had participants learn the styles of twelve artists based on a sample of six paintings by each artist. In the first condition, the artists' paintings were interleaved among paintings by other artists, while in the second condition, they presented the artists one after the other, that is, blocked. After learning about the artists and their paintings, the interleaved group was better able to identify the artist responsible for each of the series of new paintings.

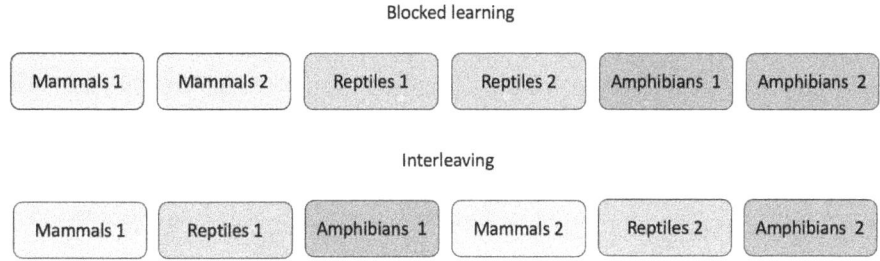

Figure 9.2 Blocked learning versus interleaving.

Interestingly, however, volunteers believed blocking had been more successful, just like the Post Office workers in Baddeley's study. This process, described by Kornell and Bjork, has become known as interleaving and is often used in conjunction with distributed practice.

Spaced learning increases the retention of newly learned information, but by introducing different yet related information into the gap, we can deepen learning further. The benefits of interleaving have been shown in several more recent studies and with different types of information. But why should interleaving produce better learning outcomes than blocking, especially as it appears to run counter to other theories of forgetting?

Initially, it was assumed that the effect seen when examples were interleaved was due to the spacing effect and due to a delay between presenting one set of information and the next. It's certainly the case that interleaving will inevitably lead to spacing, but this doesn't mean it's necessarily due to it. One explanation why interleaving works is that it forces learners to resolve the interference between different study items, therefore encouraging them to notice similarities and differences, which is why Zulkiply and Burt have dubbed interleaving the *compare and contrast effect* (Zulkiply & Burt, 2013). This then leads to the encoding of higher-order representations, which, in turn, fosters both retention and transfer. However, this also means that in some cases, interleaving and spacing are incompatible because of the time delay, making it harder to contrast items.

Interleaving, therefore, encourages learners to compare and contrast different types of related information. For example, on Monday, our teacher introduces the class to mammals (warm-blooded, have hair or fur, give birth to live young), but on Tuesday, students receive an introductory lesson on reptiles (cold-blooded, lay eggs, have scales). This forces them to compare mammals with reptiles – mammals are warm-blooded, reptiles are cold-blooded.

Sometimes, it's good to forget

While distributed practice and interleaving encourage learners to compare and contrast different study items, there's probably an added element to these techniques. Distributed practice inevitably leads to some forgetting between the first and second learning episode. Say, in the first learning session, I give you a list of words to learn. Depending on the ISI (the time between the first and second learning episode) you should have forgotten at least some words from the first study session. Re-studying forces you to recall the words that might have started to decay due to the passing of time. You might even think you've forgotten, but actually haven't. That recalling will take more mental effort, and this increased mental effort is going to result in deeper processing. If I were to ask you to recite the words from the first study session at the beginning of the second, you might recall some or all, but if I gave you a list of words and asked you to identify only those from the first study session, you should recall more. The word itself acts as a cue.

The notion that we need to forget to learn better might seem like an odd suggestion, seeing as I've spent most of the preceding chapters emphasising the need to make sure what we've learned remains in long-term memory. I've also implied that, while not wholly bad, forgetting is something we would rather prevent. Sometimes, however, forgetting can be useful. Even essential. Studies have discovered a curious phenomenon, whereby allowing us to forget what we have learned benefits us in the long term. According to The New Theory of Disuse, this is because the strength of our learning relies on both retrieval strength and storage strength (Bjork & Bjork, 1992). Retrieval strength is the measure of the ease with which we currently recall something and its relevance to the present. Retrieval strength is, therefore, measured by our current performance, such as how well we answer the questions on a test. But we've already seen that short-term retention doesn't necessarily equate to long-term learning. However, retrieval strength fluctuates, so information might have a high or a low strength. We can think of storage strength as learning, a measure of how deeply embedded information is and how easily we can recall it later. Storage strength doesn't decrease (except with brain trauma); it only accumulates. It also cannot be measured directly, only inferred, so if the information learned can be recalled in the future, then we can infer that storage strength is high.

Take, for example, the phone number of your childhood home. This is one of those items of information that often stays with us throughout our lives because of the importance parents place on it – before the days of mobile phones and landlines capable of programming names and numbers into them, people needed to commit their phone numbers to memory (and often the numbers of close friends and family). This number might not come readily to mind, but many people will still be able to recall it; the storage strength of the number is high, yet the retrieval strength may well be low. Your current phone number, on the other hand, may come readily to mind (high retrieval strength), but you might forget it over time (low storage strength). The same can be said for the number of our hotel room while on holiday – we will probably recall it while we are staying in the hotel (high retrieval strength), but the chances are the memory will fade pretty quickly once we return home (low storage strength).

As we have seen, an important goal of learning is the ability to recall what we have learned at some point in the future, that is, to ensure that storage strength is high.

But we also need to be mindful that there is still more to learning than just remembering things; we can teach a non-chess player to memorise board positions but that doesn't mean they can play chess. When we engage in study, both storage strength and retrieval strength increase, but after studying, the higher the storage strength, the slower the loss of retrieval strength – high storage strength leads to a slower rate of forgetting. This does, indeed, make sense. What appears slightly counterintuitive, however, is that when we re-study the material, the lower the retrieval strength, the greater the boost to storage strength. This might require a little unpacking.

Say I presented to you a list of words that I wanted you to learn, and then gave you a recall test a few minutes later. You recall all the words perfectly, but we already know that recall will decline over time, so when I surprise you with a repeat test a week later, you will most likely have forgotten the words. Not that you've forgotten all the words because you may recall some, but storage strength is low because you haven't had to recall or rehearse the list during the intervening period – retrieval strength has declined. However, because recall at this second time point is more difficult, the effort required to recall the list of words may well increase storage strength. If learning seems easy, then chances are retrieval strength is high, meaning that there are few gains to be obtained by revisiting the material. But if retrieval strength is low, there is a greater potential for making learning gains – forgetting is actually increasing our capacity to learn because of the effort required to recall the information – this is why self-testing can be such a powerful learning tool.

I've often witnessed behaviour in my students that runs counter to this. In the run-up to important exams, many students would use revision to increase their confidence and self-esteem by revisiting material they were already very familiar with. Confirming to ourselves that we know the material can make us feel smart, but this is often at the expense of material we don't know too well. Continually testing ourselves on information that we have already learned in a concrete and permanent way does little to increase our ability to recall; it just confirms that we know it. Not that students should never return to material they know very well, just that they shouldn't spend a disproportionate amount of effort and time on it compared to the material they don't really know. Students can, of course, reinforce known information by incorporating it into other, less known material through techniques like elaborative interrogation (for example, asking *why* questions). Perhaps a student is fully conversant with the multi-store model of memory but not so much the working memory model – by testing themselves on the similarities and differences between the two, the student will engage in both models, one that is well known and one that isn't.

Desirable difficulties

Techniques such as distributed practice and interleaving are desirable difficulties, another term coined by psychologists Robert and Elizabeth Bjork (Bjork & Bjork,

2011). One thing we always need to be aware of is that learning shouldn't be a passive process. It's true that memories come to mind with little or no effort. Sometimes they can even be intrusive, but learning is different because learning should be deliberate, effortful, and dynamic. We certainly can learn latently, as I described earlier, but when we have decided to learn something and set our goals, we need to think about how we can go about achieving our aim. Most of all, learning is difficult, and we will often struggle. But difficulty is a very important part of the process, just so long as we pitch the difficulty right.

Difficulties that at first sight appear problematic and detrimental to learning often lead to more flexible and durable learning. Such difficulties are thought to trigger encoding and retrieval processes that support learning, comprehension, and remembering. Or, in other words, deeper learning. You'll recall Craik and Lockhart's theory of depth or levels of processing from previous chapters, the notion that how we process new information in terms of elaboration leads to more durable retention than, say, simple rote rehearsal, and that different types of information are encoded differently. Deeper learning also leads to greater understanding through consolidation processes, where connections are made to other learned information and schemas emerge. However, if the learner doesn't have the background knowledge and skills to respond successfully to these difficulties, they then become undesirable, so our wannabe Hendrix needs to ensure they pitch the difficulty of the guitar lessons just right. When desirable difficulties are optimal, the brain works harder to learn the information and, while learning might appear slow, the information is successfully encoded and consolidated into long-term memory.

Learning is often predictable in terms of both place and style. This might be more pronounced in school settings, but it still applies to many other types of learning. The term for this in the research literature is *contextualised*, and we find that when learning becomes contextualised, material is more easily retrieved in that specific context. This means that performance can become less predictable if it's tested after a delay, in a different context, or both. One example would include so-called context-based retrieval, one explanation of interleaving, where people are much better at recalling information in the same room in which learning originally took place. Varying conditions of practice, as well as the environmental setting, can, however, enhance long-term retention. One study found that learning the same material in two different rooms rather than twice in the same room increased recall (Smith et al., 1978). In another study, children practised throwing beanbags at a target marked out on the floor while their vision was obscured. Half the children practised throwing at a fixed distance while the other half threw to targets that were closer or further away. After the practice session, researchers waited a while before testing the children's performance by having them throw from a fixed distance. It might be assumed that the children who had practised at a fixed distance would perform better, yet it was actually the other group who scored higher. Varying the conditions had made them more accurate with their throwing (Kerr & Booth, 1978).

Spaced, or distributed, learning, therefore, raises storage strength by allowing for a certain degree of forgetting between presentations of the material. We might, for example, learn some facts about a particular subject, put the material to one side for a while and then return to it, reminding ourselves of what we covered during the initial presentation. This reminding and recalling then makes it easier to recall the information when we revisit on the third, fourth, or fifth occasion. One of the reasons distributed practice appears to be so successful is because of these reminding mechanisms, in that each time the information is presented, the effort required to remember what was previously learned enhances retention. This means that the more often we revisit the information, the stronger the learning becomes. As the time between each learning episode increases, so does the difficulty – learning becomes more effortful. However, at some point, the lag increases so much that any benefit from the spacing effect disappears. The lag also allows for other biological factors to help with memory consolidation. Consolidation, including the formation of schemas, often takes place while we sleep; however, psychological scientists at the University of Lyon have also found that wakeful rest can be just as effective, helping people to learn faster and retain information for longer (Mazza et al., 2016).

Retrieval practice

We tend to think of testing as a means of checking our knowledge. Rarely do we consider it as part of learning. Much of the research we've already explored is based on the premise that periodically returning to learned material leads to better retention over time, but how we return to the material can make a big difference to our learning. Self-testing is also more effortful compared to alternative methods such as restudy, and this might be why students avoid it. But while restudying material provides us with the feeling of accomplishment, its passive nature is simply luring us into a false sense of progress. When we self-test, we open ourselves up to the fact that we might not know the material as much as we think we do. This, in turn, lowers our self-esteem and can negatively impact motivation. It's no wonder we avoid it. Not only that, but students tend to believe that restudy is more beneficial than self-testing (Carpenter et al., 2020). Just like in the Post Office study (described previously) and with studies into interleaving, learners tend to have a faulty appreciation of how to learn and strategies that work, what learning science calls metacognition.

As you've probably realised by now, our beliefs about learning don't always match the evidence. Several studies (discussed in Chapter 13) have found that most learners employ suboptimal strategies. Furthermore, many educators don't always know what works best for their students. Educators, as well as learners, often view testing as a result of learning, a way of assessing what has been learned. Often, they fail to consider testing (or retrieval practice) a learning strategy in its own right.

The testing effect (or test-enhanced learning) is the phenomenon whereby actively recalling or recognising information from memory leads to better retention of that information compared to other study methods like rereading or restudying (Hui et al., 2021). One common misunderstanding is that the testing effect is the result of repeated exposure to the material, but, as we've seen in previous chapters, learning and retention have much more to do with depth of processing brought about by cognitive effort. This view broadly falls into a category of explanations known as retrieval effort theories. The magnitude of the testing effect is therefore related to the increase in difficulty, depth, and effort.

One explanation why retrieval is so effective argues that engaging in retrieval leads to elaboration of the memory trace by activating semantic associations related to the to-be-learned information. Say, for example, we are given a word pair to memorise, such as Mammal – Cat. During the recall test, we are given only the first half of the pair (Mammal) and are expected to recall the second half of the pair (Cat). As part of our thought processes, we are likely to sift through possible answers, perhaps dog, lion, kitten, etc. These other animals may serve as cues, helping us remember Cat on a later test.

Similarly, the mediator effectiveness hypothesis suggests that testing might improve memory, at least in part, by promoting the effective utilisation of mediators. By mediator, we're referring to any piece of information linking a cue to a target. We tend to generate semantic associations spontaneously when attempting to retrieve a specific item. If, for example, you are trying to recall the name of the actor who played Pepper Potts in the Marvel films, other items related to the actor might help you recall the name. She was married to Robert Downey Jr's character (Iron Man) in the films but was also married to Chris Martin from the band Coldplay in real life. She also has a rather unusual line of scented candles. Using these cues will hopefully be enough for us to retrieve the name Gwyneth Paltrow. These initial spontaneously generated associations can then be employed later as cues to help us recall the name.

What this essentially means is that, rather than being an assessment of knowledge, testing forces our brains to work harder, strengthening and reinforcing neural connections. As we mentally search for the target item, we spontaneously recall similar yet erroneous items. If our answers are wrong, feedback corrects the errors, but the incorrect responses may still act as cues: *Oh, I said dog last time, but that was wrong. The answer was cat.*

Like many of the studies we've encountered, the ones looking into retrieval practice aren't without their weaknesses. Again, we find that much of the research takes place in highly artificial and controlled environments and uses university students as participants. The key to successful retrieval practice lies partly with elaboration of the memory trace through the activation of semantic associations (with obvious links to schemas). A more difficult test, therefore, might generate more possible answers before reaching the target, leading to greater elaboration.

But it's difficult to know how this would apply to non-text material, such as maps, pictures, and diagrams. So far, the research doesn't have an answer.

The notion of testing can be divisive, with many pointing to the impact it can have on young people's well-being. It's worth emphasising, however, that this refers to high-stakes testing, the tests that shape future outcomes and trajectories. Retrieval practice is a form of low-stakes testing – its purpose is to enhance learning, not to assess it. In this respect, there is no reason retrieval practice should take the form of formal tests. In fact, I'd argue that it shouldn't. We can test using questioning and quizzes and many other ways that can help us activate what we have learned. There is, of course, always an emotional component to learning, one we can't (but often do) ignore. The emotional side of learning is where we turn in the next chapter.

Deliberate practice

One aspect of our thinking that often prevents us from taking on new learning tasks is the belief that we are incapable of certain types of learning. At school, you might have assumed that your brain just couldn't get to grips with the complexities of mathematics or that your artistic ability was limited. Perhaps you fell for the hype surrounding left- and right-brain differences and decided that, because you were left-brain dominant, you would never perfect right-brain tasks. This idea of innate ability has some grounding in science – certain aspects of our abilities are, indeed, highly heritable (such as intelligence and personality), but often the environment can play an important role in circumventing these limitations.

Often, as children, we are pushed to believe that if we work hard, then we'll succeed. This isn't always the case, yet effort is a major factor in how well we do in the tasks we choose or are given. We can't all be Mozart or Da Vinci, even though we know Mozart dedicated his life from a very young age to perfecting his craft. In other words, he may have had some biological advantage, but it was the hard graft that really produced the results in the end. Psychologist Anders Ericsson spent a lifetime studying expert performance and investigating ways that we can push learning to the limits. Ericsson places greater emphasis on practice, or more specifically, deliberate practice. His most famous study involved violinists and the techniques they used to reach high standards of expertise. One finding that arose from the study was that the most accomplished students put in an average of ten thousand hours of practice by the time they were twenty. This led writer Malcolm Gladwell to propose that this was the minimum amount of time required to master any skill – the so-called 10,000-hour rule (Gladwell, 2008).

But before you calculate when you'll become a skilled guitarist, bear in mind that Gladwell's rule fails to reflect Ericsson's actual findings. Indeed, Ericsson has been critical of Gladwell's misinterpretation. The contention is that there isn't anything special about 10,000 hours. The best students in the study had put in 7,400 hours by the time they were 18, but the *7,400-hour rule* didn't really have the same marketing appeal. In addition, 10,000 hours was the average, and half the violinists hadn't even accumulated that amount of hours by the time they reached the age of 20 (Ericsson, 2008). What Gladwell perhaps failed to recognise was that Ericsson was investigating a specific type of practice (deliberate practice) and people who had become highly skilled, not just good enough or pretty competent. Gladwell viewed all practice as the same and that learning something new required us to become experts in it.

The 10,000-hour rule has also taken a bit of bashing from researchers other than Ericsson. In a 2014 review, academics found that, on average, the amount of deliberate practice accounted for just 34 percent of the variance in chess ability (Hambrick et al., 2014). Deliberate practice, therefore, did make a difference, but nowhere near enough to explain why some players became highly skilled while others didn't. Furthermore, there was a huge variation in the number of hours of deliberate practice exhibited by different standards of player. For example, grandmasters practised for between 832 and more than 24,000 hours; intermediate players actually completed 13 percent more practice than the grandmasters. A similar pattern was found with musicians, where deliberate practice only accounted for 30 percent of the variance in performance. Again, there were wide variations with some musicians failing to achieve the highest level even when practice time far exceeded 10,000 hours. Others achieved the highest level with only modest practice. A more recent study has reached similar conclusions (Macnamara et al., 2016). In their review of 34 studies investigating the practice habits and performance levels of 2,765 athletes, the review found that, at the elite level, the amount of practice was not related to performance.

The problems that surround the 10,000-hour rule don't undermine the effectiveness of deliberate practice, but do indicate that there is no magical number of hours that will transform anyone into a chess grandmaster or a concert pianist. Teasing out the nuances of these types of study does, however, tell us a little about what makes an impact. The age at which we begin to learn a new skill is an important, overriding factor and is correlated with expertise. Starting early seems to make a huge impact on how accomplished people become, and we can't totally rule out the possibility of a critical or sensitive period. We can see this in children raised in bilingual households or in countries with first and second languages.

Intelligence also makes a difference, as does working memory capacity and personality.

The crucial factor in the development of expertise (and the one overlooked by Gladwell) is that deliberate practice is not simply practice. Deliberate practice achieves a certain goal and comprises individualised training activities usually carried out alone. These activities are designed to improve aspects of performance and include individually tailored and structured feedback. In this respect, advocates aren't simply saying *work hard and practice lots and eventually you'll be an expert*; they say that with effort, hard work, structure, determination, and help, you can do pretty well at whatever you put your mind to. Nevertheless, it's still perhaps better to play to your strengths, so if you have a particular proclivity towards music, languages or playing chess, it might be perhaps better to hone your expertise here rather than attempt something in which you have little experience.

The takeaway from this is pretty simple – if you want to learn something new and become good at it, you need to put in the hours and the effort. But there is more to learning than this. Planning your route through your learning, responding appropriately when things don't go the way you planned, sticking with it, and using effective learning techniques are all part and parcel of getting to where you want to be.

Chapter summary

- Distributed practice (the spacing effect) is a more effective learning strategy than blocked learning.

- Interleaving, which involves mixing different yet related information during study, enhances learning.

- Some degree of forgetting between learning episodes can be beneficial for long-term learning. The effort required to retrieve information that has started to decay strengthens its storage strength. When retrieval strength is low, restudying the material leads to greater learning gains.

- Retrieval practice, or the act of actively recalling information from memory (also known as the testing effect or test-enhanced learning), is a highly effective learning strategy. Regularly testing oneself on learned material leads to better retention compared to passive restudying.

- Deliberate practice, characterised by focused, goal-oriented training activities with specific feedback, is crucial for developing expertise.

Further reading

Jones, K. (2019). *Retrieval practice: Research & resources for every classroom*. John Catt.
Smith, M., & Firth, J. (2018). *Psychology in the classroom: A teacher's guide to what works*. Routledge.

References

Baddeley, A. D., & Longman, D. J. A. (1978). The influence of length and frequency of training session on the rate of learning to type. *Ergonomics, 21*(8), 627–635. https://doi.org/10.1080/00140137808931764

Bjork, E. L., & Bjork, R. A. (2011). Making things hard on yourself, but in a good way: Creating desirable difficulties to enhance learning. In M. A. Gernsbacher, R. W. Pew, L. M. Hough, & J. R. Pomerantz (Eds.), *Psychology and the real world: Essays illustrating fundamental contributions to society* (pp. 56–64). Worth Publishers.

Bjork, R. A., & Bjork, E. L. (1992). A new theory of disuse and an old theory of stimulus fluctuation. In Healy, A. F., Kosslyn, K. M., & Shiffrin, R. M. (eds.) *From learning processes to cognitive processes: Essays in honor of William K. Estes* (Vol. 2, pp. 35–67). Psychology Press.

Carpenter, S. K., Endres, T., & Hui, L. (2020). Students' use of retrieval in self-regulated learning: implications for monitoring and regulating effortful learning experiences. *Educational Psychology Review, 32*(4), 1029–1054. https://doi.org/10.1007/s10648-020-09562-w

Cepeda, N. J., Vul, E., Rohrer, D., Wixted, J. T., & Pashler, H. (2008). Spacing effects in learning: A temporal ridgeline of optimal retention: Research article. *Psychological Science, 19*(11), 1095–1102. https://doi.org/10.1111/j.1467-9280.2008.02209.x

Ericsson, K. A. (2008). Deliberate practice and acquisition of expert performance: A general overview. *Academic Emergency Medicine, 15*(11), 988–994. https://doi.org/10.1111/j.1553-2712.2008.00227.x

Gladwell, M. (2008). *Outliers: The story of success*. Back Bay Books.

Hambrick, D. Z., Oswald, F. L., Altmann, E. M., Meinz, E. J., Gobet, F., & Campitelli, G. (2014). Deliberate practice: Is that all it takes to become an expert? *Intelligence, 45*, 34–45. https://doi.org/10.1016/j.intell.2013.04.001

Horvath, J. C., Horton, A. J., Lodge, J. M., & Hattie, J. (2017). The impact of binge watching on memory and perceived comprehension. *First Monday: A Peer-Reviewed Journal of the Internet, 22*(9), 1–12. https://doi.org/10.5210/fm.v22i9.7729

Hui, L., de Bruin, A. B. H., Donkers, J., & van Merriënboer, J. J. G. (2021). Does individual performance feedback increase the use of retrieval practice? *Educational Psychology Review, 33*(4), 1835–1857. https://doi.org/10.1007/s10648-021-09604-x

Kerr, R., & Booth, B. (1978). Specific and varied practice of motor skill. *Perceptual and Motor Skills, 46*(2), 395–401. https://doi.org/10.1177/003151257804600201

Kornell, N., & Bjork, R. A. (2008). Learning concepts and categories: Is spacing the "enemy of induction"? *Psychological Science, 19*(6), 585–592. https://doi.org/10.1111/j.1467-9280.2008.02127.x

Küpper-Tetzel, C. E., Kapler, I. V., & Wiseheart, M. (2014). Contracting, equal, and expanding learning schedules: The optimal distribution of learning sessions depends on retention interval. *Memory and Cognition, 42*(5), 729–741. https://doi.org/10.3758/s13421-014-0394-1

Macnamara, B. N., Moreau, D., & Hambrick, D. Z. (2016). The relationship between deliberate practice and performance in sports. *Perspectives on Psychological Science, 11*(3), 333–350. https://doi.org/10.1177/1745691616635591

Mazza, S., Gerbier, E., Gustin, M.-P., Kasikci, Z., Koenig, O., Toppino, T. C., & Magnin, M. (2016). Relearn faster and retain longer. *Psychological Science, 27*(10), 1321–1330. https://doi.org/10.1177/0956797616659930

Rohrer, D., & Pashler, H. (2007). Increasing retention without increasing study time. *Current Directions in Psychological Science, 16*(4), 183–186. https://doi.org/10.1111/j.1467-8721.2007.00500.x

Smith, M., & Firth, J. (2018) *Psychology in the classroom: A teacher's guide to what works.* Routledge.

Smith, S. M., Glenberg, A., & Bjork, R. A. (1978). Environmental context and human memory. *Memory & Cognition, 6*(4), 342–353. https://doi.org/10.3758/BF03197465

Zulkiply, N., & Burt, J. S. (2013). The exemplar interleaving effect in inductive learning: Moderation by the difficulty of category discriminations. *Memory & Cognition, 41*(1), 16–27. https://doi.org/10.3758/s13421-012-0238-9

10 Routes to remembering

How the cognitive system allocates resources is important when looking at the efficiency of human learning, so we must consider how best to work within these limitations. Deeper learning requires increased mental effort, but too much mental effort can not only overload our limited cognitive resources, but it can also negatively impact motivation and engagement. There's a lot going on here, and juggling types of learning to get the most out of learners can feel overwhelming. But learning isn't only concerned with storing information; it's also about being able to use what we have learned when we need to. We know the act of recalling strengthens this memory further. In Chapter 7, I discussed the memory cycle and how the brain may, sometimes, infinitely recall and re-consolidate learned information. In this chapter, I want to expand on some areas I discussed in Chapters 7 and 10 and offer some practical strategies to help all learners.

Build a city, not a village

Baddeley and Hitch propose a system comprising components representing phonological, or sound-based, inputs, and visual and spatial information. These components are thought to operate independently, which is why we can look at a diagram and listen to an explanation of it while keeping cognitive load to within acceptable limits (there is less competition for resources). If, however, we attempt to read the words on a screen while someone talks over them, it becomes increasingly difficult to both comprehend words and understand what is being said because competition for resources is higher. The brain processes and encodes visual information differently from auditory inputs, and by understanding this, we can exploit this knowledge for our own advantage.

I once lived in a small North Yorkshire village with a peculiar name. There was essentially one road in and one road out. This was fine because there was never much traffic (unless you got stuck behind a tractor). One day, there was an accident on the main road, and all the cars, lorries, and buses were diverted through my sleepy village. It wasn't long before traffic on the narrow country lane ground to a halt, slowing to barely a crawl. Having only one road in and out wasn't the most efficient situation in this case. Similarly, if we learn in only one way (or in one modality), we create a single route to the information we've learned, making recall less efficient and often slower. This is one reason learning styles theory is such a ridiculous idea – visual learners only recall visually, auditory ones only by sound, and kinaesthetic learners by getting up and moving about. This is a simplification, obviously, but hopefully you get the gist. Now, say I'm travelling to a large city. I look at the map and consider all the routes I could take. Some are faster, some slower, some routes use mainly motorways, others minor roads, while some routes use a combination. If there are roadworks on the motorway, I can adjust my journey to avoid them. As learners and educators, we should build cities, not villages. The more routes we create, the more likely we are to reach our destination efficiently and use what we have learned.

Picture this

During the 1960s, Canadian psychologist Allan Paivio came to an interesting yet seemingly simple conclusion: people find it easier to remember concrete nouns they can imagine compared to abstract nouns they can't. If I were to ask you to imagine a tree, you might instantly see the image of a tree in your mind. Now, try to conjure an image of the word truth. Chances are the first task will be much easier than the second because truth is a much tougher word to visualise than tree.

If I presented you with two lists of words, for example:

List 1	List 2
Tree	Truth
Car	Justice
River	Liberty
House	Ambiguity

If I then test you on your ability to recall them, you'll probably remember more from list 1 than list 2. This is because you've encoded the word *and* the image, creating two routes to the information. Now, you might have managed to represent some words in list 2 as images (such as scales for the word justice). This phenomenon is referred to as dual coding because you have encoded the words twice – once as an image, and once as a word.

Mental imagery, therefore, can enhance our ability to recall information and solve problems. Studies using mental chronometry (the measure of the time it takes to carry out various cognitive tasks) find that the ability to mentally rotate objects in the mind leads to an enhanced ability to compare objects for similarity. For example, if I were to show you a set of three-dimensional shapes, two of which were the same but viewed from a different angle, your success on the task would correlate with your ability to hold the representation of the shape in your mind (or in working memory) and rotate it until it matched one of the other shapes. Studies using brain scanning technology have found that when people engage in such tasks, the occipital cortex (the area of the brain associated with sight) is more active, implying that the brain doesn't distinguish between what we are seeing in the real world and imagining in our mind.

Paivio proposes that the human cognitive system codes information in two ways – as words and as images, reflecting our ability to deal with both language and non-verbal objects and events (Paivio & Csapo, 1971). Dual coding theory is, therefore, consistent with the multi-component working memory model devised by Baddeley and Hitch. Because we can use these two different encoding systems simultaneously, we can combine a word with its related image and create multiple pathways to the same memory. This dual coding not only results in easier access, but it also leads to deeper learning, a notion consistent with levels of processing theory. In addition, it may also help us better utilise cognitive load because it lessens the stress on a single modality. The advantages don't stop here, and there is ample evidence suggesting that learning to use both images and auditory materials externalises information for use in problem solving (Zhang & Norman, 1994), once again, optimising load (see figure 10.1).

But it's not just about combining images with text. We can also enhance learning by creating drawings that depict the content of a lesson, translating written notes into pictorial representations, or adding visual images when taking notes in lessons. In a study from 2018, researchers at the University of Waterloo in Canada discovered that drawing simple pictures might be more effective than taking notes or copying information from the board – the so-called drawing effect (Fernandes et al., 2018). Myra Fernandes found that participants asked to produce a quick (four-second) drawing of items in a list of words had significantly better recall of the words than those who wrote them down multiple times. Initially, volunteers were given lists of simple words, such as truck or shoe, but later trials included more complex concepts, such as isotope and spore, where participants were expected to recall the definition. Even with the increased complexity of the words, recall

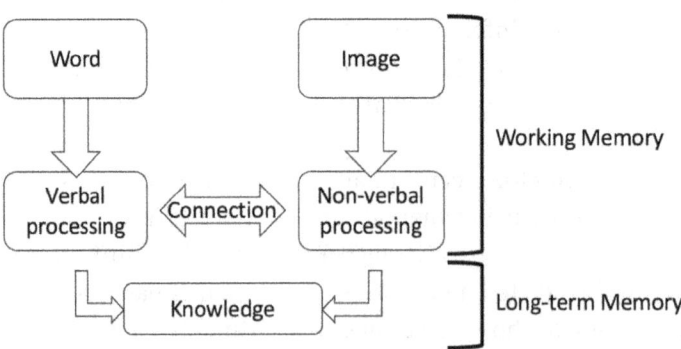

Figure 10.1 Creating more than one route to remembering using dual coding.

remained higher in the drawing condition than in the condition where participants copied out the definitions.

Another study (again from 2018) concluded that older adults who take up drawing could also see significant improvements in their memory (Meade et al., 2018). Retention of new information typically declines as people age due to the deterioration of critical brain structures involved in memory, particularly the hippocampus and frontal lobes. However, visuospatial processing regions of the brain, involved in representing images and pictures, are mostly intact in normal ageing and in dementia.

Why should drawing a concept make it easier to recall later? There are several explanations. First, as explained above, we've created more pathways to the memory, so if one pathway temporarily fails, there are others we can use as a backup. Second, drawing is a generative activity, requiring learners to elaborate on the meaning of what they have learned by translating it into a new concept. This elaboration results in deeper processing (Craik and Lockhart's framework) in that generative activities result in deeper processing. Finally, when learners use drawings to retrieve learned material, any new learning may be enhanced by connecting it with what they already know. Drawing can, therefore, be effective at activating prior knowledge, thus optimising the load placed on memory, supporting perceptual processing, and making connections more explicit (Wetzels et al., 2011).

It's good to talk

The Working Memory Model proposes a model whereby components deal separately with spatial and visual information (visuo-spatial sketchpad), and sound-based information (the phonological loop). The phonological loop processes both internal and external dialogue, so we can enhance learning by repeatedly rehearsing information. But is it better to rehearse mentally (speak the words in our head) or out loud?

Research seems to favour the latter; a phenomenon dubbed *the production effect*. Studies investigating the production effect often assess the ability of volunteers to recall word lists under different conditions. For example, participants learn words by reading them aloud, writing them down, typing them, or spelling them and, while many of these methods produce better recall than rehearsing the words silently, reading them aloud produces consistently higher results (Ozubko & MacLeod, 2010). One study also found that singing may enhance memory more than speaking (Quinlan & Taylor, 2013). A 2012 study discovered that volunteers asked to learn textbook passages by reading them aloud performed better on a fill in the blanks task a day later compared to passages read silently (Ozubko et al., 2012), while Knutson and Le Bigot found people are more likely to re-use a reference that they had spoken earlier compared to a reference spoken by someone else (Knutsen & Le Bigot, 2014).

Reading aloud creates more routes to the learned information. Not only are we generating the sound externally, but we are also hearing it.

Cognition as embodied

So far, we've looked at cognition as being wholly concerned with the brain. But is this really the case? A more recent development in cognitive science posits that cognitive processing is closely related to bodily activity and the surrounding environment. This embodied cognition may have far-reaching consequences, as it implies that we can enhance learning when the brain, body, and environment interact. For example, how do body movements, postures, and the environment interact to impact cognition? And what implications might the answer to this question have on learning and instruction?

This view isn't new. Teachers have used drama as a learning tool for a long time, yet such methods tend to be labelled progressive and often rejected by traditionalists or recent adopters of cognitive science. Certain skills learning does, of course, require physical practice – everything from learning a sport to brain surgery, but can we also adapt these methods to, for example, teach a lesson on the French Revolution? Instead of just reading about the Estates-General, students could physically stand in different areas of the room to represent the three estates. The First Estate (clergy) might stand on a raised platform. The Second Estate (nobility) could be located in a designated area with chairs. The Third Estate (commoners) might stand crowded together.

As the lesson progresses, the teacher introduces historical events. When the Third Estate declares itself the National Assembly, students physically move to the centre of the room, symbolising their assertion of power. When the king locks them out, they could be forced to move into the *Tennis Court* (another part of the room) to take the oath. The activity requires learners to physically act out power dynamics and shifting alliances, forcing them to engage multiple cognitive pathways. Bodily movement, spatial awareness, and social interaction make the lesson more memorable and, therefore, increase the likelihood of memory consolidation.

In a 2020 study, Bethan Stagg used process drama to examine its impact on primary school children's knowledge of biological classification and attitudes towards plants. Process drama can place learners in the position of an authentic scientific scenario, using instructional activities that resemble those of professional scientists. Stagg discovered that not only did the children find the experience enjoyable and engaging, but the session also led to substantial knowledge retention (Stagg, 2020).

The learning gains seen in such activities are thought to arise through several means. Physical activity encodes specific movements and gestures into long-term memory, which can then be used as triggers. Embodied cognition is also consistent with theories of generative learning, discussed in Chapter 13, and cognitive offloading (see below), which may benefit working memory (Castro-Alonso et al., 2024). Instructional frameworks that utilise physical activity, such as *Mantle of the Expert* (see further reading), aren't only about making lessons fun, but also about using multiple modalities to generate knowledge pathways.

If learning encompasses bodily movements and gestures, might this mean that handwriting (as opposed to typing on a laptop or tablet) will lead to better retention? The answer, unfortunately, isn't a simple yes or no. In studies comparing the effectiveness of handwritten note-taking and electronic methods, researchers sometimes find benefits to the former. In other studies, they find no difference between methods, while at other times they discover that any positive effect disappears when students review their notes before taking a test. But what are the overall findings?

In a meta-analysis from 2020, Mike Allen and colleagues examined 14 studies into the phenomenon, with a total of just over 3,000 participants. They discovered that using an electronic device to take notes led to a decrease in outcome measures (such as scores on a test). Indeed, 25 percent of students who used them scored below the mean. There's a potential caveat, however. Larger advantages were seen in specific subjects, including natural science and statistics, while the impact was less in subjects like psychology and education (Allen et al., 2020).

Why might writing notes by hand be better than typing them on a laptop or tablet? Maybe using an electronic device engages differently with our cognitive and psychomotor responses. Handwriting involves muscle memory – writing is automatic. We don't have to think too much about it. This, in turn, is going to place less pressure on cognitive resources. So, handwriting might reduce cognitive load. Handwritten notes also take less time, and as we've seen, time is a factor in memory selection and consolidation. If handwriting takes less time than typing, we pay more attention to what is being taught, leading to increased learning. From a more practical perspective, electronic devices with WiFi connectivity provide more opportunities for distraction (such as checking emails or social media).

But there could also be an embodied component. The act of writing might store information differently because of the bodily movements required. Many students might also include images in their notes (dual coding), as well as summarise and paraphrase elements of the lecture (generative learning). Handwriting creates a city, while using an electronic device may not. From a levels of processing perspective, handwriting forces elaboration (through summarising and paraphrasing, for example). Elaboration results in deeper processing.

There's a rather nuanced takeaway here. Handwritten notes seem to work better in most cases; we just don't know why. This is one of those many areas where researchers add that *more research is needed* to the conclusions section of their academic papers. It could be that some electronic devices are better than others, and some might be superior to handwritten notes.

Learning through imagination

Without the ability to imagine, humans wouldn't have evolved to be the species they are today. Learning and innovation require us to imagine things that don't yet exist but might one day. Similarly, planning involves holding possibilities in mind.

Imagination is key to knowledge, understanding, and learning. Research into the role of the *imagination effect*, the notion that people perform better on a test when they can imagine a procedure or concept (Leahy & Sweller, 2008), takes one of two branches: learning factual information or learning procedures and concepts.

In the first branch, researchers have observed that when they ask learners to imagine pictures while engaging with narrative facts, they recall the facts more accurately than those who are not instructed to imagine them. In one study, for example, schoolchildren read a story while actively creating pictures in their mind, while a control group used other mnemonic strategies. The researchers found that the imagination group recalled more factual details of the story than the control (Pressley, 1976). Replications using learners of similar ages have confirmed these findings. However, studies with older learners, including high school and post-secondary school students, found no significant difference (for example, Woloshyn et al., 1990). While the imagination effect may not help older learners, deploying imagination techniques appears to assist poor readers' comprehension skills (De Koning & van der Schoot, 2013).

The second branch concerns imagination's role in learning procedures and concepts. For example, students who are asked to imagine a procedure or concept perform better on tests compared to learners asked to only study the same material. Through imagination, learners construct mental representations as images to depict the content of a lesson. This might include imagining the content of a scientific text detailing the working of the human respiratory system, imagining the application of geometry rules, or imagining the utilisation of a bus schedule (Fiorella & Mayer, 2015). A 2009 study with high school students found that those who engaged in imagining each paragraph of scientific text about water molecules exhibited a better understanding compared to peers who only studied the text content (Leutner et al., 2009). It's not all positive. A 2017 study using college students found no significant difference between those participants instructed to create a mental image after reading a lesson on the human cardiovascular system and those asked to only read the material (Lin et al., 2017).

There's also a caveat here. The human ability to recreate images in the mind's eye exists on a continuum. If I were to ask you to imagine an orange, for example, you might picture it clearly in your mind, including the colour and the small indents on the skin. On the other hand, you might not create any image at all, and simply rely on the idea of an orange. Most people fall somewhere in between these two extremes; people with aphantasia cannot see anything in their mind's eye, while those with hyperphantasia can picture every detail (Zeman et al., 2015).

Elaborative interrogation: the power of why

What many of the previous techniques have in common is that they allow space for elaboration, the key ingredient of understanding. Learning should be effortful and (to some extent at least) it should make our brains hurt. How we make it effortful depends on what we are learning and our wider goals and intentions. Spaced learning, interleaving, and retrieval practice (discussed in the previous chapter) create those all-important desirable difficulties. Similarly, creating multiple pathways to learned information aids retrieval. Questions – how they are posed and what responses are expected – are an ideal way to assess knowledge, but questioning can also make us think hard about how we are going to respond, resulting in greater elaboration. Used strategically, questions can guide learners towards the most relevant information and help them remain focused on a task.

When children reach a certain age, they discover a word that drives their curiosity and pushes their learning forward. The question is *why?* As a parent or carer, this seemingly constant insistence on answers to everything can drive us to distraction, yet this behaviour is vital for healthy cognitive development. Teaching is more than the passing on of information and, as we've seen, part of the role of educators is to encourage learners to generate their own knowledge through a variety of means. This certainly includes direct instruction, but this is only part of a much wider picture.

Elaborate interrogation is a technique utilising higher-order questioning strategies that encourage learners to connect new information to existing knowledge. As we have seen, for learning to be successful, we must be able to integrate this new information into what we already know, stored as schemas. What we already know provides context for what we are learning now, but also makes this new information more readily available when we require it.

In their 1994 study, Teena Willoughby and Eileen Wood also found that elaborative interrogation encourages students to organise material to a greater extent than those who used rote repetition (Willoughby & Wood, 1994). You'll recall from Chapter 6 that the ability to categorise information increases our ability to recall it later. But it also appears that this organising and categorising increases our understanding of the material. It may well also increase the rate of transfer.

Take, for example, a lesson about the walrus. We could simply provide relevant information: *the walrus has a thick layer of blubber.* Students will then recall the statement, but in a shallow way. However, we could ask: *Why does the walrus have a thick layer of blubber?* The question requires more mental effort because learners are being asked to connect an implicit statement (that a walrus has a thick layer of blubber) with what they might already know. They may, for example, know that the walrus will have had to adapt to its cold environment. Students might also know about insulation and how this will help the walrus retain body heat. Alternatively, we could present a set of facts and ask students how they relate to the walrus.

José Moreno suggests that embedding *why* questions into texts leads to more strategic reading and, therefore, better comprehension. This ultimately results in the better recall of question-relevant information (Moreno et al., 2021). For example, rather than a text stating *chlorophyll absorbs sunlight*, we can include the question: *why is chlorophyll essential for photosynthesis?* This then prompts deeper thinking. Moreno also suggests combining embedded questions with specific instructions to answer them. Rather than the instruction *Read the text carefully*, we could write *Read the text carefully and focus on answering the why questions embedded in each paragraph*. This creates a clear goal and encourages an active search for the information relevant to the question.

Elaborative interrogation is more effective when learners have strong prior knowledge, yet less effective when prior knowledge is poor. This seems obvious. After all, if I know little about a walrus's habitat, how will I be able to answer questions about why it's covered in thick layers of blubber? To answer the question, *why is chlorophyll essential for photosynthesis?* I first need to know what chlorophyll is and what it does. The pre-teaching of key concepts is, therefore, essential. And for this, direct instruction is perhaps the most straightforward and effective route. But we can also draw on learners' prior knowledge of topics that might not be directly related to activated associated schemas. In our walrus example, we could use examples about insulation more generally, such as in our homes. Or we can draw attention to other Arctic animals.

Offloading to reduce load

So far in this chapter, I've looked at how we can make learning more effective by creating multiple routes to memory and encouraging elaboration to boost cognitive effort. But sometimes we don't have to ensure all that information stays put. We don't even have to mind all that much if some information doesn't take up relatively permanent residence in long-term memory. Forgetting can be good for learning, but so can strategically deciding what we need to remember and what we can access in other ways.

When discussing the limits of the human cognitive architecture, specifically the role of working memory, I often use as an example trying to remember a telephone number, highlighting the difficulty of attempting to hold that number in our heads until we can write it down. Telephone numbers exceed working memory capacity, although we naturally group the digits so that we can extend this. While we can often circumvent capacity limits (at least temporarily), time is never on our side. You'll hopefully recall that Pierre Barrouillet's Time-based Resource Sharing model posits we cannot process and store information simultaneously, so the chances are we'll either forget the number or recall it incorrectly.

But rarely do we need to keep a telephone number in our minds for long. Often, we'll grab a pen and write on a scrap of paper or an exposed body part. We might enter it into our phones, where it will remain until we no longer need it. Chances are, once we've offloaded the number, it will have vanished from our minds. Writing a telephone number on a scrap of paper, jotting down things we need to buy at the supermarket, or using our fingers to add up are examples of cognitive offloading. Shopping lists are perhaps the most common form of this, and many of us would be lost if we turned up at the supermarket without one. These days we might jot things down on a notes app on our phones or even leave voice reminders, but people have been cognitive offloading in some way pretty much since the dawn of our species.

There are many things we don't need to commit to memory, even though we might want to. Learning, however, requires us to remember things from facts and figures to skills. The practical implications of having to remember everything are limited – the human brain isn't just pre-wired to remember, it's also designed to forget (as we saw in the previous chapter). Everything we can hold in working memory can be offloaded, and sometimes this is the best option.

The question we need to ask is, when is the best time to offload? If I'm trying to hold that phone number in my mind, is there a point at which I have to write it down, or I'll forget it? Knowing what we do about working memory, it seems logical that people with lower working memory capacity are going to have to offload the digits before someone with a higher capacity. Or is time the crucial factor here? And yes, it all has to do with cognitive load. In studies, working memory capacity is often measured subjectively, so researchers rely on participants deciding when they reach their higher capacity. This is likely why some learners are quicker to jot information down than others. As we might assume, studies find a relationship between lower subjective working memory capacity and an increased likelihood of offloading. For example, in one study, researchers found that when participants were told not to offload in one condition but given the choice to offload in the second condition, those participants who displayed higher subjective working memory capacity offloaded less when given the option (Risko & Dunn, 2015). The ability to decide when to offload is, therefore, an important learning strategy.

What about time? Chances are, you won't offload at the start of the task, but as the task increases the load on working memory, you might decide to. But people also offload as attentional resources deplete. If you're trying to memorise a telephone number and someone starts a conversation with you, your attention is split between the two, and the load increases. As we saw in Chapter 5, splitting our attention will reduce the effectiveness of all tasks – we can either keep rehearsing the telephone number or engage in a conversation, but we can't do both. The best thing to do in this situation would be to write the telephone number down and then have the conversation. However, people may also offload when they don't need to, and this might impact learning negatively.

The problem with offloading

Do people who think they will have access to learned information later display poorer memory for them? Our memory of test items is better if we are told beforehand that we're going to be tested on the items (Middlebrooks et al., 2017), suggesting a tendency to offload if we either think we won't be tested on the information or that it will be provided for us later. The pedagogical implications of this require consideration. If, for example, students know lecture notes will be made available after the lecture, does this mean they offload most of what takes place during the lecture? Similarly, do learners pay more attention to information presented during learning if they know they'll be tested on it in the future (that *will this be on the exam?* moment)?

In one particularly interesting study, Linda Henkel identified the photo-taking impairment effect. Henkel discovered that people who took photographs of an item displayed poorer memory for those items later compared to people asked only to observe the items (Henkel, 2014). Were participants in the study offloading their memories of the items because they believed they wouldn't need to recall them later? It appears people are more likely to offload memories of items when they believe they'll have external access to them later.

The Google effect, a term coined by Betsy Sparrow and colleagues in the United States (Sparrow et al., 2011), is similar to the photo-taking impairment effect. It suggests that the internet has become a primary form of external or transactive memory where groups share knowledge and work together to complete goals. Like taking photographs on our smartphones, information that we might have once committed to memory, we now store externally. When people expect to have access to information, they have lower rates of recall of that specific information. However, they have enhanced recall of how and from where they can access the information. This might also impact the way the brain encodes and retains information. For example, there appears to be a relationship between the frequency of internet use and episodic memory. In one study, everyday internet users were found to have better immediate and delayed word recall than infrequent users, suggesting that regular internet use might enhance our ability to remember where we can find things out (Kang & Malvaso, 2024).

So, is the Google effect a good thing or a bad thing? Like most research, there's no simple answer. A 2024 meta-analysis confirmed the general principle that internet use can lead to poorer memory retention (Gong & Yang, 2024). But there's more to it than that. The effect is more pronounced when people use their phones to access information and less when using a computer. Also, people with more prior knowledge and a larger general knowledge base appear less susceptible than those with a smaller knowledge base. In this respect, we could argue in favour of the importance of prior knowledge to guide our journey through the often precarious terrain of online information.

How, then, does this impact learning? Like other forms of cognitive offloading, the Google effect might help reduce intrinsic cognitive load because we don't need to recall a fact; we just need to know where to find it. Searching for the answer on Google is less mentally effortful than trying to recall it. That said, if people become overly reliant on external storage, they may struggle to integrate knowledge into long-term memory. Having to switch constantly between retrieving and searching could lead to increased extraneous load because it creates unnecessary mental effort. Over-reliance on the internet also discourages effortful retrieval and elaboration, and, as we've seen, these are vital for deep learning to happen. It becomes less likely that information is going to take up residence in long-term memory, depriving the learner of the ability to use this information to assess, examine, and evaluate novel problems.

Cognitive offloading benefits performance but can also lead to impairments when the offloaded information isn't available at the time it's needed – if you don't have your lecture notes when you're being quizzed, there's a greater chance you won't be able to recall the information. Offloading is more likely to occur in people reporting lower subjective working memory capacity coupled with higher cognitive demands (if you believe your working memory capacity is poor, you'll be more likely to offload). However, we must bear in mind that research into cognitive offloading is still in an early stage, with most studies concentrating on cognitive load without offloading. That said, the view that people always need to commit things to memory isn't compatible with what they actually do in their daily lives, such as writing shopping lists, storing telephone numbers on their devices and jotting down notes.

Collective working memory

Cognitive offloading allows us to relieve some of the pressure placed on working memory while we carry out activities that require us to think. Rather than storing information in our limited-capacity memory stores, we are releasing this information into the outside world. Knowledge, however, is still part of long-term memory, and all that we learn once belonged to someone else – it was all part of the knowledge stored in other people's long-term memory. Some of the greatest innovations in history have involved pooling this information from many long-term memories. During the COVID-19 pandemic, medical research facilities from around the globe worked together to understand the virus and manufacture a vaccine. In a similar way, learners can work together to solve a single problem, extending both their knowledge and cognitive capacities.

Collaborative learning (or group work) has been a staple of education for centuries, loved and hated by teachers in almost equal measure. Its outcomes are often unpredictable. Group members will hopefully complete a task or solve a specific problem, while in the longer term, they might learn something about cooperation and become more skilled in their ability to work as a team. During collaborative learning, group members can access knowledge held by other members, introducing what has been termed *collective working memory* (Kirschner et al., 2011). This process reduces cognitive load by distributing interacting elements of the task among the multiple working memories of the group members. For complex tasks, collaboration becomes a scaffold for individuals' knowledge acquisition processes (Kirschner et al., 2018). However, if the scaffolding effect doesn't materialise, the task simply adds to extraneous load, a situation we need to manage.

Why might collaborative learning fail?

The act of collaboration is an evolutionary adaptation. But, as we know, humans don't always collaborate effectively. In learning, the aim of collaborative learning is to add to our knowledge by pooling cognitive resources, so collaborative learning is probably best suited to complex tasks – if all the members of a group have the same expertise, they're not going to gain all that much from the experience. Group members, therefore, come to the table with differing levels of knowledge and expertise, and collaboration allows for the sharing of these. If, however, these differences aren't recognised prior to the activity, collaboration will most likely fail. Collaborative teams, for example, are often chosen based on their specific knowledge and skill set. During the COVID-19 pandemic, for example, some working groups would have brought together experts from diverse disciplines, including virology, data science, public health, psychology, and sociology. Group members would have been informed of the parameters of the problem and how their expertise could help reach the group's goal.

Groups that have no experience of working together have a much higher rate of failure, so when putting a team together, it's often wise to consider who has worked well with whom in the past. In education settings, collaborative learning often fails because there's an absence of a precise goal – it's difficult to work together if you don't know what you're doing. Teachers will often include sets of instructions for group work, including advice on how to allocate tasks and organise information. Without guidelines, it's unlikely the group will learn very much, even though they may learn incidentally. Providing scripts can help, as can offering just-in-time support (Fischer & Hänze, 2019).

What students already know will determine whether collaborative learning is necessary. If group members are already knowledgeable about the content of the task, then it's probably not worth it. Sometimes, collaborative learning can be detrimental, and group members can experience expertise reversal, where learners with more knowledge in a specific area can no longer benefit. For high-complexity tasks, group members learn in a more efficient way than individual learners, but this isn't the case with low complexity tasks, so it's best to opt for individual learning.

Chapter summary

- Creating multiple pathways to learned information significantly enhances memory and recall efficiency.

- Active engagement and generative activities, such as drawing and speaking aloud, promote deeper processing and improve memory retention.

- Embodied cognition suggests that learning is closely linked to bodily activity and the surrounding environment, implying that engaging the body can enhance learning.

- Cognitive offloading, the act of using external resources to store information, can relieve working memory load but may also negatively impact memory retention if relied upon excessively.

- Collaborative learning, where individuals pool their cognitive resources, can extend knowledge and cognitive capacities, particularly for complex tasks, but its success depends on factors like group dynamics, task complexity, and clear goals.

Further reading

Caviglioli, O. (2019). *Dual coding for teachers*. John Catt.

Taylor, T. (2016). *A beginner's guide to mantle of the expert: A transformative approach to education*. Singular Publishing Limited.

References

Allen, M., LeFebvre, L., LeFebvre, L., & Bourhis, J. (2020). Is the pencil mightier than the keyboard? A meta-analysis comparing the method of notetaking outcomes. *Southern Communication Journal*, 85(3), 143–154. https://doi.org/10.1080/1041794X.2020.1764613

Castro-Alonso, J. C., Ayres, P., Zhang, S., de Koning, B. B., & Paas, F. (2024). Research avenues supporting embodied cognition in learning and instruction. *Educational Psychology Review*, 36(1). https://doi.org/10.1007/s10648-024-09847-4

De Koning, B. B., & van der Schoot, M. (2013). Becoming part of the story! refueling the interest in visualization strategies for reading comprehension. *Educational Psychology Review*, 25(2), 261–287. https://doi.org/10.1007/s10648-013-9222-6

Fernandes, M. A., Wammes, J. D., & Meade, M. E. (2018). The surprisingly powerful influence of drawing on memory. *Current Directions in Psychological Science*, 27(5), 302–308. https://doi.org/10.1177/0963721418755385

Fiorella, L., & Mayer, R. E. (2015). *Learning as a generative activity*. Cambridge University Press. https://doi.org/10.1017/CBO9781107707085

Fischer, E., & Hänze, M. (2019, March). Back from "guide on the side" to "sage on the stage"? Effects of teacher-guided and student-activating teaching methods on student learning in higher education. *International Journal of Educational Research*, 95, 26–35. https://doi.org/10.1016/j.ijer.2019.03.001

Gong, C., & Yang, Y. (2024). Google effects on memory: A meta-analytical review of the media effects of intensive Internet search behavior. *Frontiers in Public Health*, 12. https://doi.org/10.3389/fpubh.2024.1332030

Henkel, L. A. (2014). Point-and-shoot memories. *Psychological Science*, 25(2), 396–402. https://doi.org/10.1177/0956797613504438

Kang, W., & Malvaso, A. (2024). Frequent internet use is associated with better episodic memory performance. *Scientific Reports*, 14(1), 24914. https://doi.org/10.1038/s41598-024-75788-1

Kirschner, F., Paas, F., Kirschner, P. A., & Janssen, J. (2011). Differential effects of problem-solving demands on individual and collaborative learning outcomes. *Learning and Instruction*, 21(4), 587–599. https://doi.org/10.1016/j.learninstruc.2011.01.001

Kirschner, P. A., Sweller, J., Kirschner, F., & Zambrano, J. R. (2018). From cognitive load theory to collaborative cognitive load theory. *International Journal of Computer-Supported Collaborative Learning, 13*(2), 213–233. https://doi.org/10.1007/s11412-018-9277-y

Knutsen, D., & Le Bigot, L. (2014). Capturing egocentric biases in reference reuse during collaborative dialogue. *Psychonomic Bulletin & Review, 21*(6), 1590–1599. https://doi.org/10.3758/s13423-014-0620-7

Leahy, W., & Sweller, J. (2008). The imagination effect increases with an increased intrinsic cognitive load. *Applied Cognitive Psychology, 22*(2), 273–283. https://doi.org/10.1002/acp.1373

Leutner, D., Leopold, C., & Sumfleth, E. (2009). Cognitive load and science text comprehension: Effects of drawing and mentally imagining text content. *Computers in Human Behavior, 25*(2), 284–289. https://doi.org/10.1016/j.chb.2008.12.010

Lin, L., Lee, C. H., Kalyuga, S., Wang, Y., Guan, S., & Wu, H. (2017). The effect of learner-generated drawing and imagination in comprehending a science text. *Journal of Experimental Education, 85*(1), 142–154. https://doi.org/10.1080/00220973.2016.1143796

Meade, M. E., Wammes, J. D., & Fernandes, M. A. (2018). Drawing as an encoding tool: Memorial benefits in younger and older adults. *Experimental Aging Research, 44*(5), 369–396. https://doi.org/10.1080/0361073X.2018.1521432

Middlebrooks, C. D., Murayama, K., & Castel, A. D. (2017). Test expectancy and memory for important information. *Journal of Experimental Psychology: Learning, Memory, and Cognition, 43*(6), 972–985. https://doi.org/10.1037/xlm0000360

Moreno, J. D., León, J. A., Kaakinen, J. K., & Hyönä, J. (2021). Relevance instructions combined with elaborative interrogation facilitate strategic reading: Evidence from eye movements. *Psicologia Educativa, 27*(1), 51–65. https://doi.org/10.5093/PSED2020A20

Ozubko, J. D., Hourihan, K. L., & MacLeod, C. M. (2012). Production benefits learning: The production effect endures and improves memory for text. *Memory, 20*(7), 717–727. https://doi.org/10.1080/09658211.2012.699070

Ozubko, J. D., & MacLeod, C. M. (2010). The production effect in memory: Evidence that distinctiveness underlies the benefit. *Journal of Experimental Psychology: Learning Memory and Cognition, 36*(6), 1543–1547. https://doi.org/10.1037/a0020604

Paivio, A., & Csapo, K. (1971). Short-term sequential memory for pictures and words. *Psychonomic Science, 24*(2), 50–51. https://doi.org/10.3758/BF03337887

Pressley, G. M. (1976). Mental imagery helps eight-year-olds remember what they read. *Journal of Educational Psychology, 68*(3), 355–359. https://doi.org/10.1037/0022-0663.68.3.355

Quinlan, C. K., & Taylor, T. L. (2013). Enhancing the production effect in memory. *Memory, 21*(8), 904–915. https://doi.org/10.1080/09658211.2013.766754

Risko, E. F., & Dunn, T. L. (2015). Storing information in-the-world: Metacognition and cognitive offloading in a short-term memory task. *Consciousness and Cognition, 36*, 61–74. https://doi.org/10.1016/j.concog.2015.05.014

Sparrow, B., Liu, J., & Wegner, D. M. (2011). Google effects on memory: Cognitive consequences of having information at our fingertips. *Science, 333*(6043), 776–778. https://doi.org/10.1126/science.1207745

Stagg, B. C. (2020). Meeting Linnaeus: improving comprehension of biological classification and attitudes to plants using drama in primary science education. *Research in*

Science and Technological Education, 38(3), 253–271. https://doi.org/10.1080/02635143. 2019.1605347

Wetzels, S. A. J., Kester, L., & Van Merriënboer, J. J. G. (2011). Adapting prior knowledge activation: Mobilisation, perspective taking, and learners' prior knowledge. *Computers in Human Behavior*, *27*(1), 16–21. https://doi.org/10.1016/j.chb.2010.05.004

Willoughby, T., & Wood, E. (1994). Elaborative interrogation examined at encoding and retrieval. *Learning and Instruction*, *4*(2), 139–149

Woloshyn, V. E., Willoughby, T., Wood, E., & Pressley, M. (1990). Elaborative interrogation facilitates adult learning of factual paragraphs. *Journal of Educational Psychology*, *82*(3), 513.

Zeman, A., Dewar, M., & Della Sala, S. (2015). Lives without imagery – Congenital aphantasia. *Cortex*, *73*(June), 378–380. https://doi.org/10.1016/j.cortex.2015.05.019

Zhang, J., & Norman, D. A. (1994). Representations in distributed cognitive tasks. *Cognitive Science*, *18*(1), 87–122. https://doi.org/10.1016/0364-0213(94)90021-3

The forgotten variable
Emotions and learning

As a child, I was very poor at maths. There was something about it I just didn't get, and not being able to understand it caused me no end of anxiety. I was much more comfortable with History and English, Biology was okay, but I found Physics baffling. When presented with a mathematical equation, my brain would freeze, as though every single neuron had ceased to fire. Today, I suspect I would be seen as suffering from maths anxiety, a habitual type of anxiety that can negatively impact performance. This negative impact hints at one way a person's emotional state can affect their ability to recall learned information and engage in critical higher-order thinking – or the use of executive functions.

There are probably many reasons I developed a fear of maths. Perhaps there was a genetic component? My parents were never skilled mathematicians, although my maternal grandfather was an engineer. He must have had a pretty good grasp of maths, surely? My early education was also quite disruptive, and by the time I was eleven, I'd attended six schools across three countries, so perhaps it was the instability of my early educational experiences? As we've seen, competency in maths requires good foundations, and it's hard to accomplish this when you're constantly on the move. The worse I convinced myself I was at maths, the more anxious I became. But how did this anxiety impact my ability to tackle mathematical tasks? I'll try to answer this a little later.

This chapter is about how emotions can help and hinder learning. There are many aspects of emotions, well-being, and mental health that are important, both in educational settings and wider contexts. It's not the purpose of this chapter to debate, discuss, and analyse the current state of mental health – I'm neither qualified nor experienced enough to discuss such complex matters. That is not to deny the existence of a mental health crisis, or that psychological well-being should have a place in schools, colleges, and other educational establishments. But my aim here is to look at how emotional states impact cognition, specifically learning, so this chapter's remit is quite narrow, admittedly.

What are emotions?

Deciding precisely what constitutes an emotion isn't as simple as you might think, and pinpointing a single definition proves problematic. According to some accounts, there are potentially over 90 different definitions (Cabanac, 2002). There's a general consensus that an emotion is a mental state, a notion supported by our own experiences – we know when we are sad, angry, anxious, or happy. We are also quite skilled at detecting these mental states in others, even though we often get it wrong. The problem is that many people laugh when they are nervous and cry when they are happy, so people don't react uniformly to the same emotion. But this doesn't exactly tell us what emotions are. Like learning, emotions rely heavily on proxies, such as observable behaviour.

Neuroscientist Antonio Damasio proposes a neurological definition of emotion as *complex programs of acting triggered by the presence of certain neural systems* (Damasio, 2011). Psychologists view emotions as three interrelated constructs: affective tendencies, core affect, and emotional experience. The most relevant of these three constructs to learning is perhaps core affect – the way we feel at any particular time. Core affect is also straightforward to measure through self-completion questionnaires, where individuals are asked to rate a feeling in terms of valence (a continuum ranging from pleasant to unpleasant) and arousal, or our bodily activation (such as heart rate), ranging from low to high. So, if a student were asked to rate their levels of anxiety just before an exam, they might rate valence as unpleasant and arousal as high. If we measured the student's heart rate, chances are we'd find it elevated. What we think of positive emotions, therefore, will have positive valence, while negative emotions will be closer to the unpleasant end of the scale (but I'll explain later why the distinction between positive and negative emotions isn't a useful one).

We also don't really know how many emotions there are. Anger, sadness, and happiness might be obvious, but what about curiosity, interest, or boredom? As far as research is concerned, there is no real consensus. Furthermore, emotions are also dependent upon the language with which we name them. For example, sometimes we might feel happy, yet that happiness is tinged with melancholy. While some languages may have words that depict these nuanced emotions, many do not. There appears to be general agreement among many researchers that there are six or eight pure emotions: anger, disgust, fear, happiness, sadness, and surprise (and perhaps joy and anticipation), with all other emotions being elements of these. American psychologist Robert Plutchik proposes that basic emotions can be blended, much in the same way we can blend colours, to produce many more (Plutchik, 2001; Teigen, 1994). Anxiety, for example, isn't always considered an emotion but a state that combines thoughts, feelings, and physical sensations that arise because of a perceived threat. Anxiety certainly includes emotion (such as fear and surprise), and for this reason, we can often treat it as if it were an emotion.

There's a widely held view that emotions are either positive or negative and that our goal in life should be to maximise the former and minimise the latter. But is anxiety, for example, always a bad thing? Anxiety and fear certainly serve a useful evolutionary purpose; it's unlikely our distant ancestors would have lasted very long if they weren't afraid of that rapidly approaching sabre-toothed tiger. Anxiety increases arousal, preparing our body for fight or flight, a vital survival instinct. How can something that protects us from harm be negative? The fight-or-flight response is designed to be short-lived, and once the danger has receded, our body returns to its default position. If the anxiety is prolonged (such as chronic long-term anxiety), we remain in an overly alert state, which in turn negatively impacts several bodily systems, including cognition and immune functioning. So, some anxiety is good, at least when our life depends on it. Another positive is that arousal produced via the stress response can help us concentrate and remain focused, but only to a point – once we get too anxious, our ability to function suffers. This is commonly known as Yerkes-Dodson law, first proposed by Robert Yerkes and John Dillingham Dodson (Yerkes & Dodson, 1908).

The same can be said for all emotions; that is, they are neither intrinsically positive nor negative. Psychologist Reinhard Pekrun uses the terms activating and deactivating emotions rather than positive and negative. Emotions serve a purpose, but only if they occur under the right conditions (Pekrun, 2006). Boredom, for example, might lead us to shift our attention away from the task at hand, but it might also result in increased creativity or motivate us to find something else to do. Pekrun describes such emotions as achievement emotions because the emphasis is on pursuing academic goals (Pekrun et al., 2007). An activity might, for example, result in curiosity if the student finds the task interesting, or boredom or frustration if task demands are mismatched (too easy or too difficult). Outcome-related achievement emotions arise when the task has reached completion, and the outcome is known, resulting in emotions such as joy or pride at a favourable result or anger and frustration at the seemingly insurmountable task demands (Smith, 2017).

It's likely that my difficulties with maths were, in part at least, the result of my levels of anxiety exceeding the sweet spot (Yerkes-Dodson Law) and my emotional reaction to what I believed were too high task demands. But there's much more to emotions than anxiety, and emotional states are going to impact people differently. How, then, are emotions linked to learning and the way we understand the cognitive architecture associated with it? If memory is vital for learning, then we need to begin our investigation here.

Broaden and build

Emotions, of course, have wider consequences for our health and well-being, as well as our ability to bounce back following adversity (or resilience). This then most likely impacts people's capacity to learn. Psychologist Barbara Fredrickson's

Broaden and Build framework views emotions as having an evolutionary function related to human survival (Fredrickson, 2001). Fear, for example, acts as a survival mechanism, allowing us to escape or avoid potentially life-threatening situations. Anxiety keeps us vigilant and constantly on the lookout for danger. Anxiety triggers the stress response, resulting in the production of adrenaline and cortisol, which leads to the dampening down of non-essential functions so that we can divert resources to areas where they are most needed, assisting us with our fight or (most likely) flight. This response narrows our potential responses to the situation – we can attack or run. We don't need to think because higher order cognitive functions are less important. Instinctual processes take over.

According to Fredrickson's framework, negative emotions will narrow our options, while positive emotions broaden them. Fear will give us fewer options than, for example, curiosity. Curiosity is a broad emotion that builds what Fredrickson describes as thought-action repertoires, a kind of psychological capital that we can nurture and deploy when situations arise. Imagine a student struggling to solve a challenging maths problem. If the learning environment fosters positive emotions, such as through encouragement, humour, or the joy of small successes, the student may approach the problem with more creativity and persistence. These positive emotions can encourage the learner to think beyond rigid, habitual responses and explore alternative strategies. Faced with the prospect of giving up, they might, for example, visualise the problem differently, break it down into smaller parts, or ask for collaborative input from peers. Over time, these experiences of positive engagement help to build self-efficacy and resilience. If they later face another problem, they have a store of previous successes on which to draw, increasing confidence and the feeling that they are equipped to tackle it. This, in turn, can counteract the physiological and psychological effects of anxiety.

Emotions and memory

Brain mechanisms that give rise to conscious emotions aren't all that different from those that give rise to cognition. They are also processed in a similar way, differing only in terms of the inputs into the brain's cortical-based general neural networks. Multiple regions of the brain are involved in the simplest and most mundane memory tasks, and when we add potent emotions to the mix, millions of neurons increase in activity (Palombo et al., 2016). For example, when people recall past events, neural activity increases in the amygdala, medial temporal lobe, anterior and posterior midline, and the visual cortex. These areas are involved in several functions, from emotional activation to literally seeing the experience in our mind's eye. The amygdala plays a major role in memory, decision-making, and emotional response. Cognition and emotion are working together.

Emotions can trigger memories, even when we don't want them to. Involuntary memories can surface when we hear a song, detect a smell or taste food from our childhood, such as Marcel Proust's depiction in *In Search of Lost Time*. Then, the simple act of biting into a biscuit triggered long-dormant memories of childhood. Similarly, in Haruki Murakami's book *Norwegian Wood*, the Beatles song of the same name allows the protagonist, Toru Watanabe, to recall Naoko, his first love, vividly.

Music is a powerful memory cue; just think about a time you've heard a song from your youth and the feelings and memories the song triggers. Often we can't even describe the emotion that arises, but seemingly without warning, our minds are filled with recollections and moments that we thought we'd forgotten long ago. Professor Catherine Loveday is a neuroscientist at the University of Westminster, a memory researcher with a tendency to approach her well-worn discipline from unusual and often highly creative directions. One of her particular interests is how songs from our past impact our recollections of our lives and, in turn, engage emotional responses. Music really takes hold during the teenage years, so somewhere in my memory are the punk bands of my youth and the grunge and Britpop of my late teens and early twenties. Songs appear to cluster around significant times in my life, mainly my younger years, but also more recently. Loveday would call these clusters my *reminiscence bump*; episodic autobiographical memories organised like a Spotify playlist, each characterised by its own soundtrack.

In an intriguing study, Loveday transcribed thousands of hours of the popular long-running BBC Radio 4 programme Desert Island Discs, where guests pick their favourite records to take with them should they be shipwrecked on a deserted island. The songs chosen often cluster around specific moments in the lives of the guests, suggesting that aspects of the environment influence our episodic memories, including the music we listen to. Interestingly, the only group of people who tended not to display a reminiscent bump were politicians of all persuasions. Former UK Prime Minister David Cameron, for example, included everything from Mendelssohn to The Killers, while former Labour Party leader Ed Miliband chose both Sir Hubert Parry's Jerusalem and Robbie Williams' Angels. It was difficult to find a reminiscence bump in either of these men's choices, leading to the suggestion that the lists were carefully curated by public relations experts who wanted both men to appeal to the widest demographic (Loveday et al., 2020).

Emotions and cognitive structures

Emotions can, therefore, help us recall the past. But they can also hinder learning. For many years, researchers studying cognitive processes viewed them as a nuisance, as confounding variables capable of wreaking havoc on even the most carefully planned experiment. Mary Helen Immordino-Yang and Antonio Damasio of the Brain and Creativity Institute at the University of Southern California liken emotions to a toddler in a china shop, interfering with the orderly rows of stemware on the shelves. But Immordino-Yang and Damasio also think we've got emotions all wrong, especially when it comes to learning.

Emotions have an important role to play in processes such as attention, memory, and decision making, but are also linked to factors like motivation. Immordino-Yang and Damasio put the case for emotion in learning a little more forcefully, insisting that any competent teacher recognises that emotions and feelings affect students' performance and learning, adding, educators often fail to consider that the high levels of cognitive skills taught in schools (including reasoning and decision making, language, reading and mathematics) do not function as rational disembodied systems, influenced but detached from emotion and the body (Immordino-Yang & Damasio, 2007).

Like the researcher attempting to control for emotions, teachers and learners often view emotions as an irritating part of the learning process. Emotions certainly don't fit with the view that the human brain is like a computer, adding further weight to arguments against the computer analogy. Computers don't have emotions. Computers don't get anxious. They don't get distracted. You can't hurt a computer's feelings with a careless word. Yet emotions are real. We experience their impact every moment of every day. Emotions impact all mental processes, including cognitive load. In his 2019 review of Cognitive Load Theory, John Sweller explores potential avenues of investigation (Sweller et al., 2019). These include emotions, stress, and uncertainty, topics I've previously covered in The Emotional Learner and Becoming Buoyant (Smith, 2017, 2020).

Emotions and cognitive load

Once again, we return to the same old problem, that of limited cognitive resources. This time, however, it's our emotional responses to learning situations that lead to unmanageable load. We, therefore, can't exclude emotions from our discussions about learning. However, rather than attempting to eliminate them from the learning environment (if doing so was even possible), we need to accept them and manage the ones that are going to cause the most problems. This is not just an issue in the classroom. There are many occupations that require people to work in highly charged environments and make split-second, often lifesaving, decisions. Emotional responses often govern these environments.

Anxiety, therefore, may restrict the capacity of working memory by competing with cognitive processes that are trying to get the job done (Moran, 2016). One study explored the impact of heightened emotions in medical professionals tasked with recognising heart murmurs. Participants with emotional states categorised as invigorating reported increased cognitive load, while those categorised as tranquil reported decreased cognitive load (Fraser et al., 2012). Another study found that inducing positive emotions during a learning task decreased the perceived difficulty of the task, but inducing positive emotions before the learning task increased the mental effort participants invested during the task (Um et al., 2012).

We know from previous research that people with a propensity towards higher levels of anxiety (known as trait anxiety) perform worse on formal tests than their less anxious peers. Tests of performance are always going to be stress-inducing, but anxiety does place added pressure on our already limited mental resources. Research has also discovered that cortisol, a hormone released in the brain during times of stress, influences memory consolidation and memory retrieval, only in different directions. It may, then, aid in the initial stages of learning, when new information is consolidated into previous learning, but prevent this information from being recalled when required (Smith, 2017, p.144).

Increasing task demands increases cognitive load. As the complexity of the task increases, cognitive resources have an incrementally harder time dealing with it. But it's not only the demands of the task but also what Hwan-Hee Choi and colleagues in the Netherlands describe as environmental causal factors. The primary environmental factors that add to load are stress and uncertainty, and while some stress has a positive impact, too much will make learning more difficult (Choi et al., 2014).

In a 2022 meta-analysis, researchers investigated how a particular type of anxiety (maths anxiety) impacted working memory. The analysis included data from 57 studies, amounting to 66 unique samples and over 16,000 participants. Findings confirmed a relationship between maths anxiety, maths performance, and working memory (Finell et al., 2022). Maths anxiety is defined as a feeling of tension and anxiety that interferes with the manipulation of numbers and the solving of mathematical problems in ordinary life and academic situations (Ashcraft, 2002). It's thought to be influenced by environmental, intellectual, and personal factors, starting as early as six years old and persisting into adulthood.

The reasons people might develop maths anxiety are multifaceted. Unlike many other academic subjects, mathematics relies heavily on foundational knowledge and skills learned very early in formal education (and perhaps earlier). Gaps in this knowledge can lower confidence at later stages. The importance of maths skills is also universally held, placing the need to be proficient at a much higher cultural level. There's also a tendency to view maths as difficult and that people are good at it or not, emphasising the belief that such skills are innate.

Attitudes towards our own intellectual and academic abilities build over time (what psychologists call academic self-concept). Prior experiences shape later views about ability. Therefore, early negative experiences shape our current views. We might then claim that we've always been bad at maths and therefore will always be bad at maths, reducing our confidence in our abilities to complete mathematical tasks – a concept referred to as self-efficacy. Attributions about the reason we are bad at maths (such as *I'm stupid* or *I've never been good at maths*) combine with low self-efficacy (*because I've always been bad at maths I won't be able to solve this equation*).

Emotions and attentional control theory

How, then, can we attempt to explain the mechanisms by which anxiety raises cognitive load towards unmanageable levels? Attentional control theory (ACT), developed by Michael Eysenck, a psychologist at Royal Holloway, University of London, proposes that anxiety acts as a distracter that depletes the cognitive capacity needed for solving complex problems (Eysenck et al., 2007). ACT emphasises the impact of anxiety on executive function, leading to an increased focus on threat-related stimuli, impairing attentional processes and working memory.

You'll recall from Chapter 5 that attention and working memory are closely entwined and that we are often compelled to select what we pay attention to from a multitude of inputs. But other stimuli distract us and add to the mental load. Distracters can be external and internal, including worrying thoughts and negative self-evaluation. Our brains, therefore, are constantly juggling demands for our attention. Attention, within the premise of ACT, can be goal-directed (or top-down) or distraction-orientated (bottom-up). The Frontoparietal Network (FPN), a network of brain regions in the frontal and parietal lobes of the brain, is thought to be responsible for top-down attentional control. It's where we direct our attention in pursuit of a specific goal. If we are given a task to complete, it ensures that we focus on each step and ignore distractions. The FPN is like a conductor in an orchestra, making sure that all the instruments play in harmony and produce a cohesive symphony. It, therefore, plays a vital role in supporting executive functions through the interaction with working memory, planning and decision-making, and inhibitory control.

Distractive (bottom-up) processing is associated with the Default Mode Network (DMN). The DMN is involved in self-referential thinking, mind-wandering, and internally directed thoughts. These can interfere with attentional control mechanisms. Unsurprisingly, the DMN is more active in people with high trait anxiety. While the FPN attempts to keep us focused and on track, the DMN tries its best to distract us.

A third network, known as the Cingular Opercula Network (CON), attempts to resolve conflicts that arise between our goals and our distractions, acting as a kind of arbitrator between the FPN and the DMN. Because the DMN dominates in more anxious people, the CON must work much harder to resolve any conflict by redirecting attention back to the goal. While this may help maintain performance effectiveness, it comes at the cost of mental effort and reduces processing efficiency.

Processing effectiveness is the quality of performance on a task. If I were to give you a series of mathematical equations to solve, your processing effectiveness could be calculated by the number of equations you solved accurately. Processing efficiency is the relationship between the effectiveness of your performance (the number of correct answers) and the effort or resources expended to achieve that level of performance. A decrease in efficiency means that you're going to be employing more resources just to maintain the same level of performance. You'll have to work much harder to achieve the same result.

Maths anxiety may initially arise because of several factors, as already discussed. From then on, it is often self-sustaining. A child in the early stages of formal education, for example, may struggle because of limited working memory capacity. This could be exacerbated because of factors, including those from within the teaching environment. Young children rapidly develop a sense of how they perceive themselves within academic settings (academic self-concept), so a child who struggles early will develop the belief that they aren't good at maths. This, then, increases levels of anxiety around the subject, impacting factors such as motivation and self-efficacy. Consequently, raised levels of anxiety lead to increasingly poor performance, and the cycle begins again. The early years of formal education are, therefore, vital in identifying those children who may struggle and providing the tools to assist them.

Emotions and cognitive load theory

From a cognitive load theory perspective, emotions represent extraneous cognitive load. You'll recall extraneous cognitive load as being any element unrelated to the learning task. These elements are going to compete for resources – it doesn't make any difference if they are memory limitations, distractions, or emotions. But emotions may also affect intrinsic cognitive load, although the mechanisms by which they do this are less well understood. It most likely relates to emotional regulation, the ability to keep emotions in check. This may also involve elements of academic buoyancy, or academic resilience, which I'll discuss a little later.

According to Jan Plass of New York University and Slava Kalyuga from the University of New South Wales, emotions are also likely to influence motivation. Motivation affects mental effort, so it's going to impact the extent to which we integrate new information with currently stored schemas. Plass and Kalyuga also suggest that emotions affect memory by both broadening and narrowing cognitive resources (the broaden and build framework described previously). However, if levels of anxiety are too high, this limits motivation and cognitive engagement, and there is a greater chance of abandoning the task. When we are under positive affect, information in long-term memory is more readily available, while negative emotions increase extraneous load (Plass & Kalyuga, 2019).

Is it realistic, then, to propose that strategies purported to manage load also reduce unhelpful levels of anxiety? This is certainly what cognitive load theory would imply. Take, for example, a student displaying behaviours consistent with maths anxiety. If study materials are over-cluttered, include complex language, and are generally designed in such a way as to place unwarranted stress on limited cognitive resources, it would be likely that the student would experience higher levels of anxiety. Our student is under attack from all sides: the complexity and poorly designed materials, and fear and worry brought about by their inherent anxiety over maths.

One study from 2015 set out to investigate this hypothesis (Gillmor et al., 2015). The researchers included several techniques common within CLT, including (but not limited to) simplifying language and reducing word counts, the use of diagrams to represent spatial information, directing attention with signals and cues, removal of extraneous visuals and texts, and asking the question first and ordering answer options logically (known as sequencing).

Results suggested a negative correlation between anxiety and performance, with higher anxiety levels linked to lower performance (consistent with previous findings). However, they didn't find any statistically significant differences in average reported state anxiety between students who received the reduced load items and those who received the traditional test items. It would seem, in this study at least, that reducing load on test items has little impact on anxiety levels. It's worth noting, of course, that this was a correlational design, so we can't infer causation. Additionally, the researchers used self-report measures of anxiety (the State-Trait Anxiety Inventory for Children). Other methods of anxiety measurement, such as galvanic skin response or eye tracking, might yield alternative results. It's clear that much more research is needed in this area for any definitive findings to emerge.

Emotions and academic buoyancy

Another aspect worth considering is resilience. While resilience as a topic of research can be problematic (not least due to varying definitions of the term), learning-specific resilience, or academic buoyancy, has the advantage of a solid research base. Academic buoyancy is mostly associated with the work of Andrew Martin, an educational psychologist at the University of New South Wales (Martin has also developed a theory of instructional design aimed at managing cognitive load, discussed in Chapter 13).

Academic buoyancy is the ability of students to successfully deal with academic setbacks and challenges that are typical of the ordinary course of school life (such as poor grades, competing deadlines, exam pressure, and difficult schoolwork) (Martin & Marsh, 2008). Martin's previous research into motivation and academic achievement identifies six factors that are shown to be present in successful students. Referred to as the 5Cs, they include Confidence (or self-efficacy), Coordination (or planning), Control, Composure (low anxiety), and Commitment (persistence, conscientiousness, or grit).

While a full discussion of academic buoyancy is beyond the scope of this book (see Smith, 2020, for an in-depth critique), it's highly likely that these 5Cs play an important role in the way emotions impact learning. Feelings of confidence and control over one's learning have been found to make a significant difference to learners' ability to bounce back following disappointment. The inclusion of composure, or low anxiety, is supported by research discussed already in this chapter. They also represent skills that, on the whole, can be learned.

Managing load, therefore, might not only be a matter of how we design materials and present information, but also about minimising emotional states that add pressure to an already overstressed system. While CLT generally places the emphasis on how we design learning environments (it is, in essence, a theory of instructional design), there may be some mileage in nudging learners' behaviour towards more adaptive traits. Potential for new avenues of research, perhaps.

I have focused this chapter primarily on the role of anxiety as a deactivating emotion. But, just as anxiety can raise cognitive load, other emotions may keep it manageable. Certainly, gradual exposure to anxiety-provoking situations has been shown to reduce any negative impact. For example, Sonal Arora from Imperial College London looked at how surgeons could reduce anxiety by mobilising their imagination and mental practice before performing a surgical procedure (Arora et al., 2011).

The study recruited 20 novice surgeons, randomly assigned to either a mental practice group or a control group. Both groups underwent training on virtual reality laparoscopic cholecystectomy and completed five simulated procedures. Prior to each session, the first group engaged in thirty minutes of guided mental practice of the procedure, while the control group engaged in an unrelated activity. The research team measured stress levels before and after the surgical procedure using questionnaires, heart rate, and salivary cortisol levels. They found that the mental practice group exhibited lower stress levels than the control group.

While this was a small study with only 20 participants, the findings offer some interesting insights about potential stress-reducing practices. Arora suggests that the use of imagination could prove useful in high-stress environments, such as athletes preparing for competitions or emergency responders facing critical incidents. But it may also be useful in situations where learners are facing high-stakes examinations.

Our emotions are always going to impact how efficiently people learn. Sometimes emotions can hinder learning, while at other times they can aid it. But the notion that some emotions are positive and others negative is often unhelpful, and we should really think of emotional states in respect to the utility, that is, do they activate or deactivate the ability to learn? One way they do this involves our limited cognitive resources, the depletion of which can increase load to a point where learning becomes unmanageable. Finding ways of dealing with how instructional materials and the wider learning environment can help learners better manage this cognitive load, plus internal states (including emotions), will need careful consideration.

When we have some insights into how emotions impact learning, be that from a cognitive load perspective or not, we then have a much better opportunity to design instructional environments that can take emotions into consideration. Motivation, for example, is often a symptom of poor emotional regulation (the ability to keep our emotions in check, such as staying relatively calm under pressure or curtailing our more excitable side). Emotional regulation is situation-specific, so sometimes some emotions are useful, but detrimental at others. Procrastination and self-handicapping (the tendency to sabotage our efforts) are emotional at their core. We'll look a little more at some of these areas in the next chapter.

Chapter summary

- Emotions profoundly influence learning and cognitive processes, affecting the ability to recall information and engage in higher-order thinking.
- Emotions serve important functions in learning, and the traditional view of categorising them as simply 'positive' or 'negative' is not always helpful.
- Emotions are intricately linked with memory and contribute to cognitive load.
- Maths anxiety is presented as a specific example of how negative emotions can create a cycle of poor performance and avoidance in learning.
- Managing the impact of emotions on learning requires a multifaceted approach, including instructional design and fostering academic buoyancy.

Further reading

Bethune, A. (2018). *Wellbeing in the primary classroom*. Bloomsbury.
Smith, M. (2018). *The emotional learner: Understanding emotions, learners and achievement*. Routledge.

References

Arora, S., Aggarwal, R., Moran, A., Sirimanna, P., Crochet, P., Darzi, A., Kneebone, R., & Sevdalis, N. (2011). Mental practice: Effective stress management training for novice surgeons. *Journal of the American College of Surgeons, 212*(2), 225–233. https://doi.org/10.1016/j.jamcollsurg.2010.09.025
Ashcraft, M. H. (2002). Math anxiety: Personal, educational, and cognitive consequences. *Current Directions in Psychological Science, 11*(5), 181–185. https://doi.org/10.1111/1467-8721.00196
Cabanac, M. (2002). What is emotion? *Behavioural Processes, 60*(2), 69–83. https://doi.org/10.1016/S0376-6357(02)00078-5
Choi, H.-H., van Merriënboer, J. J. G., & Paas, F. (2014). Effects of the physical environment on cognitive load and learning: Towards a new model of cognitive load. *Educational Psychology Review, 26*(2), 225–244. https://doi.org/10.1007/s10648-014-9262-6
Damasio, A. (2011). Neural basis of emotions. *Scholarpedia, 6*(3), 1804. https://doi.org/10.4249/scholarpedia.1804
Eysenck, M. W., Derakshan, N., Santos, R., & Calvo, M. G. (2007). Anxiety and cognitive performance: Attentional control theory. *Emotion (Washington, DC), 7*(2), 336–353. https://doi.org/10.1037/1528-3542.7.2.336

Finell, J., Sammallahti, E., Korhonen, J., Eklöf, H., & Jonsson, B. (2022). Working memory and its mediating role on the relationship of math anxiety and math performance: A meta-analysis. *Frontiers in Psychology*, *12*(January), 1–14. https://doi.org/10.3389/fpsyg.2021.798090

Fraser, K., Ma, I., Teteris, E., Baxter, H., Wright, B., & Mclaughlin, K. (2012). Emotion, cognitive load and learning outcomes during simulation training. *Medical Education*, *46*(11), 1055–1062. https://doi.org/10.1111/j.1365-2923.2012.04355.x

Fredrickson, B. (2001). The role of positive emotions in positive psychology: The broaden-and-build theory of positive emotions. *American Psychologist*, *56*(3), 218–226. https://psycnet.apa.org/journals/amp/56/3/218/

Gillmor, S., Poggio, J., & Embretson, S. (2015). Effects of reducing the cognitive load of mathematics test items on student performance. *Numeracy*, *8*(1). https://doi.org/10.5038/1936-4660.8.1.4

Immordino-Yang, M. H., & Damasio, A. (2007). We feel, therefore we learn: The relevance of affective and social neuroscience to education. *Mind, Brain, and Education*, *1*(1), 3–10.

Loveday, C., Woy, A., & Conway, M. A. (2020). The self-defining period in autobiographical memory: Evidence from a long-running radio show. *Quarterly Journal of Experimental Psychology*, *73*(11), 1969–1976. https://doi.org/10.1177/1747021820940300

Martin, A. J., & Marsh, H. W. (2008). Academic buoyancy: Towards an understanding of students' everyday academic resilience. *Journal of School Psychology*, *46*(1), 53–83. https://doi.org/10.1016/j.jsp.2007.01.002

Moran, T. P. (2016). Anxiety and working memory capacity: A meta-analysis and narrative review. *Psychological Bulletin*, *142*(8), 831–864. https://doi.org/10.1037/bul0000051

Palombo, D. J., McKinnon, M. C., McIntosh, A. R., Anderson, A. K., Todd, R. M., & Levine, B. (2016). The neural correlates of memory for a life-threatening event. *Clinical Psychological Science*, *4*(2), 312–319. https://doi.org/10.1177/2167702615589308

Pekrun, R. (2006). The control-value theory of achievement emotions: Assumptions, corollaries, and implications for educational research and practice. *Educational Psychology Review*, *18*(4), 315–341. https://doi.org/10.1007/s10648-006-9029-9

Pekrun, R., Frenzel, A. C., Goetz, T., & Perry, R. P. (2007). The control-value theory of achievement emotions: An integrative approach to emotions in education. In P. A. Schutz & R. Pekrun (eds.), *Emotion in Education* (pp. 13–36). Elsevier Academic Press. https://doi.org/10.1016/B978-012372545-5/50003-4

Plass, J. L., & Kalyuga, S. (2019). Four ways of considering emotion in cognitive load theory. *Educational Psychology Review*, *31*(2), 339–359. https://doi.org/10.1007/s10648-019-09473-5

Plutchik, R. (2001). The nature of emotions: Human emotions have deep evolutionary roots, a fact that may explain their complexity and provide tools for clinical practice. *American Scientist*, *89*(4), 344–350.

Smith, M. (2017). *The emotional learner: Understanding emotions, learners and achievement*. Routledge.

Smith, M. (2020). *Becoming buoyant: Helping teachers and students cope with the day-to-day*. Routledge.

Sweller, J., van Merriënboer, J. J. G., & Paas, F. (2019). Cognitive architecture and instructional design: 20 years later. *Educational Psychology Review, 31*(2), 261–292. https://doi.org/10.1007/s10648-019-09465-5

Teigen, K. H. (1994). Yerkes-Dodson: A law for all seasons. *Theory & Psychology, 4*(4), 525–547. https://doi.org/10.1177/0959354394044004

Um, E. R., Plass, J. L., Hayward, E. O., & Homer, B. D. (2012). Emotional design in multimedia learning. *Journal of Educational Psychology, 104*(2), 485–498. https://doi.org/10.1037/a0026609

Yerkes, R. M., & Dodson, J. D. (1908). The relation of strength of stimulus to rapidity of habit formation. *Journal of Comparative Neurology & Psychology, 18*, 459–482. https://doi.org/10.1002/cne.920180503

 Balancing minds, metacognition, and motivation

Learning happens in varied environments – school classrooms, university, and college lecture theatres, online, at work, in isolation and among groups of people, large and small. Learning also happens across the lifespan, from those first steps to retired folk attending a part-time Spanish language class. Employers send their staff on training courses, and continuing professional development is the buzzword of the century. We might retrain for a new career later in life or take up a hobby that requires us to develop new skills. Learning isn't confined to childhood and adolescence but continues in some form or another throughout our lives.

Learning in later life benefits people and not just in terms of slower cognitive decline. For example, in a 2005 study, Donald Roberson and Sharan Merriam studied learners aged between 75 and 87 in the rural area of South Georgia in the United States. They discovered their participants benefited from a sense of purpose and control, both of which tend to diminish in older age (Roberson & Merriam, 2005). Adult learners are also more self-directed than younger ones. Self-directed learning is a process whereby individuals take responsibility for defining their learning objectives and selecting methods to achieve them, aligning their efforts with personal goals or the demands of their individual context. A key aspect of this approach is its highly personalised nature – both the learning methods and goals are tailored to the learner's specific life circumstances. In this process, learners are not only central participants but also integral to shaping the context in which their learning occurs. Self-directed learners display several important characteristics, such as the ability to set themselves clear goals and to monitor their own learning process, skills referred to as metacognition.

Learning is more than cognition, yet we can't remove cognition from the learning equation. Memory, of all types, allows learning to happen, and as we've seen with case studies of individuals like Henry, if there is no memory, there is no learning. Certain aspects of cognition decline as we age, such as working memory, yet older individuals have more prior learning to draw upon than younger learners.

In this chapter, I want to investigate other factors that make learning happen, ones that are often dismissed because they can't always provide the certainties that we might expect from the learning sciences. In the previous chapter, we looked at emotion and the way internal states are deeply entwined with each other. Emotion also fuels other so-called non-cognitive skills such as motivation, which provides a continuous feedback loop between planning, goal setting, resilience, and many strategies and skills that may not, at first, appear to relate all that much to processes such as cognitive load and attention. I also want to investigate the notion that people change; that a disengaged school dropout can flourish later in life, given the right opportunities and motivations. People change as they mature, both because of experience and the development of brain structures. We also change as a direct result of education, and we all begin that journey at different stages, with different motivations, needs, and abilities. While previous chapters have attempted to find a common thread running through all learning, here I want to emphasise that learners are far from homogenous.

Changing brains

We know that learning changes our brains by making new connections between neurons. The most notable changes take place during the first few years of life, but continue in some respects, at least until our early 20s. There is, of course, an inevitable decline as we age, but that shouldn't prevent us from viewing learning as a lifelong endeavour.

The increase in connections during the early years of life is called synaptogenesis and can last for several months, depending on the species of animal. Synaptogenesis is followed by a process called cognitive pruning, when unused connections are removed, probably because they don't serve any useful purpose. Once complete, the density of these connections should have reached adult levels.

It was once thought that this process resulted in the establishment of critical developmental periods, after which specific types of learning (such as language) became, if not impossible, highly improbable. However, this view was predicated on studies of infant monkeys where researchers found that brain density declined to adult levels at around three years. But three years is also the age at which monkeys reach sexual maturity – much earlier than humans. As we've seen in previous chapters, applying the findings from non-human animal studies to humans can often lead us in the wrong direction. Advances in brain imaging techniques, such as fMRI, mean that we can now study living human brains rather than relying on brains post-mortem or those of non-human animals. Such advances have provided a much clearer picture of how the brain develops and why it declines.

We now assume that humans may pass through a sensitive stage, after which learning might become more problematic, but far from impossible. Indeed, studies of feral children, those children who have, for various reasons, spent much of their early years isolated from human contact, find that even if they cannot master language in early infancy, they can gain these skills later. We also saw in Chapter 2 that cognitive decline can slow considerably through learning new skills, and that all learning changes the structure of our brains regardless of our maturing years.

More recent research using fMRI technology has discovered that the teenage brain continues to develop, albeit only in specific brain regions. The visual cortex, for example, should be fully developed by around ten months. Synaptic density then declines because of cognitive pruning, reaching adult levels by about ten years old. Development in the frontal cortex is much slower, lasting well into the teenage years, while the pruning process is much slower. Synaptic density doesn't peak until about 11 years old, and pruning continues into the early 1920s (see Smith, 2017, for a full discussion). The development of the frontal cortex is associated with the emergence of executive function, a set of abilities vital to successful learning, including many of the abilities described in previous chapters.

Brain development is, of course, a gradual process – we don't wake up one morning and proclaim that our frontal cortex is fully developed, and we've suddenly transformed from petulant teen to a fully cognisant adult. Changes are subtle and can only be evidenced over time. Similarly, cognitive decline is more of a creep than a sudden surprise, and it's unlikely we'll see it coming. While there are age ranges for such development, these are guides rather than absolutes, and there are always going to be differences between people in how fast and how well these changes take place.

Higher-order thinking: the role of executive functions

I've mentioned executive functions in previous chapters without elaborating on what we mean by the term. Robert Logie describes executive function as including any cognitive abilities that involve the control of other, simpler abilities (Logie, 2016). These include memory and attention. But executive function is also about planning and goal setting, as well as the ability to manage thoughts, actions, and emotions so that we can achieve what we have set out to do.

There are thought to be three major components to executive function: working memory, cognitive flexibility, and inhibitory control. These three components result in the emergence of related skills, including paying attention, organising, and planning, initiating tasks, staying focused on tasks, and self-monitoring.

Working memory

As discussed throughout the previous chapters, working memory contributes significantly to learning outcomes. While some might attribute academic achievement to measures of intelligence, working memory is a much better predictor of success (Alloway & Alloway, 2008). Working memory skills at age 5 are the best predictor of literacy and numeracy six years later, accounting for a higher variance than IQ (Alloway & Alloway, 2010). IQ and working memory are moderately associated with each other, but there appears to be minimal overlap, suggesting that working memory is more than simply a proxy for intelligence.

Working memory is a relatively stable construct, as we have seen in studies of capacity and duration. This means that those learners who display low working memory capacity at the beginning of formal education are likely to remain at that level, further adding to the view that teaching should take such limitations into account when designing learning environments. Compared to IQ, working memory remains relatively impervious to environmental influences, such as socio-economic status and years spent in pre-school education.

Although relatively stable, working memory follows a developmental trajectory. Capacity increases substantially during childhood, with smaller increases between around 20 and 39. There's then a slight decline between around 50 and 85, but the decline is much slower than the increases seen in childhood. This means that people in the 60s are performing at a similar level to those in their 20s, at least in terms of completing working memory tasks. Even those in the 70s and 80s are performing as well as teenagers (Alloway & Alloway, 2013).

The picture is very different when it comes to fluid intelligence, however. Fluid intelligence is thought to be related to brain development (or cortical thickening) between the ages of 6 and 12. In old age, this volume decreases, and by the time we're 80 years old, we may have lost over 2 percent of brain volume. It's hypothesised that this is why we see a sharp decline in fluid intelligence after about 65 and a further decline in those over 80.

Cognitive flexibility

One important aspect of learning is the ability to adjust our behaviour according to a change in the environment. When faced with multiple tasks or when we have to shift our perspective from one task to another, the ease with which we can do this is going to impact how well we learn. We refer to this ability as cognitive flexibility or cognitive shifting (Dajani & Uddin, 2015).

Learners in formal educational settings are expected to accomplish this every day. They may, for example, attend to a teacher speaking, writing on the board, and transferring knowledge from them to those in the room. If they single out a pupil and ask a question, the individual will need to switch from listening to engaging with the question, perhaps frantically attempting to wrench a response from their memory. Similarly, switching from the rules of listening to those of engaging in a learning task, either individually or as part of a group, requires a change in behaviour to suit the new environment. But cognitive flexibility isn't only about switching – it's also about mixing. The teacher will mix tasks. Not only will they be engaging in direct instruction, but they might also consider a question to ask and to whom they should ask it. In addition, they might scan the classroom, remaining mindful that pupils appear engaged, are behaving appropriately, and aren't covertly checking their social media notifications under the desk. We usually describe this as multitasking, an activity we are rarely very skilled at, as I explained in Chapter 5. Cognitive flexibility, therefore, includes both switching costs (the difficulty or time to change from one task to another) and mixing costs (the difficulty or time to maintain multiple tasks in mind).

The more effectively learners can switch and mix, the more efficient their learning. For example, a 2013 meta-analysis found that shifting ability was a good predictor of mathematics and reading achievement in children (Yeniad et al., 2013), while a 2014 study found that cognitive flexibility predicted early reading skills (Colé et al., 2014). Studies have also found a connection between cognitive flexibility and critical thinking skills (Karakuş, 2024). As critical thinking skills increase, so does cognitive flexibility.

Like other aspects of executive function, cognitive flexibility changes throughout the lifespan. However, switching costs don't follow the same trajectory as mixing costs. The cost of switching, for example, decreases with age, and higher switching costs equate to poorer performance. Those who find it hard to alter their focus from a task requiring one set of rules and goals to one with a different set will not learn as efficiently compared to those who are more skilled at changing their focus of attention. Because of a less mature attentional system that is tuned to deal with single tasks, adolescents and younger adults experience greater difficulty switching than their older peers. Switching, therefore, is going to lead to increased mental effort because the learner must disengage from the previous task and activate the rules and goals of the new task. Reconfiguring attentional focus increases cognitive load because task switching requires holding information about both the previous and new tasks in working memory.

While switching costs decrease with age, mixing costs increase. This means that as we age, we become less efficient at maintaining multiple tasks in mind. While younger people may see increased cognitive load during switching tasks, older people will see increased cognitive load from mixing costs. However, as we saw earlier, multitasking is always going to increase load, negatively impacting all tasks. We really want to avoid multitasking unless we are engaging in skills that have become automatic.

Reducing task switching

Because switching costs are higher in younger learners, teachers might want to manage the resulting increased cognitive load. This can be accomplished within a CLT paradigm by adhering to the strategies discussed previously. But there are also methods teachers can utilise that aren't directly attributed to CLT. Perhaps the most straightforward method would be to minimise unnecessary task switching. Abrupt changes from one task to another can add to load because learners must switch quickly from one set of rules to another. This is particularly relevant in situations where learners are moving from one subject to another in short succession. A seven-year-old, for example, is going to find it difficult to move from a reading or writing task directly to a mathematical task. Leaving short intervals between tasks or matching similar tasks together could help to reduce the costs of switching.

Teachers can also provide clear and predictable routines. When transitions from one task to another are well-structured and expected, students experience lower cognitive load associated with task switching (see Smith, 2020, for a comprehensive discussion on routines and goal pursuit). If learners know a transition is approaching, this can help to reduce the demand placed on attentional resources. This can be accomplished using cues and signals in preparation for the switch. With older learners, the physical change from one lesson to another (changing classrooms, teachers, and sometimes peers) can be enough to accommodate the switch.

Finally, consistent task structures can help with switching costs. When a task is presented with a familiar format, students don't need to learn a new format or new rules associated with the task. If, for example, a teacher uses the same task structures for all lessons, these structures provide a blueprint that learners automatically activate when presented with the task. Learners won't have to think about what they are meant to do or how they are expected to accomplish a task, reserving cognitive resources for the task itself. One potential way to accomplish this is through carefully scripted lesson planning.

Inhibitory control

Inhibitory control refers to the ability to stop a thought, behaviour, or action when an alternative response, or no response, is needed for optimal outcome (Holmboe et al., 2021). The research literature often divides inhibitory control into motor inhibition, interference inhibition, and cognitive inhibition. Motor inhibition is our ability to inhibit some kind of pre-planned motor response. If we're driving and we think the light ahead is about to turn red, we might instinctively speed up. We might, however, think to ourselves, *that's really not a great idea because knowing my luck I won't make it and that camera on top of the pole will catch me.* In such a scenario, we inhibit our original response (pedal to the metal), take our foot off the accelerator, and apply the brake – we initially intended to speed up, but we inhibited that initial response and slowed down.

Interference inhibition is perhaps the type of inhibitory control most common to formal learning environments, as well as our day-to-day lives. It represents our capacity to ignore distractions and focus on the task at hand. Classrooms, however well controlled, can be filled with distractions. A learner, for example, might find it hard to focus on a task because other learners are talking or other forms of low-level disruption. But such distraction can be external and internal, so attempting to quieten our inevitable internal dialogue also requires a level of attentional control. Consequently, learners with a higher capacity for interference inhibition can focus more on their learning despite external distractions. On the flip side, those with less effective inhibitory control will become more distracted, even by low-level disruption.

Our third category, cognitive inhibition, refers to the ability to resist proactive interference. Higher levels of cognitive inhibition support flexible thinking because it allows us to pause, think, and adapt. Say a student comes up with an idea for a project. They conduct some preliminary research only to discover that the evidence cannot support their initial hypothesis. What our student needs to do is reject their original assumption and adapt the project to consider fresh evidence. In the language of cognitive psychology, they are required to update their schema with the new information before continuing. This is a more cognitively demanding task than one might initially think. Often, even when presented with evidence that goes against our pre-held beliefs, we continue to reject it. Just try to change the mind of someone who believes the Earth is flat, and you'll immediately understand how hard it can be. For example, a 2014 study found that providing facts to people who believed vaccines to be unsafe actually reduced their uptake (Nyhan, 2021). Changing our mind about some deep-seated beliefs requires effort, especially when the evidence overwhelmingly goes against what we believe to be true.

As you might expect, inhibitory control improves gradually during childhood. Younger children are more easily distracted, impulsive, and less able to focus their attention for long periods than their older peers. However, there is also a decline in inhibitory control after around our mid-thirties.

But how does inhibitory control impact that most crucial aspect of learning – working memory? From a CLT perspective, cognitive inhibition is a moderator of cognitive load. Learners with better inhibitory function are going to experience less mental effort when carrying out a task, and less mental effort equates to lower cognitive load. However, we'd also expect that those who are less able to inhibit distractions are going to report higher levels of mental effort. In studies, this is exactly what we find. These results are also consistent across different teachers, so it appears to be a generalised effect of inhibition on cognitive load (Yeigh, 2014).

We can also examine the role of cognitive inhibition through the lens of attentional control theory (ACT), a model we last met when discussing maths anxiety. CLT and ACT are complementary theories, seeing as they both deal with ways to manage mental resources. While the former emphasises the role of working memory limitations during instruction and learning, ACT focuses on how anxiety and other emotional states affect attentional control (or the function of the central executive, in Baddeley and Hitch's model of working memory), and how this then influences cognitive processes and load. You'll recall that in the ACT model, attention is regulated by both goal-directed (top-down) and stimulus-directed (bottom-up) systems. Anxiety then modulates the balance between these two systems. Inhibition is a function of the central executive, which helps to minimise interference (or distraction) from anything that isn't directly related to the task. An imbalance between goal-directed and stimulus-directed systems is likely to result in deficits in performance.

ACT can provide an adjunct to CLT by addressing both the instructional impact of cognitive load on working memory and how anxiety and emotions impact the balance between different attentional systems. If we take, as an example, a learner tackling a maths problem from a CLT perspective, the teacher is concerned about how the problem is presented to the learner. If the task instructions are unclear or contain lots of irrelevant information, this will place pressure on extraneous load and hinder learning because the learner will need to inhibit distractions (including irrelevant information) and attempt to make sense of over-complicated instructions. The learner will be better able to manage cognitive load if the teacher simplifies the task goals and instructions, as well as breaks the problem down and makes explicit connections to prior learning. These steps should result in more efficient consolidation into pre-stored schematic networks.

Levels of trait anxiety will impact how the same learner copes with the task. Higher trait anxiety will create difficulties in blocking out distractions (this is the stimulus-driven system coming into play). This then leads to difficulties focusing on completion of the maths problem (the goal-directed system). The imbalance between the two systems reduces efficiency, slowing completion time, but not necessarily leading to reduced accuracy.

Metacognition: learning how to learn

At the start of this chapter, I noted that older learners benefit from increased metacognitive skills, including self-regulation and the ability to set and pursue specific learning related goals. Metacognition doesn't always get the attention it deserves, perhaps because, as American developmental psychologist John Flavell puts it, it's *a fuzzy concept of multifarious definitions* (Flavell, 1979). You might be unfamiliar with the term but aware of the concept. Perhaps you call it self-regulated learning, thinking skills, or learning to learn? This fuzziness is perhaps why metacognition hasn't taken hold in the same way as other concepts like CLT. Or perhaps it's seen as a little too 'faddy', useful only to occupy teachers for a few hours on a training day?

Flavell offers a definition that attempts to circumvent this fuzziness, describing it as a regulatory system involving knowledge, experiences, goals, and strategies. Some definitions seem a little more clinical, such as a second- or higher-order thinking process which involves active control over cognitive processes (Mevarech & Kramarski, 2014, p.36). Others are much simpler: Our ability to know what we know and know what we don't know (Costa and Kallick, 2009). You can probably see why Flavell considered it fuzzy.

Perhaps not surprisingly, I'm going to adopt the definition offered in Psychology in the Classroom as: any type of thinking about thinking… including, thinking about our own memory abilities, or about the process we use when solving a problem, or about our own planning and organisational skills (Smith & Firth, 2018, p.58). This is a much broader definition than some others but allows us to fully grasp how metacognition encompasses both thinking about the task in hand, (including, knowledge, ability, resources, and cognitive, affective, and physiological state) and metacognitive regulation and awareness (such as monitoring, planning, regulating to optimise performance during the task, and evaluating and reflecting on the cognitive process after the performance).

Metacognition is perhaps one of the most underrated skills in learning, and one of its strengths is that it can be taught. It also does what it claims to do and much more besides. In studies, metacognition has been found to be a powerful predictor of academic performance, but for it to be useful, learners must first understand how to use it effectively. It improves consistently in the early years and becomes more explicit and effective with age. For example, a three-year-old becomes more aware of their own knowledge states when they start using verbs like *to think* or *to know*. Furthermore, a six-year-old can already reflect with some accuracy on their own thinking (Schraw & Moshman, 1995). The older children are, the more accurately they can predict their future performance. This early metacognitive development is thought to serve as a basis for higher-order thinking processes that mature later, resulting in individuals becoming gradually more aware of their own knowledge and increasingly better at selecting the more efficient strategy for the task at hand.

As you can see, metacognition isn't domain-specific, so it can add value across the curriculum and improve outcomes in various subjects. That said, it's particularly beneficial in mathematics (Dignath et al., 2008). Furthermore, we can see the benefits throughout the academic lifespan, from primary school to university.

Knowledge can be metacognitive too, depending on how we use it. If I have an understanding about how memory works and its relationship to learning, I can use the knowledge to make my learning more effective and efficient. However, I can also use my understanding of planning, goal setting, procrastination, and motivation to ensure I remain on the right track. This would involve an awareness of how humans learn, the processes involved, and how and why these processes might derail learning. One of the more interesting outcomes of metacognition is its ability to correct misleading information. It's surprisingly easy for us to assimilate false information into current schemas, and this is even more relevant today with the increase in so-called fake news. A study from 2020 found that introducing metacognitive reflection into a reading task reduced the number of judgement errors (Salovich & Rapp, 2020).

Bailey, Dunlosky, and Hertzos investigated the use of a metacognitive training package for use at home. They looked at older adults (between 60 and 89 years) and tailored their training to focus on age-related cognitive decline. Often, such interventions involve mnemonic training, which has been found to be beneficial for older adults. However, this study used an intervention developed by John Dunlosky and his colleagues that included two interrelated self-regulation strategies: self-testing and study time allocation. They found the take-home manual benefited participants regardless of whether they had used the strategies in the past (Bailey et al., 2010).

But how might we apply metacognitive strategies? There are many techniques from which we can choose, although the most effective tend to involve planning, evaluation, and monitoring. These would include techniques centred on behaviour management and behaviour change, such as goal setting, habit formation, self-reflectiveness, and nurturing academic-specific resilience, or academic buoyancy

(Smith, 2020). But it's not only about implementing these changes; it's also about understanding why they improve learning outcomes. For example, understanding why distributed practice, interleaving, and retrieval strategies work better than the alternatives enhances our metacognitive awareness by increasing our general knowledge about learning. We can then choose strategies most likely to improve learning outcomes.

Motivation

For people to learn, they first require the drive to do so. This is certainly more so in formal or quasi-formal settings. Motivation obviously shifts depending on the purpose of the task, so an infant's desire to speak is both driven by evolution and the need to communicate. Others might be driven to learn a new language out of necessity (moving to a different country where their native language isn't the norm), a desire to communicate with the locals when on holiday, or just as a way of stretching ourselves and our language skills. In formal educational settings, motivation is often external (or extrinsic) in that students are compelled to learn rather than choose to do so. Motivation has been a topic of interest to psychology since at least the days of behaviourism, and there have been many theories developed to explain why some people are driven to achieve their goals while others are less so. We might grumble at the lack of drive in the younger generation (a gripe that dates back to at least Plato's days), yet we remain fully aware that young people are motivated to pursue personal interests, often to the point of obsession. But are older learners more motivated than younger ones?

Many older learners may well be motivated differently, for example, because they have a personal desire to know more about a certain topic (intrinsic motivation) rather than through external rewards or the need to avoid sanctions (extrinsic motivation). Some years ago, I designed and delivered an introductory psychology course for adult learners under the umbrella of *learning for pleasure*, for which participants were charged a small fee. They would arrive at 6.30 each evening and remain engaged and attentive until 9 (with a short half-time break). Their reasons for being there were varied, but they attended because they wanted to, not because they were compelled to. We might explain this behaviour in terms of extrinsic versus intrinsic motivations (the difference between being compelled to do something and wanting to do something). However, the adult learners in my class might also have wider goals in mind.

Motivation is the process that initiates, guides, and maintains goal-orientated behaviours (Smith, 2017, p.96). Learning represents the pursuit of a goal, and our internal states and desires drive us towards those goals. Such goals vary, so we might be motivated to achieve something (such as learning Spanish for our upcoming trip to Barcelona), to prevent something (revising for an exam to prevent failure), or to make something happen in the present (take a painkiller to stop a headache). Whatever the need, the process usually comprises three characteristics: activation, persistence, and intensity. Activation is the initial trigger of a specific behaviour – if we feel hungry, we might seek food. Persistence is our continued effort, or how long we're prepared to stick to pursuing our goal. We might call this resilience, mental toughness, or grit, but they all amount to the same process. Finally, intensity refers to the strength of our response to the activity. There are many theories and models of motivation, some that emphasise internal and external reward mechanisms, and others that take goal pursuit as the primary drive. There may well be other factors at play, such as personality.

Self-determination theory

Edward Deci and Richard Ryan view motivation in terms of different types, stressing the importance of intrinsic motivators over extrinsic ones. They suggest that people have three basic psychological needs: the need for competence, the need for relatedness, and the need for autonomy.

The need for competence refers to our desire to control our immediate environment and outcomes. People want to know how things are going to turn out, and they want to know the results or consequences of their actions. The need for relatedness is our desire to interact with, be connected to, and experience caring for other people. The need for autonomy is the urge to be a causal agent and have a choice over what we do. If autonomous motivation concerns choice, then controlled motivation relates to the lack of choice. Ryan and Deci describe it as behaving with the experience of pressure or demand towards specific outcomes that come from forces perceived to be external to the self. Autonomy, however, doesn't mean acting independently; it merely means acting with choice, so it can mean acting alone but also acting interdependently with others. The fundamental premise of Ryan and Deci's theory involves the role of these self-determining factors, hence, *self-determination theory* or SDT (Ryan & Deci, 2000).

SDT is a theory of human motivation, emotion, and development concerned with factors related to growth-orientated processes in people. The theory's primary concern is with the factors that promote or prevent people from intrinsically engaging in positive behaviours. To be intrinsically engaged, we need to feel that our actions are based on choice and free will, even if such feelings are illusionary. People's motivation can be affected in many ways, and we all often feel unmotivated towards tasks we view as less rewarding. Motivation ebbs and flows but is often at its highest point when we feel the activity we are engaged in is being done because we want to do it, rather than us being told to, or coerced into doing it.

According to SDT, the more controlled the learning environment, the less likely learners are to employ intrinsic forms of motivation. This doesn't mean that extrinsic reward systems don't work, just that the interpersonal learning context needs to remain informational and supportive, rather than critical and authoritarian. Learning environments that encourage autonomy have been found to result in greater learning and performance outcomes than controlling styles. In addition, feedback given in a controlling context can reduce intrinsic motivation (Smith, 2017).

Autonomy-supportive learning environments, therefore, might help support activating emotions (referred to in the previous chapter), such as interest and curiosity, as well as foster feelings of value (both personal and value of the task), persistence, and academic buoyancy (Smith, 2020). These factors relate to learners' feelings of control (or perceived locus of causality). In other words, the more a learner feels in control of their learning, the better they cope with the demands of the task and any setbacks that might arise. This then impacts other factors such as cognitive load, as we'll see later.

Achievement goal theory

The goals we set ourselves influence our subsequent behaviour, not a revelatory notion in itself, but one that binds future aspirations to the present. The main premise of achievement control theory is that our goals influence our behaviour within achievement settings, including school, colleges, and universities. Goals represent our future intentions or valued outcomes; they are something we want to achieve. Edwin Locke suggests that for us to achieve our goal, we must: be committed to the goal, have the requisite ability to attain it (if we do not, then our first goal should be to acquire this ability), and be free from conflicting goals (Smith, 2020). There's a link here to both prior knowledge and metacognition, as goal pursuit involves planning (a metacognitive strategy) and the knowledge of what we already have. If we lack the knowledge and understanding to achieve our goal, the first thing we need to do is gain it – we need to know what we know and what we don't.

Hulleman defines achievement goals as cognitive representations of desired outcomes that direct behaviour in different ways based on how an individual conceptualises competence (Hulleman et al., 2016). Competence, therefore, plays a central role in motivation because how competent we feel about reaching our goals, or how confident we are in our ability to do something effectively, sufficiently, or successfully, is going to influence how we approach a task. There's a connection to self-efficacy here: how confident we are in our ability to successfully complete a task. But how we attribute the causes of our perceived competence is also going to play a significant role. Do we, for example, believe that outcomes rest on something internal (such as intelligence) or external (hard work and resilience)? Overconfidence can lead to the illusion of knowledge, often leading to unrecognised incompetence, the so-called Dunning-Kruger effect (Kruger & Dunning, 2009).

According to the dichotomous model, one of several models within achievement goal theory, we can divide goals into two kinds: mastery and performance goals. The primary aim of mastery goals is to develop and increase competence or develop skills. Conversely, performance goals motivate us to demonstrate our competence relative to others (Smith, 2017). Mastery goals tend to be more beneficial than performance goals, as striving for competence and skills leads to deeper learning than wanting to do better than peers. A learner concerned with demonstrating their performance relative to others is more likely to choose easier tasks requiring less mental effort, and less mental effort is associated with shallower learning.

The trichotomous model takes this premise a little further. Andrew Elliot proposes further distinctions, differentiating between performance approach, performance avoidance and mastery goal orientations (Elliot & McGregor, 1999). A performance approach goal orientation is the attempt by the individual to demonstrate competence, while a performance avoidant orientation is the attempt to avoid being seen as incompetent. These goal orientations change the way learners view achievement situations. Learners who adopt a performance goal orientation avoid challenging tasks as a way of demonstrating competence (the chances of looking competent while engaging in an easy task are much higher than in a more difficult one). Performance avoiders, however, are much more likely to withdraw from the entire learning process. It has also been linked to other outcomes, including shallow processing, poor retention of information, and a decrease in overall performance (Smith, 2017, p.39).

These attitudes, or attributions, to learning fuel motivation. They also feed into our implicit theories of learning. Carol Dweck, for example, suggests that those who attribute success to internal, fixed qualities (such as the view that intelligence cannot be improved) become less motivated and are more likely to develop a performance goal orientation, while learners who consider intelligence to be more malleable develop a mastery goal orientation. Dweck popularised this notion in her theory of growth and fixed mindsets (Dweck, 2000).

The need for cognition

Need for cognition (NFC) is less of a motivational strategy and more of a motivational trait. In other words, it's an internal state that drives us towards a desire to think hard. Let me ask you a question: Would you rather take a test or receive a mild electric shock? The question might seem somewhat baffling. After all, who would choose to get electrocuted? Then again, think about the things you might put off that are mentally challenging and the methods you choose to avoid doing them. We often use terms associated with physical pain when we've completed or are engaging in a task that requires the expenditure of cognitive effort, so we might say, *I've done so much studying today my brain hurts*. We have a tendency to avoid mental effort, which means we face a major challenge when it comes to learning something new that's going to test our mental capacity. This isn't just about motivation and procrastination; it really does seem like the task is going to cause us pain, so much so that we might prefer physical pain. In one study, for example, Todd Vogel and his co-researchers discovered that participants were more likely to choose to have a scalding hot object placed on their skin than complete a memory task (Vogel et al., 2020). In another study, researchers found people would much rather subject themselves to an electric shock than to be left alone in a room with nothing but their own thoughts (Wilson et al., 2014). Is thinking so aversive that we would choose pain instead? It's an interesting proposition, but one that both tallies with our experiences while leaving a great deal of room for manoeuvre. Many people enjoy crosswords and puzzles that require a great deal of mental effort, even though how individuals measure their own levels of effort differs. Similarly, many of us enjoy learning new things and deliberately place ourselves in a position where our intellect will be tested. Memory tests are quite boring, as is sitting alone in a room with little to do, so perhaps it's the boring tasks that cause us the most pain? I must admit that sitting down and tackling German grammar isn't always an exciting activity, but I'm not sure I'd choose pain as a suitable replacement.

We can observe this behaviour in classrooms too. Some students appear to experience a certain joy from engaging in mentally taxing tasks, while others will either try their hardest to avoid any kind of mental effort or, when given a choice, opt for the simpler of the tasks offered. The tendency to take on hard tasks represents a person's *need for cognition*. NFC is defined as the tendency to engage in and enjoy effortful thinking (Bruinsma & Crutzen, 2018). Someone high in NFC possesses the tendency to engage in and enjoy activities that require thinking and reflecting. Such individuals can actively mobilise cognitive resources and employ them effectively. This means they also have a preference and tolerance for tasks with a higher cognitive load. Those low in NFC are more likely to enjoy tasks that are simpler and thus require less mental effort and, therefore, lower cognitive load.

Traits are relatively stable over the lifespan, and this is also the case for NFC. It does, however, increase over time in line with the development of cognitive capacities, including working memory, and peaks in our late teens and early 20s. There's a slight decline between around 25 and 50, after which the decline accelerates slightly. This later downturn is most likely the result of declines in working memory and other cognitive resources, as well as a reduction in motivation to engage in effortful cognitive tasks. But we also know that people become less cognitively flexible, or stuck in their ways, so are more likely to engage in tasks based on what's worked in the past rather than actively seeking new strategies. This implies that people high in NFC are also better at employing metacognitive strategies.

Motivation and cognitive load

I've hinted above that motivation may be a determining factor in the management of cognitive load. For example, those high in NFC can cope better with higher load than those who are lower in NFC. The same appears to be the case with other aspects of motivation. For example, cognitive load can be viewed as a motivational cost (Feldon et al., 2019). People who exhibit a growth mindset report lower cognitive load (Xu et al., 2021), and instructional strategies that focus on increased autonomy-support lead to more manageable levels of cognitive load (Evans et al., 2024).

David Feldon and colleagues examined the relationship between cognitive load and motivation through the lens of expectance-value-cost theory (EVCT). When we face the prospect of a new task, we tend to make a decision about taking on the task based on its costs versus its benefits. If the costs are too high, we are less likely to try. But there's more to it than a simple cost-benefit analysis. When we approach a task, we often think to ourselves, *how likely am I succeed in this task?* The more confident we are (or the higher our self-efficacy), the higher our motivation to engage. This is the expectancy portion of EVCT. We might then consider the value of the task. *Is it worth doing in the first place? Does it add value to my learning and understanding?* Finally, we consider the cost involved – *is it going to make my brain hurt? Am I likely to fail at the task and then deal with the shame and guilt of having failed?* Our aim is, therefore, to lower the cost – the higher the cost, the higher the mental effort required and, thus, the higher the perceived cognitive load. Feldon suggests educators can help lower the cost through the deployment of learning strategies related to cognitive load theory, such as prior-knowledge and clear instructions, but also making the task relevant to the learner by emphasising the task's value and why it's necessary within a wider context (Feldon et al., 2019). This might be communicated in very simple terms (it'll be on the exam), or regarding later learning (knowing this now will help you complete more advanced tasks later).

There's also some evidence that a growth mindset results in a more manageable cognitive load. Kate Xu and colleagues (including John Sweller) found that those participants categorised as having a growth mindset reported lower perceived intrinsic and extraneous cognitive load than those with a fixed mindset (Xu et al., 2021). In addition, those with some prior knowledge of the to-be-learned topic reported higher mastery-goal orientation. The mechanisms linking growth mindset and cognitive load are quite speculative, however. If we believe that intelligence is malleable rather than a fixed entity, the likelihood is that we also subscribe to the view that we can improve with effort. Success, therefore, becomes a manifestation of attribution style (*I succeeded because I tried very hard*) rather than because *I'm just really intelligent*. If failure is also about poor strategising, success is related to employing the right strategies when they are needed (metacognition). This then leads to increased motivation, reduced frustration, and improved learning.

What about the role of intrinsic and extrinsic motivation on cognitive load? You might think the two are unconnected. Paul Evans, yet another researcher at the University of New South Wales, found that motivation can also be an outcome of strategies used to lower or manage cognitive load (Evans et al., 2024). Evans investigated a framework devised by Andrew Martin called *load reduction instruction* (discussed in the following chapter) and found that extraneous cognitive load can negatively affect motivational processes. This seems logical, particularly through the lens of SDT. If cognitive load is too high, we are much more likely to give up and assume we can't complete the task successfully. But if cognitive load can be managed effectively, we are much more likely to press on. Teaching that helps to regulate cognitive load, therefore, increases learners' feelings of competency and self-efficacy. Similarly, teaching styles that focus on autonomy support are associated with reduced intrinsic and extraneous cognitive load, leading to increased motivation and engagement. On the flip side, controlling or chaotic teaching styles can increase cognitive load. This is most likely because autonomy support directs learners' attention towards the learning activity.

Chapter summary

- Learning is a continuous process throughout life, extending beyond childhood and adolescence and is influenced by a variety of factors beyond just cognition.
- Executive functions are critical for successful learning. These functions include working memory, cognitive flexibility (the ability to switch and mix tasks), and inhibitory control (the ability to stop thoughts, behaviours, or actions when needed).
- Metacognition, defined as thinking about one's own thinking, is a powerful and teachable skill that enhances learning. It involves awareness of one's knowledge and the ability to regulate cognitive processes through planning, monitoring, and evaluating learning.
- Motivation is essential for initiating, guiding, and maintaining goal-oriented learning behaviours. Theories such as SDT, which highlight the needs for competence, relatedness, and autonomy, and achievement goal theory, focusing on mastery and performance goals, provide frameworks for understanding what drives learners.
- Motivation and cognitive load are interconnected. Learners with a higher NFC can cope better with higher cognitive load.
- Factors like autonomy-supportive learning environments can lead to more manageable levels of cognitive load and increased motivation. Educators can lower the perceived cost of learning by making tasks relevant, providing clear instructions, and building on prior knowledge.

Further reading

Firth, J. (2025). *Metacognition and study skills*. David Fulton.
Martin, A. (2010). *Building classroom success*. Continuum.
Smith, M. (2020). *Becoming buoyant: Helping teachers and students cope with the day to day*. Routledge.

References

Alloway, T. P., & Alloway, R. (2008). Working memory: Is it the new IQ? *Nature Precedings*. https://doi.org/10.1038/npre.2008.2343.1
Alloway, T. P., & Alloway, R. (2010). It is better than you think: Fluid intelligence across the lifespan. *Nature Precedings*. https://doi.org/10.1038/npre.2010.4655.1

Alloway, T. P., & Alloway, R. G. (2013). Working memory across the lifespan: A cross-sectional approach. *Journal of Cognitive Psychology, 25*(1), 84–93. https://doi.org/10.1080/20445911.2012.748027

Bailey, H., Dunlosky, J., & Hertzog, C. (2010). Metacognitive training at home: Does it improve older adults' learning? *Gerontology, 56*(4), 414–420. https://doi.org/10.1159/000266030

Bruinsma, J., & Crutzen, R. (2018). A longitudinal study on the stability of the need for cognition. *Personality and Individual Differences, 127*, 151–161. https://doi.org/10.1016/j.paid.2018.02.001

Colé, P., Duncan, L. G., & Blaye, A. (2014). Cognitive flexibility predicts early reading skills. *Frontiers in Psychology, 5*. https://doi.org/10.3389/fpsyg.2014.00565

Costa, A. L., & Kallick, B. eds. (2009). Assessing habits of mind. In *Learning and leading with habits of mind* (Vol. 16, pp. 190–220). Association for Supervision and Curriculum Development.

Dajani, D. R., & Uddin, L. Q. (2015). Demystifying cognitive flexibility: Implications for clinical and developmental neuroscience. In *Trends in neurosciences* (Vol. 38, Issue 9, pp. 571–578). Elsevier Ltd. https://doi.org/10.1016/j.tins.2015.07.003

Dignath, C., Buettner, G., & Langfeldt, H.-P. (2008). How can primary school students learn self-regulated learning strategies most effectively? *Educational Research Review, 3*(2), 101–129. https://doi.org/10.1016/j.edurev.2008.02.003

Dweck, C. S. (2000). Self-theories: Their role in motivation, personality, and development. In *Essays in social psychology*. Psychology Press. https://www.amazon.de/dp/1841690244

Elliot, A. J., & McGregor, H. A. (1999). Test anxiety and the hierarchical model of approach and avoidance achievement motivation. *Journal of Personality and Social Psychology, 76*(4), 628–644. https://doi.org/10.1037/0022-3514.76.4.628

Evans, P., Vansteenkiste, M., Parker, P., Kingsford-Smith, A., & Zhou, S. (2024). Cognitive load theory and its relationships with motivation: A self-determination theory perspective. *Educational Psychology Review, 36*(1). https://doi.org/10.1007/s10648-023-09841-2

Feldon, D. F., Callan, G., Juth, S., & Jeong, S. (2019). Cognitive load as motivational cost. *Educational Psychology Review, 31*(2), 319–337). https://doi.org/10.1007/s10648-019-09464-6

Flavell, J. H. (1979). Metacognition and cognitive monitoring: A new area of cognitive–developmental inquiry. *American Psychologist, 34*(10), 906–911. https://doi.org/10.1037/0003-066X.34.10.906

Holmboe, K., Larkman, C., de Klerk, C., Simpson, A., Bell, M. A., Patton, L., Christodoulou, C., & Dvergsdal, H. (2021, 12 December). The early childhood inhibitory touchscreen task: A new measure of response inhibition in toddlerhood and across the lifespan. *PLoS One, 16*. https://doi.org/10.1371/journal.pone.0260695

Hulleman, C. S., Barron, K. E., Kosovich, J. J., & Lazowski, R. A. (2016). Expectancy-value models of achievement motivation in education. In Lipnevich, A. A., Prekel, F., & Roberts, R. D. (Eds) *Psychosocial skills and school systems in the twenty-first century: Theory, research, and applications* (April 2018, pp. 241–278). Springer https://doi.org/10.1007/978-3-319-28606-8

Karakuş, i. (2024). University students' cognitive flexibility and critical thinking dispositions. *Frontiers in Psychology, 15*, 1420272. https://doi.org/10.3389/fpsyg.2024.1420272

Kruger, J., & Dunning, D. (2009). Unskilled and unaware of it: How difficulties in recognizing one's own incompetence lead to inflated. *Journal of Personnality and Social Psychology, 77*(6), 1121–1134.

Logie, R. H. (2016). Retiring the central executive. *Quarterly Journal of Experimental Psychology, 69*(10), 2093–2109. https://doi.org/10.1080/17470218.2015.1136657

Mevarech, Z., & Kramarski, B. (2014). *Critical maths for innovative societies.* OECD. https://doi.org/10.1787/9789264223561-en

Nyhan, B. (2021). Why the backfire effect does not explain the durability of political misperceptions. *Proceedings of the National Academy of Sciences of the United States of America, 118*(15). https://doi.org/10.1073/pnas.1912440117

Roberson, D. N., & Merriam, S. B. (2005). The self-directed learning process of older, rural adults. *Adult Education Quarterly, 55*(4), 269–287. https://doi.org/10.1177/0741713605277372

Ryan, R., & Deci, E. (2000). Intrinsic and extrinsic motivations: Classic definitions and new directions. *Contemporary Educational Psychology, 25*(1), 54–67. https://doi.org/10.1006/ceps.1999.1020

Salovich, N. A., & Rapp, D. N. (2020). Misinformed and unaware? Metacognition and the influence of inaccurate information. *Journal of Experimental Psychology: Learning Memory and Cognition, 47*(4), 608–624 https://doi.org/10.1037/xlm0000977

Schraw, G., & Moshman, D. (1995). Metacognitive theories. *Educational Psychology Review, 7*(4), 351–371. https://doi.org/10.1007/BF02212307

Smith, M. (2017). *The emotional learner: Understanding emotions, learners and achievement.* Routledge.

Smith, M. (2020). *Becoming buoyant: Helping teachers and students cope with the day to day.* Routledge.

Smith, M., & Firth, J. (2018). *Psychology in the classroom* (First edition). Routledge.

Vogel, T., Savelson, Z., Otto, A. R., & Roy, M. (2020). Forced choices reveal a trade-off between cognitive effort and physical pain. *ELife*, Nov, 17, 1–18. https://doi.org/10.7554/eLife.59410

Wilson, T. D., Reinhard, D. A., Westgate, E. C., Gilbert, D. T., Ellerbeck, N., Hahn, C., Brown, C. L., & Shaked, A. (2014). Just think: The challenges of the disengaged mind. *Science, 345*(6192), 75–77. https://doi.org/10.1126/science.1250830

Xu, K. M., Koorn, P., de Koning, B., Skuballa, I. T., Lin, L., Henderikx, M., Marsh, H. W., Sweller, J., & Paas, F. (2021). A growth mindset lowers perceived cognitive load and improves learning: Integrating motivation to cognitive load. *Journal of Educational Psychology, 113*(6), 1177–1191. https://doi.org/10.1037/edu0000631

Yeigh, T. (2014). Cognitive inhibition and cognitive load: A moderation hypothesis. *International Journal for Cross-Disciplinary Subjects in Education, 5*(3), 1744–1752. https://doi.org/10.20533/ijcdse.2042.6364.2014.0243

Yeniad, N., Malda, M., Mesman, J., Van Ijzendoorn, M. H., & Pieper, S. (2013). Shifting ability predicts math and reading performance in children: A meta-analytical study. *Learning and Individual Differences, 23*(1), 1–9. https://doi.org/10.1016/j.lindif.2012.10.004

13 Designs for learning

In the preceding chapters, I have presented a cognitive view of learning, drawing heavily on what we currently understand about how the brain registers, stores, and recalls information. Learning is viewed as a dynamic process where learners actively construct knowledge rather than passively ensuring that information remains in long-term memory. While learning represents a change in long-term memory, that change is multifaceted and involves a variety of mechanisms. Learning is as much constructivist as it is cognitive. Remembering is an act of reconstruction.

From this evidence, it's possible to highlight those methods that are most likely to work for most people. But learning isn't as homogenous as we might think, and hopefully I've also emphasised differences between learners. For example, working memory capacity, attention, motivation, and emotional regulation are just a few aspects that differ. All these will impact how individuals approach a learning task and how successful they are at completing it. Knowing how learning happens can help us design environments that potentially benefit all learners, just as long as we remain mindful that they will bring different traits, skills, and strengths to the table.

The limited impact of learning science

The question about how people learn and how they might learn more effectively has a long and successful history. Yet despite the evidence, educators often promote less effective methods while learners use techniques that are far from optimal. In 2013, a team of researchers (including John Dunlosky and Daniel Willingham) published the results of an investigation into the efficacy of a range of study techniques and whether students were making the most of those found to work. Most students were choosing suboptimal methods of study. For example, studies have confirmed that strategies such as highlighting, underlining, and re-reading are ineffective, yet they were the preferred method for most learners. The most effective (such as retrieval practice, elaborative interrogation, and distributed learning) were the most effective, but the least used (Dunlosky et al., 2013).

Was this a case of students not knowing the best techniques or educators promoting inefficient methods? Fast-forward a couple of years, and a paper by Kayla Morehead, a psychologist from Kent State University, found that teachers and lecturers were endorsing both effective strategies (such as practice testing) and so-called learning myths (including learning styles). The implication here is that even educators aren't always aware of what works and what doesn't. Neither do many appear informed about which are learning myths, and which are evidence-backed strategies (Morehead et al., 2015).

It turns out that even when students know which strategies are the most effective, they don't always use them. A study conducted by Rachael Blasiman in 2017 discovered that students who said they planned to use certain strategies over the coming months rarely did. Even when they said they were going to self-test, for example, in the end, they reverted to the less effective strategies, including rereading and highlighting (Blasiman et al., 2017). Such learning strategies are passive, in that they do little to enhance the strength of the memory within the brain's cognitive architecture. They only provide us with the illusion of learning.

What are we then to take from these studies? Most of this research has involved undergraduate students (often psychology undergraduates), so it might be difficult to claim that such results could be replicated using different groups. Understanding how younger learners approach their learning may well be more useful, as it's likely that university students have inherited their study techniques from earlier educational experiences. To help correct this imbalance, researchers in the Netherlands investigated the study strategies used by 318 Dutch-speaking secondary school students and, just as importantly, they looked at the strategies these young learners used when studying alone beyond the influence of their teachers (Dirkx et al., 2019).

In their study, Kim Dirkx and her colleagues took Dunlosky's 2013 paper as the starting point for their investigation. However, rather than having students identify a pre-set list of strategies, Dirkx and her co-researchers didn't limit the number of strategies participants could say they used. They then categorised the strategies to see if they could place them into one of the groups from the Dunlosky study. They then further divided them into those the students used as the primary method and those they used less regularly.

The most used strategies were rereading and summarising, for both the primary method and the less regularly used. Very few students (0.3 percent) used highlighting as their primary method but over 25 percent said they used it. Practice testing was only used as the primary method by just over 8 percent of students, but this rose to slightly over 60 percent as a strategy used less often. Less than 1 percent of respondents used distributed and interleaved practice as their primary strategy, while in the less often used category, just under 4 percent of students used distributed practice while only 0.3 percent used interleaving. This is most likely because few teachers use interleaving and distributed practice, perhaps because it takes time to see results. In fact, both strategies might even appear to lead to less learning in the short-term, even though long-term gains are often higher.

In addition, students reported methods that didn't fit into these categories, including copying, thinking of real-life examples, cramming, and completing practice problems. Apart from this last technique, where just over 7 percent said this was a primary method and nearly half said they used it less often, there were a relatively small number who chose these other strategies.

You might think that over the years, teachers and students have become more skilled at promoting and using the techniques that work best, after all, studies into strategies such as spaced learning and retrieval practice span decades. Unfortunately, this doesn't appear to be the case. In a study published in 2025, Fatema Sultana and her colleagues investigated the learning strategies used by nearly 400 secondary school students across 29 UK schools (Sultana et al., 2025). They found that students mainly used less effective strategies, such as making notes, repeated reading, and highlighting. Higher utility strategies, including retrieval practice and spaced learning, were much less common. Many students saw retrieval practice as a way to assess their knowledge, rather than a learning method in its own right. Indeed, students didn't really understand what the best strategies were or how to use them. Many students were revising for tests the night before, minimising the possibility of them using spaced methods. Teachers tended to promote both higher and lower utility strategies. On a more positive note, many of the students in the study were eager to learn about more effective study methods.

Often, students aren't rejecting the best strategies – they simply don't know what the best strategies are. However, the illusion of learning might go some way to explaining why people reject strategies that work better. But there's probably more to it than that. Another possibility is cognitive bias, or errors in thinking. In this respect, the choice not to use the most effective strategy could be a form of status quo bias or comfort-driven inefficiency. People feel safer and more secure in familiar surroundings. They also cling to behaviours and habits for the same reason, even if these behaviours and habits are damaging to their goals (Smith, 2020).

What the science says: a brief recap

Learning is more than remembering facts. When we claim that learning is a change in long-term memory, we perhaps oversimplify a set of complex neurological and behavioural processes that do much more than store information. We combine new information with what we already know, contextualise it, alter it, strip it down to its bare bones so that we can use it in a multitude of ways. While the neurological system available to us is highly evolved and efficient, it's also operating with limited resources. Both our ability to attend and our ability to remember come with limitations of capacity and duration, so any attempt to learn more effectively must take these into consideration. Capacity limits are contained within what we call cognitive load, which is really just an overly technical way of saying that our brains (as sophisticated as they are) are limited in their ability to handle multiple inputs. We don't need science to tell us this, of course, because we all experience cognitive overload every day. What models of memory do, however, is provide a blueprint from which we can design environments that make effective learning more likely. There are also limits placed on our ability to attend to tasks, and we can't generally split our attention between different tasks unless some functions have developed a high degree of automaticity. Attention and working memory are closely linked, with Cowan viewing working memory as our focus of attention and having a capacity of around four pieces of information (or chunks).

What we also know from personal experience is that with practice, we can become better at doing something. When we start learning to drive a car, we are faced with multiple tasks, and our progress is slow. With practice, however, the task becomes easier because many of the skills required to drive reach a high level of automaticity. However, even experienced drivers must pay greater attention at times and will have to sharpen their focus to get safely around that multi-lane roundabout or remain mindful of pedestrians stepping into the road. When we start learning to drive, cognitive load is high. As we become more experienced and tasks become automatic, this load decreases.

This is also true for other types of learning. When our ability to write becomes automatic, we don't have to think as hard about how to form letters and words. Similarly, we automatically read items in our environments without consciously intending to, such as adverts, signage, and headlines on the front page of newspapers. We are accessing acquired skills and knowledge effortlessly, allowing us to use this information to inform new learning.

The view that learning can be viewed in terms of the resources available has been encapsulated within cognitive load theory (CLT). CLT provides a useful framework by which educators can design learning environments to help manage load. Models such as attentional control theory can help minimise the impact of deactivating emotional states that can increase mental effort beyond manageable limits.

We also know that learning is generative and that we need prior knowledge to help us effectively process incoming information. But we also know that prior knowledge can sometimes hinder new learning. Increasing cognitive effort is desirable, especially in the later stages of learning, as it can result in deeper processing and therefore a greater chance that new information will become a relatively permanent fixture of long-term memory (the general goal of learning). However, we also don't want to increase cognitive load too far, so we must implement strategies that optimise load without overloading. The emphasis isn't on eliminating load, but on managing it.

Levels of learning

In Chapter 1, I discussed the use of memorisation and linked it to the depth of processing. While memorisation is a useful and even vital learning strategy, it invariably results in shallow processing. If we divide different learning strategies into those resulting in shallow, intermediate, and deep processing, we can see how using multiple techniques ultimately produces more effective results.

Shallow learning involves a focus on how information looks or sounds and doesn't require integration into prior knowledge. It also doesn't involve critical thinking. An example of shallow learning would be rote memorisation. Intermediate learning involves recognising relationships and structures rather than simple surface features. It still lacks depth of understanding, but is useful as a bridge between, say, rote learning and more conceptual, meaningful cognitive engagement. Deep learning emphasises the why rather than the what, and involves analysis, evaluation, and synthesis. Deep learning fosters greater long-term retention and the ability to transfer knowledge to new situations (see Table 13.1).

When designing learning environments or advising learners on the most effective strategies, we need to take all these factors into consideration. Learning environments and models of instructional design should be guided by the following principles.

- Active processing and cognitive engagement.
- Building on prior knowledge.
- Checking understanding through regular feedback and error correction.
- Managing cognitive load (including emotion-related load).
- Guided independent practice.

While there are several models of instructional design that fulfil these requirements, I want to summarise three that have a strong evidence base: Generative learning theory (Fiorella & Mayer, 2015), Rosenshine's principles of instruction (Rosenshine, 2012), and load reduction instruction (LRI) (Martin, 2016). While I don't intend to discuss and evaluate these frameworks in detail, a brief overview is useful to place them within the topic of the previous chapters and situate them within the cognitive sciences and wider learning science paradigm. For a much deeper analysis of these principles, refer to the further reading section at the end of the chapter.

Generative learning

Fiorella and Mayer view learning as involving the active construction of meaning from new information via mentally reorganising it with existing knowledge. This active cognitive processing then results in the development of an understanding of new material that can be applied to new situations (transfer). I discussed the view that learning involves the active construction of meaning through schema construction in Chapter 6 and prior learning in Chapter 8. Meaningful learning involves the interaction of generation, motivation, and memory. Generation builds connections between distinct elements of to-be-learned material and between these new elements and prior knowledge, assimilating them into and updating stored schemas.

Table 13.1 Examples of shallow, intermediate, and deep learning methods

Depth	Example
Shallow	**Rote learning:** Based on repetition without understanding. Example, learning a list of vocabulary words or multiplication tables. **Auditory recognition:** Paying attention to the sound or pronunciation of a word. Example, learning a song or rhyme without understanding the meaning of the lyrics. Simple association. Linking items based on surface-level features rather than conceptual relationships. Example: associating two words because they look similar. **Passive reading/listening:** Reading or listening without actively engaging with the material or analysing its meaning. Example: Skimming a text or passively listening to a lecture.
Intermediate	**Pattern recognition:** Identifying relationships or sequences within the information. Example: Recognising spelling or phonetic patterns in language ('e' rules – Hat/Hate). Grouping similar items together (animals – mammals, reptiles, and amphibians). **Phonemic learning:** Processing sound structures of words beyond auditory recognition. Example: Learning through rhyme, alliteration, and syllable patterns. Decoding words when learning to read. **Basic categorisation:** Organising information into simple groups based on shared characteristics. Example: sorting vocabulary words into parts of speech (noun, verb, etc.). Grouping objects by colour, size, and shape in early education.
Deep	**Semantic understanding:** Focus placed on meaning. Example: explaining a concept in our own words, analysing themes and messages in literature. **Critical thinking:** Evaluating information, questioning assumption, and forming judgements. Example: analysing arguments in an essay. Comparing different theories to determine strengths and weaknesses. **Emotional engagement:** Using emotion to deepen connection or understanding. Example: Relating to characters in a story or historical figures to explore motivations. Exploring personal implications of philosophical or ethical questions.

Motivation refers to the learners' willingness to invest effort towards understanding the material (Chapter 11). Finally, memory is, as we've seen, the store of learners' prior knowledge and experience.

To support generative learning, Fiorella and Mayer propose that any new to-be-learned information should progress through three stages: selection, organisation, and integration (referred to as the SOI model). The first stage involves attention (Chapter 5), in which the learner selects the most relevant incoming sensory information for further processing in working memory. The learner then organises this selected information meaningfully. This sense-making takes place in working memory. Finally, the information links to prior learning via integration into long-term memory (schema formation). All learning methods and techniques, therefore, should include this process.

The aim of learning, therefore, is to ensure we can select the relevant information for processing, that we can organise this information effectively, and that we can integrate this new information with prior knowledge to generate deep understanding. To ensure this, Fiorella and Mayer propose the use of eight primary strategies: summarising, mapping, drawing, imagining, self-testing, self-explaining, teaching, and enacting, all of which adhere to the SOI framework.

Summarising

We can memorise a text and recite it verbatim, but this won't represent understanding (as discussed in Chapter 1). However, summarising the main points of a lesson in our own words requires deeper processing because we have to select the most salient points and organise these so that they make sense. Once we have accomplished this, we can integrate the information into our prior knowledge.

Mapping

By creating concept maps based on lesson content and linking key concepts together using lines and arrows, we can make further sense of the material. We can also create knowledge maps, a more sophisticated form of spatial diagram where links are confined to predetermined types, such as *this leads to..., this is part of....* Finally, we can use graphic organisers to categorise information more tightly. In these organisers, we might include a matrix that compares and contrasts information, cause-and-effect flowcharts, and hierarchies for classification.

Drawing

As discussed in Chapter 9, we can strengthen the access to a memory by exploiting different modalities, such as pairing written or verbal stimuli with images. This is perhaps the most common form of dual coding. Textbooks, PowerPoint presentations, and many other learning tools do this. It's fine for me to describe, say, a multi-component model of memory, but combining this with a diagram provides a visual representation that supports understanding and leads to a more resilient memory that's easier to recall. Indeed, when I mention the model, you might even see the diagram in your mind's eye before fully retrieving the concept from long-term memory. However, you'll recall from the previous discussion on CLT, that any diagram or illustration must accompany the written or verbal explanation – learners will need to see both at the same time, rather than, for example, placing the explanation on one page of a textbook and the illustration several pages ahead. This might seem obvious now that we understand how cognitive load operates, but we've all seen badly designed textbooks that don't take these concerns into account.

Imagining

Imagination, discussed in Chapter 10, allows the learner to mentally select the relevant information and organise it in working memory. This information is then integrated into long-term memory. However, we must remain mindful that people's ability to imagine isn't uniform, although it's likely that those less able to create images in their mind have developed successful compensatory tactics.

Self-testing

Self-testing (or retrieval practice) is, without doubt, the most useful and simple of strategies. It's also been found to be more effective than re-reading or re-studying material (Karpicke & Roediger, 2008), two techniques found to be most common among a range of learners. As in the study described above, learners are likely to view testing as a way to assess what they know, and less likely to understand it as a powerful learning strategy.

Learners can engage in retrieval practice in many ways, from answering practice questions to quizzing themselves on key aspects of a topic using, for example, flashcards.

Retrieval practice also meets the SOI requirements, in that learners select and recall the relevant information, organise it in working memory and then integrate it with prior knowledge. As we saw in Chapter 7, this process involves the reconsolidation of information and leads to stronger neural connections.

Self-explaining

Like summarising and self-testing, self-explaining requires learners to recall what they have learned, but this time explain the contents of the lesson to themselves during learning. Self-explaining is most effective when learners can select the most important information and restate it in their own words and generate inferences to organise the material.

Teaching

When learners teach others, it's important that they select the most relevant information, organise it coherently in ways others can understand, and provide enough elaboration so that the new information can be successfully integrated with prior learning and existing knowledge. Experienced and novice teachers alike understand the preparation that goes into teaching others. Many may have also discovered that preparing to teach a topic acts as a learning experience in itself.

Enacting

Engaging in task-relevant movements during learning, such as manipulating objects or performing gestures, activates embodied cognition and helps learners to connect abstract concepts to concrete actions (for example, trainee surgeons practising the movements involved in complex procedures). Enacting, according to Fiorella and Mayer, might be more effective when learners have greater prior knowledge.

Rosenshine's principles of instruction

Barak Rosenshine's principles of instruction attempt to take evidence from cognitive science and apply it to instructional design. Like generative learning theory, Rosenshine's principles promote active processing and engagement, aiming for meaningful learning over methods that result in shallow learning (such as rote memorisation). Similarly, what the learner already knows plays a vital function in strengthening connections and ensuring new information can be successfully integrated into schematic structures. Deeper learning is encouraged through elaboration, just like the strategies proposed by Fiorella and Mayer.

Begin lessons with a brief review of previous learning

Reviewing previous learning has several benefits. Daily reviews strengthen learning and encourage fluent recall while correcting any errors in understanding. Reviewing material also helps learners develop effortful recall needed to solve novel problems or understand new material. Remember that one goal of learning is to automate certain procedures so that less load is placed on mental resources. Automaticity aids in this goal. Rosenshine suggests that teachers should allocate five to eight minutes to review previous material.

Present new material in small steps with student practice after each step

Because of working memory limitations, presenting too much new information results in raising cognitive load beyond manageable levels. This is supported by evidence presented in previous chapters but is also something we experience on a daily basis. If someone is explaining a complex concept to us (or just providing directions to the Post Office), we often find ourselves asking them to slow down or back up and repeat themselves. Formal learning is no different. Similarly, echoing the instructions back to the person helps us to fully understand their instructions and correct any errors. It's therefore important to have learners practice what they have learned.

Ask lots of questions and check responses

Questioning is the bedrock of successful learning and helps learners practice new information, correct errors, and connect new information to prior knowledge. Rosenshine also suggests asking learners to explain the process of answering the questions, encouraging self-reflection, and building metacognitive skills.

Provide models

Teachers should model answers or think aloud when solving problems. This, along with the effective use of worked examples, helps learners zero in on specific problem-solving steps, which, in turn, helps to prevent cognitive overload.

Guide student practice

Learners should be encouraged to rephrase, elaborate, and summarise new material. This allows for the successful consolidation of new information in long-term memory. Rehearsal, as we have seen, strengthens neural connections and helps us retrieve and use newly learned information or apply it to problem-solving.

Check student's understanding

Long-term memory stores information, and it matters little if that information is correct or not. It's easy to assimilate incorrect information into schemas, so ensuring errors don't stick is essential for effective learning.

Obtain high success rates in classroom instruction

In studies, more effective teachers obtain higher success rates (regarding the quality of responses during guided learning practice and individual work). Obtaining high success rates might require teachers to extend the time needed to teach a topic if most students haven't grasped concepts or performed well. Rosenshine suggests maintaining a success rate of 80 percent.

Provide scaffolds for difficult tasks

Learners should be supported with adequate scaffolding, which can be withdrawn gradually as learners grow in confidence.

Require and monitor independent practice

According to Rosenshine, students need to engage in extensive and successful independent practice for skills and knowledge to reach a level of automaticity. To this end, students need to overlearn the material. Overlearning pertains to studying or practising beyond the point where one can recall the information or perform an action accurately. Studies suggest that continuing to practice beyond the point of confidence further strengthens neural pathways while reducing the amount of effort and consequently reduces cognitive load (Shibata et al., 2017). By overlearning, students improve retention and enhance performance, while becoming increasingly confident in their ability to complete the task.

Independent practice should focus on the same material as guided practice, ensuring the latter is used as preparation for the former. During independent practice, teachers should circulate, monitor, and supervise learners. Collaborative and cooperative learning can prove beneficial, but bear in mind the limits of this outlined in Chapter 10.

Weekly and monthly reviews

Regular reviews help students to bind different components of knowledge into patterns or chunks. This, as we've seen, can take pressure off working memory (or reduce cognitive load), thereby freeing up resources for reflection and problem-solving. In addition, reviewing information will further strengthen connections through the formation and updating of schemas.

Load reduction instruction

LRI is a framework developed by Andrew Martin, an educational psychologist at the University of New South Wales. Martin is perhaps best known for his work on motivation and academic buoyancy (see Chapter 12 and Smith, 2020) and perhaps accepts the premise proposed by Claxton that learning isn't only about load reduction – it's also about factors such as motivation and self-efficacy (Claxton, 2021).

LRI is an instructional approach that focuses on reducing cognitive load through a series of practical strategies encompassed within stages. LRI aligns closely with CLT by applying its key principles. The framework also aligns well with the notion of levels of processing, as each stage allows for deeper learning, culminating in more independence. What LRI does (that CLT doesn't) is offer practical strategies like support, scaffolding, and guidance, tailored to instructional design and teaching practices. CLT is much broader in its approach, describing a theoretical framework that explains how cognitive load impacts learning and memory. In this respect, LRI is perhaps more useful for teachers than CLT.

Martin's aims are two-fold. The first aligns with CLT, in that LRI helps learners manage the requirements of the task in terms of available cognitive resources. The second aim is to boost motivation and engagement by creating a learning environment that enhances these qualities. LRI assumes that in the early stages of learning a new topic, learners have less prior knowledge to draw from. Because of this, instruction must remain simple and direct. For example, if I were to skip the first 12 chapters of this book and jump directly to the current chapter, you would have a hard time understanding many of the specialist terms. The earlier chapters in this book act as a foundation for later ones. At the start of learning anything new, it's preferable to begin with small steps, be it playing a song on guitar, running your first 5K, or getting to grips with the complexity of quantum physics.

LRI comprises five principal strategies (difficulty reduction, support and scaffolding, practice, feedback, and guided independence), rising incrementally in difficulty and complexity. Early stages are dominated by direct instruction to reduce difficulty. This is the search for the sweet spot, where material is neither too easy nor too challenging. Learning is supported through scaffolding, including the extensive use of worked examples. Learners then practice what they have learned, repeating important concepts multiple times. Teachers provide constructive feedback before allowing students to work independently once they understand the material and encourage independent practice.

These strategies help learners build a solid foundation of knowledge, explore concepts independently, manage cognitive load, transition from novice to expert, gradually shifting responsibility from teacher to learner and ultimately facilitating the acquisition of robust schemas. However, these five strategies aren't necessarily incremental stages and should remain flexible. Martin describes LRI as a framework that can be adapted to different learners, subjects, and tasks.

Stage 1: Reducing the difficulty of instruction during initial training

The first stage of the LRI framework sets the scene for later learning by providing the foundations on which to build knowledge and understanding. Pre-training is the term Martin uses to describe how educators introduce the core elements of the task or topic. This might include identifying relevant names, definitions, and functions. Educators also use modelling to show how learners should complete a task. Educators share examples of good practice with learners or provide clarity on what constitutes good work and how they can achieve it.

Tasks should be broken down into bite-sized chunks. Learners can then be encouraged to complete each chunk separately and view the completion of each chunk as a success. This builds motivation and self-efficacy. Prior learning should be assessed periodically and at the outset of each new task or lesson.

At this point, educators can correct errors and misconceptions. Regular, spaced reviews should then be used to ensure understanding, perhaps at the start of each week.

Stage 2: Instructional support and scaffolding

We know from Chapter 5 that the human cognitive system doesn't handle multiple inputs of the same kind very well. When we attempt multitasking, both tasks suffer. One aim of instructional design should therefore be the reduction of split attention, where the learner must focus on more than one stimulus. We know that switching between stimuli increases cognitive load and impacts other executive functions negatively, so it would make sense that reducing this is going to help learners manage these mental resources, especially in the earlier stages of learning something new. For example, if we present a learner with a mathematical diagram and separately issue the equation or formula to find, say, the angle, the learner is required to switch between the diagram and the equation. However, by integrating the equation into the angle itself on a diagram, there is going to be less switching between the task elements. Similarly, we can exploit the dual-coding effect by teaching to different modalities, such as integrating text into images or narration into animations.

But we must also remain mindful that irrelevant information is going to impact how hard learners need to work. Avoiding information directly unrelated to the task will help reduce load, while providing cues to help learners locate or focus on the most relevant information helps with load management. For example, we might ask students to watch out for a particular event or focus their attention on a particular character. We could also identify a major theme within a text and explicitly connect the task instructions to the theme.

A powerful strategy is to provide worked examples. These demonstrate to the learner precisely what is required, avoiding any confusion over the purpose of the task. They can be coupled with templates that help learners remain on track. For example, writing templates can help students structure essays logically.

Stage 3: Ample structured practice

Deliberate practice, including rehearsal, relevant to the specific skill or task, helps learning embed. As we saw in previous chapters, we can prevent time-based decay through repetition and while this represents shallow learning, it ensures that relevant information is available to assist in deeper learning and understanding later. Imagining and mentally rehearsing material can be used with other methods. For example, reading information on a concept, turning away, and mentally reinstating the details of the learning.

As well as deliberate practice (including mental practice), educators should employ guided practice methods that help learners through the process of learning and problem-solving. This can be done using prompts or by presenting a partial solution to a problem that students can then complete.

Stage 4: Appropriate provision and instructional feedback

Feedback should provide concrete and specific information on the answer or the quality of the application. We know that errors and misconceptions are difficult to correct as they often require the updating of pre-stored schemas. Furthermore, schemas can, in some cases, distort new information. As well as feedback, educators should also feed forward, offering ways in which the solutions to a task or the application of a skill can be improved.

Stage 5: Independent practice and guided autonomy

One purpose of the early stages of learning is to ensure skills and knowledge become automatic, allowing the learner to better use this knowledge to complete similar tasks. For example, rote learning of multiplication tables results in automaticity if not deep learning (we can learn our seven times table without understanding multiplication). However, the automaticity arising from sufficient rehearsal results in faster and more efficient application to related tasks and problem-solving – we don't have to think as hard about the answer to seven times seven, so we have greater available cognitive capacity to apply the knowledge to a more complex task.

Once skills and knowledge have become automated or fluent, educators should encourage learners to attempt similar problems, tasks, or skills independently. Following this, learners should engage in guided discovery learning and be encouraged to take on new tasks and move their learning in new directions. This could include applying this learning to real-world problems.

Common threads

The three examples summarised here have several overlapping features. First, they all represent some kind of explicit instruction. Explicit instruction is a rather vague term and can be used in different ways (and is often synonymous with direct instruction), but essentially refers to any teacher-led method of instruction. This covers a wide variety of methods and needn't be viewed as one where there is little student input or autonomy. Some forms of explicit instruction may be more rigid than others, with highly predictable and set routines, often employing detailed lesson plans that rarely deviate. LRI follows a specific trajectory from direct instruction to guided discovery learning.

All three examples have been designed to manage cognitive load; in that they accept that mental resources are limited. People learn more effectively when they aren't overwhelmed by too much information or by information that is too complex. This helps to reduce task difficulty while also implementing elements of challenge (or desirable difficulties). LRI and Rosenshine's principles also stress the importance of scaffolding.

What they also do is combine elements of cognitive science with the notion of constructivism, introduced in Chapter 3. You'll hopefully recall that I described modern cognitive psychology as adopting elements of the constructivist approach, with the emphasis on knowledge construction and generative learning. All view knowledge as integrating new knowledge and experiences with prior knowledge and experiences. Learners are, therefore, active creators of their own knowledge rather than passive recipients.

While all three frameworks are certainly useful, they are not without their weaknesses. The methods they promote aren't new, and teachers have been using many of the techniques for decades. Scaffolding, for example, originated with the work of Jerome Bruner in the 1960s and was, itself, inspired by the work of Lev Vygotsky (Margolis, 2020). Indeed, many of the techniques represent not only common sense, but what teachers have been doing for some time. While Rosenshine's principles represent a tick list of techniques, Martin's LRI allows for flexibility, assuming teachers are more than capable of using the framework in light of the learners they are currently teaching. More broadly, Rosenshine's principles appear to oversimplify often complex and nuanced aspects of memory, retention, and schema formation, often drawing on evidence that is out of date. This isn't always the fault of Rosenshine, as research into many areas of learning, such as CLT, has moved rapidly over the past decade or so. It does highlight, however, the need to consider the changing evidence-based landscape and the need to adjust these frameworks accordingly. Of the three frameworks presented here, LRI shows the greatest utility and future promise.

Chapter summary

- Learning is an active and constructivist process where learners build knowledge by engaging with information and integrating it with their existing understanding. This involves dynamic mechanisms in the brain related to registering, storing, and recalling information. Remembering itself is viewed as an act of reconstruction.

- Despite significant research in learning science identifying effective learning strategies, learners and sometimes educators often favour less effective methods like highlighting, underlining, and rereading. This might be due to a lack of understanding, the illusion of learning from passive methods, or cognitive biases.

- Effective learning strategies promote deeper processing of information, moving beyond shallow memorisation to involve understanding relationships, critical thinking, analysis, evaluation, and synthesis.

- Designing effective learning environments and instruction requires careful consideration of cognitive load, ensuring it is manageable for learners with limited cognitive resources. Instructional design should aim to optimise load rather than eliminate it, considering factors like prior knowledge and the need for active processing and engagement.

- Several evidence-based instructional design models draw on cognitive science principles to guide effective teaching and learning. These include generative learning theory, which emphasises the active construction of meaning through the selection, organisation, and integration of information. Rosenshine's principles of instruction provide practical strategies for effective teaching, such as reviewing prior learning, presenting new material in small steps, and frequent questioning. LRI focuses on reducing cognitive load through strategies like difficulty reduction, scaffolding, and guided practice, ultimately aiming for independent learning. These models often share common threads like explicit instruction, managing cognitive load, and incorporating constructivist elements.

Further reading

Ashman, G. (2020). *The power of explicit teaching and direct instruction*. Corwin.

Zoe, E., & Enser, M. (2020). *Fiorella and Mayer's generative learning in Action*. John Catt.

References

Blasiman, R. N., Dunlosky, J., & Rawson, K. A. (2017). The what, how much, and when of study strategies: Comparing intended versus actual study behaviour. *Memory*, *25*(6), 784–792. https://doi.org/10.1080/09658211.2016.1221974

Claxton, G. (2021). *The future of teaching and the myths that hold it back*. Routledge.

Dirkx, K. J. H., Camp, G., Kester, L., & Kirschner, P. A. (2019). Do secondary school students make use of effective study strategies when they study on their own? *Applied Cognitive Psychology*, January, 952–957. https://doi.org/10.1002/acp.3584

Dunlosky, J., Rawson, K. A., Marsh, E. J., Nathan, M. J., & Willingham, D. T. (2013). Improving students' learning with effective learning techniques: Promising directions from cognitive and educational psychology. *Psychological Science in the Public Interest*, *14*(1), 4–58. https://doi.org/10.1177/1529100612453266

Fiorella, L., & Mayer, R. E. (2015). *Learning as a generative activity*. Cambridge University Press. https://doi.org/10.1017/CBO9781107707085

Karpicke, J. D., & Roediger, H. L. (2008). The critical importance of retrieval for learning. *Science*, *319*(5865), 966–968. https://doi.org/10.1126/science.1152408

Margolis, A. A. (2020). Zone of proximal development, scaffolding and teaching practice. *Cultural-Historical Psychology*, *16*(3), 15–26. https://doi.org/10.17759/chp.2020160303

Martin, A. J. (2016). *Using load reduction instruction to boost motivation and engagement*. British Psychological Society.

Morehead, K., Rhodes, M. G., & DeLozier, S. (2015). Instructor and student knowledge of study strategies. *Memory, 24*(2), 257–271. https://doi.org/10.1080/09658211.2014.1001992

Rosenshine, B. (2012). Principles of instruction research-based strategies that all teachers should know. www.ibe.unesco.org/fileadmin/user_upload/

Shibata, K., Sasaki, Y., Bang, J. W., Walsh, E. G., Machizawa, M. G., Tamaki, M., Chang, L. H., & Watanabe, T. (2017). Overlearning hyperstabilizes a skill by rapidly making neurochemical processing inhibitory-dominant. *Nature Neuroscience, 20*(3), 470–475. https://doi.org/10.1038/nn.4490

Smith, M. (2020). *Becoming Buoyant: Helping teachers and students cope with the day to day*. Routledge.

Sultana, F., Watkins, R. C., Al Baghal, T., & Hughes, J. C. (2025). An evaluation of secondary school students' use and understanding of learning strategies to study and revise for science examinations. *Education Sciences, 15*(1). https://doi.org/10.3390/educsci15010101

Smarter learning

From the outset, the aim of this book has been to present a view of learning based on evidence from cognitive psychology. No single discipline can claim to have all the answers, the mystical silver bullet to solve everything. The evidence presented here goes some way to achieving this aim, yet there is much we don't understand, and at times, it seems like many of the pieces of our puzzle have slipped down the back of the sofa. Hopefully, the preceding chapters have made the most of the pieces that have not.

The pursuit of smarter learning

How memory and cognition work is crucial for effective learning. This statement I believe to be self-evident. Not only do I believe it to be self-evident, but over a century of research and innovation supports this proposition. But science doesn't exist in a vacuum, nor are its findings frozen in time. For every study cited here to support a cognitive view of learning, there are many more that have failed and some that are, even now, languishing in filing cabinets or existing as little more than footnotes in obscure academic journals. While I have attempted to retain an element of criticality here, I remain fully cognisant of my biases. Finding what works is an ongoing process of refining and applying evidence-based strategies, not a one-time solution. We do not yet know, for example, the changes rapid technological innovation will bring. Will the expansion of artificial intelligence mark a new era of learning, or will learning become less important in a world where cognitive offloading becomes the norm? Making predictions about the future is fraught with difficulties, yet I am as certain as I can be that humans will always need and crave knowledge. I doubt AI will ever take that from us.

Cognition is the activity of knowing

Hopefully, the preceding chapters have successfully conveyed the multifaceted nature of learning, while emphasising the vital role played by cognitive processes.

All thinking requires cognition, and we can trace learning to the complex workings of the brain. Emotions and motivation might not fall neatly in line with our understanding of cognition, yet without the ability to think, there would be no emotions, no motivation or planned behaviour, no imagination or innovation. To know, we must remember. This, too, is self-evident.

Foundational principles: understanding the building blocks of effective learning

Memory is the bedrock of learning, and how effectively we encode and store information dictates how readily we can access what we have learned. While learning certainly represents a change in long-term memory, the mechanisms by which this happens are complex and nuanced. People don't remember things in the same way or with the same accuracy. Individual differences in working memory capacity impact the limits of what we can learn at any one time.

These limits are encapsulated within cognitive load and further extrapolated within cognitive load theory. One aim of effective teaching and learning is the management of cognitive load, including the reduction of factors that may result in raised extraneous load. Is CLT the most important theory for educators to understand? It's certainly one important theory, but it's only one piece of the puzzle.

Prior knowledge aids current and future learning. Schemas allow for the consolidation of new information into pre-existing structures, allowing learners to organise new learning so that it makes sense within a wider contextual framework. This also raises the potential for transfer, where we can apply previous learning to novel situations. Similarly, the strategic use of context improves memory and comprehension.

The human factor: emotion, motivation, and metacognition

Current trends in education focusing on cognitive science often neglect the influence of so-called non-cognitive factors. In Chapters 11 and 12, I've attempted to correct this imbalance by emphasising that all learning related phenomena are cognitive in nature. Regarding emotion, viewing emotions as activating and deactivating allows us to move away from the oversimplistic negative-positive emotion dichotomy. A more productive way of approaching emotions, I propose, is one where specific emotional responses are assessed within the context in which they arise. Learning can be stressful, but it can also invigorate and promote active curiosity. Emotions also impact memory consolidation and recall, including the development of schemas. Emotions are, therefore, part of the human cognitive architecture and impact thinking and learning. They also impact cognitive load by both reducing and increasing mental effort. By managing emotions, we also manage load, which we can examine through the lens of attentional control theory (Chapter 11).

Motivation is perhaps more complex and nuanced than other aspects of learning. While theories emphasising the role of intrinsic and extrinsic factors are useful, goal theories of motivation might be better placed to explain peaks and troughs that arise during specific learning episodes and in the longer term. Learning goals provide us with an end result, allowing us to break larger goals into manageable sub-goals and provide useful timeframes for when we should reach our goal, be that at the end of lesson, the end of topic, or the final days of formal education. Motivation is further fuelled by self-efficacy (the confidence in our ability to achieve our goal), attribution (including the perceived importance of the goal), and academic buoyancy (our ability to tolerate setbacks and to endure when things get tough). Motivation may also be fuelled by innate factors related to personality, including a person's need for cognition.

Knowing how we learn and our ability to adjust our learning fall within the sphere of metacognition. The previous chapters, for example, can be used as blueprints for successful learning, improving our ability to reflect on the methods and techniques we might currently use and promote. However, often our metacognitive awareness is faulty, and our confidence in suboptimal methods can lead us to cling to techniques that simply aren't working. Hopefully, the evidence presented throughout this book can convince you that scientifically validated methods of learning exist and are more effective than those many students currently rely upon.

Designing effective learning environments and instruction

Learning should be active and generative, yet methods that result in shallow processing remain useful, especially in the early stages of learning something new. The models of instructional design outlined in Chapter 13 incorporate the areas covered in previous chapters and encourage generative learning, adhering to the key principles of constructivism. All include tools and techniques that help learners organise and assimilate new learning into current schemas, encouraging permanent and readily available knowledge. However, as no framework is foolproof and as more evidence becomes available, these frameworks must adapt accordingly. But the emphasis on deep learning techniques doesn't exclude those methods that result in shallow learning, including rote memorisation. Furthermore, while we might hold generative learning frameworks in higher regard, there is always a place for alternative tools.

Explicit instruction is one such tool and, far from being a simple memorisation technique, ensures solid foundations. This is particularly important in subjects such as mathematics, where good foundational knowledge not only improves learning outcomes but also limits anxiety. As we saw in Chapter 8, good foundational knowledge can also reduce the attainment gap, advantaging those learners who are more susceptible to underachievement. Like Explicit instruction, appropriate support, such as the strategic use of scaffolding and guided practice, helps build knowledge from the ground up while prior learning operates top-down.

Overcoming barriers to effective learning

As we saw in Chapter 13, most learners adopt ineffective learning strategies. More worrying, perhaps, educators are often unaware of what strategies work best. The reliance upon methods with little or no empirical support (such as rereading and highlighting) implies that the wealth of evidence available isn't making its way into the classrooms and lecture theatres or, indeed, onto the training courses attended by educators. The need for quick, shallow learning to pass exams may play a part. While evidence supports self-testing and wider aspects of retrieval practice, educational systems around the world rely heavily on testing as an assessment method. This reliance may, in some circumstances, favour quick yet shallow forms of learning where what we have learned in school fades rapidly following these assessments. Effective learning strategies promote long-term deep learning, and there might be some mileage in the view that the need for deep learning isn't always compatible with the high-stakes testing culture.

Learning myths persist despite attempts to counter them. The most resilient of these myths is learning styles, a notion that runs counter to what we understand about how learning happens. While not directly related to learning, other beliefs can work against attempts to improve learning. Humans don't use only 10 percent of their brain; people aren't left- or right-brained, and listening to Mozart won't make any difference to your intelligence. More importantly, the time we spend studying is less important than the quality of the learning. There is no 10,000-hour rule, and we all learn at different rates. One of the principal aims of this book has been to replace many of these myths with workable, evidence-based alternatives.

Learning improvement is an ongoing venture

Research into learning never stops. Every day, we learn a little more about how the brain deals with new information and why it so often fails to recall things we thought we'd learned. Many of the advances have come from neuroscience, and one day we'll inevitably view learning through the lens of brain science and discard the cognitive models so beloved by many today. We're not there yet, and there are many hard problems to overcome on the way. Perhaps the most enlightening discovery of recent years is that the brain continues to learn throughout the lifespan and that the brain creates new neurons well into old age. Lifelong learning, therefore, has many benefits, and learning shouldn't be viewed as confined to formal education.

It's crucial that learners and educators stay informed and remain critical consumers of learning strategies. Many of the ideas we cling to are now outdated, having been successfully challenged and replaced as research continues. Many of the ideas raised in the previous chapters, such as embodied cognition, were dismissed in the not-too-distant past but are now supported by a plethora of scientific evidence.

We don't yet know everything about learning, but what we know has the scientific support to make it useful. A model might be wrong and the language we use inadequate, but that doesn't necessarily negate its utility. However, the models we choose can inform our view. For example, Cowan's embedded process model emphasises the role of attention and sees working memory as activated long-term memory, while other models might view memory as more compartmentalised, with a lesser emphasis on attention. Similarly, we can view motivation within a self-determination framework, where we place the emphasis on extrinsic and intrinsic rewards, or from a purely goal-directed position.

Hopefully, the preceding chapters have provided a critical picture of the learning sciences from a cognitive psychology standpoint. In the introduction, I emphasised the messiness of learning research and stand by the view that to fully appreciate what we have learned from more than a century of investigation, we also need to appreciate this messiness. But there are coherent threads that run through all research, from Ebbinghaus to the present, and while some may be more relevant than others, it all helps to create a picture of how learning happens and how we can learn better, be smarter, and gain the tools and skills to negotiate the wealth of information, including misinformation, around us.

Index

Note: **Bold** page numbers refer to tables and *italic* page numbers refer to figures.

Abelson, Robert 93
abstraction 97, 123
academic buoyancy 168, 169, 182, 211
academic self-concept 168
accommodation 45
achievement emotions 162
achievement goal theory 185–186
activated long-term memory 63, 76, 79, 213
activating *vs.* deactivating emotions 162, 185, 211
amygdala 48, 102, 163
analogies and metaphors 123–124
Anderson, Richard 93
anterior cingulate cortex (ACC) 103
anxiety 31, 75–79, 160–171, 180–181; and explicit instruction 211
Arora, Sonal 170
artificial intelligence (AI) 2, 37, 42, 93, 209
assimilation 45, 62, 74
Atkinson, Richard *56, 56–58*
atomistic *vs.* holistic epistemic state 17
attention 75; and classroom displays 80–81; selective 76–77
attentional control theory (ACT) 167–180
attribution theory 118, 211
Ausubel, David 113
automaticity 66, 195, 200, 202, 205

Baddeley, Alan 43, 57, 67, 71, 128–129
Barrouillet, Pierre 57, 73; *see also* time-based resource sharing model
Bartlett, Frederic 86–88, 92
behaviourism 29, 37–41
Bergman, Erik 87
big 5 personality theory 31
binding 103, 115
biologically primary knowledge 22–23, 32
biologically secondary knowledge 22–23
Biran, Maine de (François-Pierre-Gontier de Biran) 51
Bjork, Elizabeth 135
Bjork, Robert 132, 135
blank slate theory, criticism of 29
Blasiman, Rachael 193
boredom 31, 76, 161, 162
Brewer, William 193
Broadbent, Donald 42, 43, 56; model of attention 77–78
broaden and build framework 162–3
Brown, John 71
Brown-Peterson technique 71
Bruner, Jerome 206

Cattell-Horn-Carrol theory of intelligence 30–31
central executive 59, 81, 102, 103, 181
Choi, Hwan-Hee 166

Chomsky, Noam 42, 43
chunking 71; *vs.* grouping 116–117
cingular opercula network (CON) 167
Claparède, Edouard 55
Claxton, Guy 5, 23, 63, 75, 98, 99, 202
cocktail party problem 77
cognitive decline 28, 32–35, 174–176, 183
cognitive flexibility 108, 110, 176, 177–179
cognitive load 43, 72–73, 81, 103, 119, 124, 144, 146, 149
cognitive load theory (CLT) 73–75, 85, 98
cognitive offloading 148, 152–155
cognitive surprise 24–25
collaborative learning 155–157, 202
collective working memory 155
computer metaphor 4, 56
conditioning 38–40
confirmation bias 16
conscientiousness 31, 169
consolidation 103, 107, 125, 137; and re-consolidation 106, 199
constructivism 45, 206, 211
context-dependent memory 9, 67, 87
contextualised learning 136
context variability theory 67
core affect 161
core knowledge 22, 25
Coronel, Jason 94
Cowan, Nelson 53, 57, 62–63, 71, 79, 81, 116, 195; *see also* embedded processes model
Craik, Fergus 18–19, 51, 61
critical thinking 19, 23, 178, 196, **197**
cued recall 67–68, 87–89, 96, 105, 106, 132, 138
Cunitz, Anita 72
curiosity 76, 151, 161–163, 185, 210

Damasio, Antonio 161, 164–165
Deci, Edward *see* self-determination theory
declarative *vs.* non-declarative memory 14, 53–55, 92
default mode network (DMN) 167
deliberate practice 125, 139–140, 205
desirable difficulties 135–137, 151, 206
dichotic listening technique 76–77, 115

digit span 60, 70–71, 116–117
Dirkx, Kim 193
distinctiveness 108
distributed practice (spacing effect) 129, 132, 133, 135, 137, 183, 193
dorsolateral prefrontal cortex 102
drawing effect 146, 198
dual coding 59, 145, 146
dual trace theory *see* fuzzy trace theory
Dunlosky, John 182, 192, 193
Dunning-Kruger effect 185
Dweck, Carol 186

Ebbinghaus, Hermann 69–70; criticisms of 85–87
einstellung effect 118–119
elaborative interrogation 135, 150–151, 192
element interactivity 98
Elliot, Andrew 186
embedded processes model 62, 76, 79, 97
embodied cognition 45, 148, 200, 212
emotion 160–171; and academic buoyancy 169–170; and cognitive load theory 168–169; and memory 164
emotional regulation 168, 170–171, 192
encoding 52, 67, 75, 81, 89, 102–107, 115, 121
engagement 5, 23, 80, 144, 168, 196
engram 101
episodic buffer 59, 103
episodic memory 14, 53–55, 62, 87–88, 96, 154
era of evolutionary adaptation (EEA) 22
Ericsson, Anders 96, 117, 139–140
Evans, Paul 188
executive function 176–181
expectance value cost theory (EVCT) 187–188
explicit instruction 205, 211
extraneous cognitive load 74, 154, 155, 168, 181, 188; and emotions 168
extrinsic *vs.* intrinsic Motivation 183–184, 188
eyewitness testimony 60
Eysenck, Michael 167

familiarity 11–13
feedback 125, 138, 140, 185, 203, 205; and feed forward 205
Feigenson, Lisa 108
Feldon, David 107–108
Fiorella, Logan 113–114, 196–200; see also generative learning theory
fixed mindset 186, 188
Flavell, John 181
fluid intelligence 30–31, 124, 177
forgetting 66–81; interference 66, 67–68, 120; temporal decay 66, 68, 72, 89, 96, 205
forgetting curve 69–70, 72, 85, 98
Fredrickson, Barbara 163
frontoparietal network (FPN) 167
fuzzy trace theory 104–105

Galton, Francis 70
garden path sentences 90
Gardner, Howard 31
Geary, David 22–23, 32
generative learning theory 196–200
germane cognitive load 74
gestalt psychology 41, 45, 118
gist memory 59, 104–106
Gladwell, Malcolm 139–40
Glanzer, Murray 72
Godden, Duncan 67, 87
google effect 154
Grant, Harry 67
Greve, Andrea 109
growth vs. fixed mindset 186–188
Groot, Adriaan de 95–96
guided discovery learning 205
guided practice 202, 204, 211

Harlow, Harry 41
Hebb, Donald 41–42
Henry (memory patient) 48–50
heritability 32
hidden curriculum 3
hippocampus 28, 33–34, 48–49, 54, 102–103, 107, 110, 147
Hitch, Graham 43, 57, 81, 89, 101–102, 146
Hooke, Robert 51, 69

illusion of explanatory depth 16–17
imagination 22, 31, 50; and generative learning 199; imagination effect 149–50
immediate digit span see digit span
Immordino-Yang, Mary Helen 164–165
implicit learning 11, 55
implicit theories of learning 186
independent practice 196, 202–203, 205
induction learning 18, 132
infantile amnesia 32
information processing model 43, 44, 56
inhibitory control 167, 176, 179–180
intelligence quotient (IQ) 30–32, 176, 177
interleaving 132–133, 136, 151, 183, 193
intrinsic motivation 183, 185
isolation effect 108–109

Jacobs, Joseph 70
James, William 22, 51, 53, 70
Johnson, Marcia 89
Jones, Mary Cover 38
Jost, Adolf 69
Jost's Law of Forgetting 70

knowing how vs. knowing that 13–14
knowledge, definition of 12–13
knowledge is power hypothesis 113–114
Köhler, Wolfgang 41
Kornell, Nate 132–133

language learning 22, 25–26, 32; and the brain 23, 28, 34
Lashley, Karl 101
latent learning 11, 40
learning myths 6, 193, 212
learning science(s) 1–3, 6, 45–46
learning sets 41
learning styles (learning myth) 6, 145, 193, 212
levels of processing theory 18, 61–62, 97, 98, 136, 146, 149, 202
Levine, Jerrold 72
little Albert study 38, 55
load reduction instruction 188, 196, 202–206

localised theory *vs.* distributed theory of memory 101–102
Locke, Edwin 185
Lockhart, Robert 18, 61
Loftus, Elizabeth 60
long-term memory 5, 8, 14, 18, 52, 53, 55, 59–64, 67, 68, 72, 79, 87, 96–98, 116, 117, 155
Loveday, Catherine 164

Maguire, Eleanor *see* taxi driver study
mantle of the expert 148
mapping *see* generative learning theory
Martin, Andrew 169, 188, 202–203; *see also* academic buoyancy; load reduction instruction
Martin, George R. R. 90
Massachusetts Institute of Technology (MIT) 42
maths anxiety 160, 166, 168, 180
Matthew effect 114
Mayer, Richard 113–114, 196–198, 200
mediator effectiveness hypothesis 138
memorisation *see* rote learning
memory 48–65; *see also* forgetting; long-term memory; working memory
memory cycle 103–107, 110, 125
memory errors 121
Mendel, Gregor 123
mental chronometry 145
mental maps 40, 45
mental practice 170, 204
Merriam, Sharan 174
Merton, Robert 114
metacognition 117, 174–189, 210–211
Miller, George 2, 42–43, 57, 70, 116
Miller's magic number seven 70, 79
Milner, Brenda 48
mindset (Dweck theory) 187–188
misconceptions 118, 125, 204, 205
mixing costs 177–178
modal model of memory *see* multi-store model of memory
Moore, Thomas Verner 1
Morehead, Kayla 193

motivation 79, 183–189; and cognitive load theory 168, 187, 188; and emotions 165; and generative learning 196–197; and load reduction instruction 203
MRC Cognition and Brain Sciences Unit 43, 109, 128
multiple-choice questions 12, 17
multiple intelligences, theory of 31
multi-store model of memory 56
multi-tasking 177–178, 204
Murakami, Haruki 164
myelin 27, 34
Myers Briggs type indicator (MBTI) 31

nature-nurture debate 29
need for cognition (trait) 186–187
Neisser, Ulric 1, 37, 42, 63
neural networks 45, 101, 163
neurogenesis 33
New Theory of Disuse 134
noetic *vs.* autonoetic consciousness 13
non-declarative memory 54–55

Oberauer, Klaus 78
occipital cortex 146

Palinko, Oskar 72–73
parietal cortex (PAR) 103, 167
Pavlov, Ivan 37
Pearlstone, Zena 89
Pear, Thomas 86
Pekrun, Reinhard 162
perception 1, 2, 22, 42, 43, 78
Perception and Communication (Broadbent book) 43
performance goal *vs.* mastery goal orientation *see* mindset
Perkins, Nellie 70
personality 29, 31, 32, 184, 211
Peterson, Lloyd and Margaret 71
phantom recollection principle 105
phonological loop 59, 81, 89, 147
photo-taking impairment effect 154–155
Piaget, Jean 45, 92
place (sign) learning 40
primacy and recency effect 69, 72, 86

prior knowledge 188; and negative mediators 118–121; and positive mediators 115–118
problem solving 22, 23, 41, 96, 117–118, 122, 201, 205
procedural memory 14, 31, 55, 92–93, 102
processing effectiveness *vs.* processing efficiency 167
procrastination 171, 182, 186
production effect 147
Proust, Marcel 164
pruning (cognitive process) 175–176
psychometrics 31

radical behaviourism 29
Raynor, Rosalie 38
recognition *vs.* recall 11
rehearsal 52, 56, 66, 71–72, 85, 201, 204
relational memory 91
reminiscence bump 164
replication 85–86
resilience 162–163, 168–169, 175, 184; and academic buoyancy 182
retrieval practice 137–139, 151, 192, 194, 199
Roberson, Donald 174
Roediger, Henry 87–88, 98
Rosenshine's principles of instruction 196, 200–202
rote learning 62, 124, 136, 151, 196, **197**, 205, 211
Ryan, Richard 184; *see also* self-determination theory

scaffolding 155, 201–204, 206
Schank, Roger 93
schema theory 87, 92–99; and the brain 102–110; and knowledge production 113–114, 118, 121, 124–125
Schmidt, Stephen 108
Scoville, William Beecher 48
selective attention *see* attention
select, organise, integrate (SOI) model 114, 198–199
self-determination theory (SDT) 184–185; and cognitive load 188

self-efficacy 163, 166, 185, 202, 211
self-explaining 199
self-testing *see* retrieval practice
semantic memory 53–55, 88
Semon, Richard 101
Shallice, Tim 60
shallow *vs.* deep processing *see* levels of processing theory
Shiffrin, Richard *56,* 56–58
short-term memory 43, 49, 52–54, 56, 57; capacity of 70–71; difference between working memory 81
Skinner, B. F. 29, 38–39, 41
SLIMM framework 107, 109
social learning 11
spacing effect *see* distributed practice
Sparrow, Betsy 154
Stahl, Aimee 108
status quo bias 194
Stevenson, Harold 40
stimulus-response behaviour 38–39, 42, 49
storage strength *vs.* retrieval strength 134–135, 137
Stout, George 59–60
stress response 162–163
Sultana, Fatema 194
Sweller, John 74, 165, 188
switching costs 178–179
synaptogenesis 33, 175

taxi driver study 28, 54, 101–102, 103
ten-thousand-hour rule 139–140, 212
testing effect 138
Thorndike, Edward 39, 122; Thorndike's law of effect 39
time-based resource sharing model 73, 152
tip-of-the-tongue (TOT) phenomenon 12
Tolman, Edward 39–40, 92
top-down attention 167
transfer of learning 121–122; high road 122; low road 122
Treisman, Anne 78
Treyens, James 93
Tse, Dorothy 106
Tulving, Endel 13–14, 51, 53–54, 89

valence (emotions) 161
verbatim memory 104–106
visuo-spatial sketchpad 59, 81, 89, 147
Vogel, Todd 186
Von Restorff, Hedwig 108
Vygotsky, Lev 45, 206

Warrington, Elizabeth 60
Watson, John B. 29, 32, 38, 41
Why don't students like school? (book by Daniel Willingham) 52

Wiliam, Dylan 75
Willingham, Daniel 52, 192
word length effect 71, 86, 88
worked examples 201, 203–204
working memory 57, 59–64; and attention 75–81; and cognitive load 72–75
working memory model 43, 57

Xu, Kate 188

Yerkes-Dodson law 162

For Product Safety Concerns and Information please contact our EU representative GPSR@taylorandfrancis.com
Taylor & Francis Verlag GmbH, Kaufingerstraße 24, 80331 München, Germany

www.ingramcontent.com/pod-product-compliance
Lightning Source LLC
Chambersburg PA
CBHW062137160426
43191CB00014B/2312